D0016300

WITHDRAWN

PENGUIN BOOKS

MAYA

Charles Gallenkamp was born in Dallas, Texas, and educated at the University of Texas and the University of New Mexico. He has conducted archaeological research in the southwestern United States, Mexico, and Central America under the auspices of various museums and foundations. In addition to several previous books, he has written articles that have appeared in national magazines and newspapers. He frequently lectures on archaeology and pre-Columbian art, and he served as Exhibition Coordinator for the highly acclaimed "Maya: Treasures of an Ancient Civilization."

CHARLES GALLENKAMP

MAYA

The Riddle and Rediscovery of a Lost Civilization

THIRD REVISED EDITION

PENGUIN BOOKS

PENGUIN BOOKS
Published by the Penguin Group
Penguin Books USA Inc.,
375 Hudson Street, New York, New York 10014, U.S.A.
Penguin Books Ltd, 27 Wrights Lane, London W8 5TZ, England
Penguin Books Australia Ltd, Ringwood, Victoria, Australia
Penguin Books Canada Ltd, 10 Alcorn Avenue,
Toronto, Ontario, Canada M4V 3B2
Penguin Books (N.Z.) Ltd, 182–190 Wairau Road,
Auckland 10, New Zealand

Penguin Books Ltd, Registered Offices:
Harmondsworth, Middlesex, England

First published in United States of America
by David McKay Company, Inc. 1959
Revised and expanded edition first published in the United States
of America by David McKay Company, Inc. 1976
Second revised edition published in Penguin Books
by arrangement with David McKay Company, Inc. 1981
Third revised edition first published in 1985
by Viking Penguin Inc.
Published in Penguin Books 1987

10   9

LIBRARY OF CONGRESS CATALOGING IN PUBLICATION DATA
Gallenkamp, Charles.
   Maya, the riddle and rediscovery of a lost civilization.
   Published in conjunction with an exhibition organized by the
Albuquerque Museum opening Apr. 1985.
   Bibliography: p.
   Includes index.
   1. Mayas—Antiquities.   2. Indians of Mexico—Antiquities.
3. Indians of Central America—Antiquities.   4. Mexico—
Antiquities   5. Central America—Antiquities.   I. Albuquerque
Museum.   II. Title.
F1435.G16   1987   972'.01   87-8771
ISBN 0 14 00.8831 8

Printed in the United States of America
Set in Times Roman
Designed by Barbara DuPree Knowles
Map by Paul Pugliese

CHARLES GALLENKAMP

MAYA

The Riddle and Rediscovery
of a Lost Civilization

THIRD REVISED EDITION

PENGUIN BOOKS

PENGUIN BOOKS
Published by the Penguin Group
Penguin Books USA Inc.,
375 Hudson Street, New York, New York 10014, U.S.A.
Penguin Books Ltd, 27 Wrights Lane, London W8 5TZ, England
Penguin Books Australia Ltd, Ringwood, Victoria, Australia
Penguin Books Canada Ltd, 10 Alcorn Avenue,
Toronto, Ontario, Canada M4V 3B2
Penguin Books (N.Z.) Ltd, 182–190 Wairau Road,
Auckland 10, New Zealand

Penguin Books Ltd, Registered Offices:
Harmondsworth, Middlesex, England

First published in United States of America
by David McKay Company, Inc. 1959
Revised and expanded edition first published in the United States
of America by David McKay Company, Inc. 1976
Second revised edition published in Penguin Books
by arrangement with David McKay Company, Inc. 1981
Third revised edition first published in 1985
by Viking Penguin Inc.
Published in Penguin Books 1987

10 9

LIBRARY OF CONGRESS CATALOGING IN PUBLICATION DATA
Gallenkamp, Charles.
   Maya, the riddle and rediscovery of a lost civilization.
   Published in conjunction with an exhibition organized by the
Albuquerque Museum opening Apr. 1985.
   Bibliography: p.
   Includes index.
   1. Mayas—Antiquities.   2. Indians of Mexico—Antiquities.
3. Indians of Central America—Antiquities.   4. Mexico—
Antiquities   5. Central America—Antiquities.   I. Albuquerque
Museum.   II. Title.
F1435.G16   1987   972'.01   87-8771
ISBN 0 14 00.8831 8

Printed in the United States of America
Set in Times Roman
Designed by Barbara DuPree Knowles
Map by Paul Pugliese

PREFACE

Since the first edition of this book was published in 1959, the science of Maya archaeology has been dramatically altered by a continual flow of new information. Intensive investigations have focused on a broad spectrum of questions, aided by large-scale excavations at numerous sites, breakthroughs in hieroglyphic decipherment, important ethno-historic studies, and innovative approaches to the interpretation of data gleaned from this research. As a result of these efforts, archaeologists have steadily enlarged our understanding of the nature and scope of Maya civilization, and many previously held concepts have undergone sweeping revisions.

In order to incorporate essential aspects of these developments, this book was updated in two subsequent editions that appeared in 1976 and 1981. In 1985, the quantity of new material made it necessary to compile a Third Revised Edition, with an expanded text and additional photographs. Moreover, this edition was originally published in conjunction with a major exhibition of Maya art organized by The Albuquerque Museum, for which I had the good fortune to act as Exhibition Coordinator. Entitled *MAYA: Treasures of an Ancient Civilization*, this show constituted the most comprehensive panorama of Maya artistic achievements ever assembled, and it visited six cities in the United States and Canada during a two-year tour in 1985–87.

Obviously no synthesis of Maya archaeology would be possible without drawing upon the writings of many explorers, scientists, and historians—as I have done in the past—and some measure of my continued indebtedness to these sources is reflected in the Bibliography. To those individuals whose assistance I have acknowledged in previous editions of this book, I again express my appreciation. In the preparation of this Third Revised Edition, I would especially like to thank James Moore, the Director of The Albuquerque Museum, for his generous support and encouragement, as well as the staff and Board of Directors of both The Albuquerque Museum and The Albuquerque Museum Foundation. I am also grateful to my associates in the Maya Exhibition Project, Jon D. Freshour and Marilyn Stebbins, for their assistance with a variety of tasks connected with this book, and to the members of the exhibition's Curatorial Committee: Flora S. Clancy, Assistant Professor of Art History, University of New Mexico; Clemency C. Coggins, Research Associate, Peabody Museum of Archaeology and Ethnology, Harvard University; T. Patrick Culbert, Professor of Anthropology, University of Arizona; Peter D. Harrison, Adjunct Associate Professor of Anthropology, University of New Mexico, and Research Associate, Middle American Research Institute, Tulane University; and Jeremy A. Sabloff, Professor of Anthropology, University of New Mexico. Finally, I owe a special debt of gratitude to Regina Elise Johnson for her invaluable help in researching, editing, and typing the manuscript.

Charles Gallenkamp
ALBUQUERQUE, NEW MEXICO

ACKNOWLEDGMENTS

Grateful acknowledgment is made to the following for permission to use selections, photographs, and drawings from other sources:

American Antiquity: "Lowland Maya Archaeology at the Crossroads," by Joyce Marcus.

Archaeology: From "The Mystery of the Temple of the Inscriptions," by Alberto Ruz Lhuillier, *Archaeology,* Volume 6, Number 1, 1953.

Carnegie Institution of Washington: Bonampak, Chiapas, Mexico, by Karl Ruppert, J. Eric S. Thompson, and Tatiana Proskouriakoff.

Cornell University Press and Orbis Publishing Limited: From *The World of the Ancient Maya,* by John S. Henderson. Copyright © 1981 by Cornell University.

The Curtis Publishing Company: "The Mystery of the Mayan Temple," by Alberto Ruz Lhuillier and J. Alden Mason, from *The Saturday Evening Post.* Copyright 1953 by The Curtis Publishing Company.

Explorers' Journal: "Balankanche-Throne of the Tiger Priest," by E. Wyllys Andrews.

Harper & Row Publishers, Inc.: The Lost Civilization: The Story of the Classic Maya, by T. Patrick Culbert.

Middle American Research Institute, Tulane University: From *The Ethno-Botany of the Maya,* by Ralph L. Roys.

New York Graphic Society: Mexico: Pre-Hispanic Paintings, Preface by Jacques Soustelle.

Peabody Museum of Archaeology and Ethnology, Harvard University: From *Relación de las Cosas de Yucatán,* by Diego de Landa, translated and edited by Alfred M. Tozzer. Peabody Museum Papers, Volume 18. Copyright 1941 by the President and Fellows of Harvard College.

Rutgers University Press: From *Ancient Maya Civilization,* by Norman Hammond. Copyright © 1982 by Rutgers, The State University of New Jersey. From *Incidents of Travel in Central America, Chiapas, and Yucatan,* by John Lloyd Stephens, edited by Richard L. Predmore.

School of American Research and the University of Utah: From *The Florentine Codex: General History of the Things of New Spain,* by Bernardo de Sahagún, translated and edited by Arthur J. O. Anderson and Charles E. Dibble.

Scientific American: From "The Rise of a Maya Merchant Class," by Jeremy A. Sabloff and William L. Rathje, Volume 233, Number 4, 1975.

Stanford University Press: From *The Ancient Maya,* Fourth Edition, by Sylvanus G. Morley and George W. Brainerd; revised by Robert J. Sharer. Copyright 1947, 1956, 1983 by the Board of Trustees of the Leland Stanford Junior University.

Thames and Hudson Ltd.: From *Tula: The Toltec Capital of Ancient Mexico,* by Richard A. Diehl. Copyright © 1984 by Thames and Hudson Ltd.

Edward H. Thompson, North Falmouth, Massachusetts: From *People of the Serpent,* by Edward H. Thompson.

University of Oklahoma Press: From *Incidents of Travel in Yucatan,* by John Lloyd Stephens, edited by Victor W. von Hagen. From *Popol Vuh: The Sacred Book of the Ancient Maya,* from the translation of Adrian Recinos. English version by Delia Goetz and Sylvanus G. Morley. Copyright © 1950 by the University of Oklahoma Press. From *The Rise and Fall of Maya Civilization,* Second Edition (enlarged), by J. Eric S. Thompson. Copyright 1954, 1966 by the University of Oklahoma Press. From *An Album of Maya Architecture,* by Tatiana Proskouriakoff. New edition copyright © 1963 by the University of Oklahoma Press.

University of Pennsylvania Museum: From *The American Collections of the University Museum: The Ancient Civilizations of Middle America,* by J. Alden Mason.

CONTENTS

Illustrations follow pages 82 and 114.

MAYA

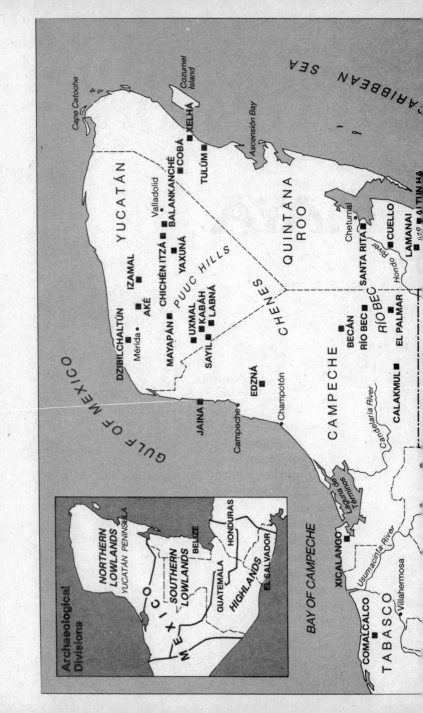

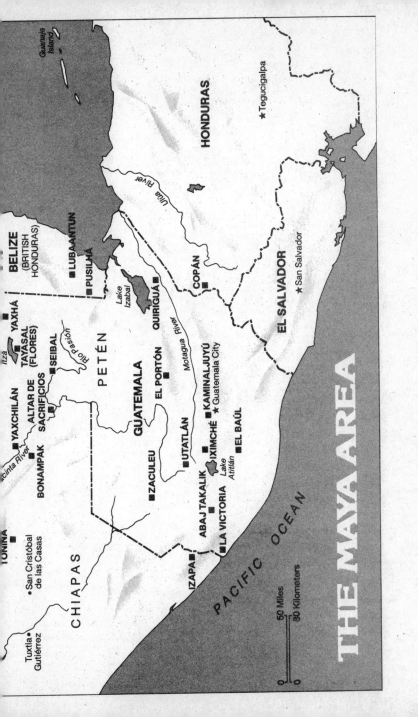

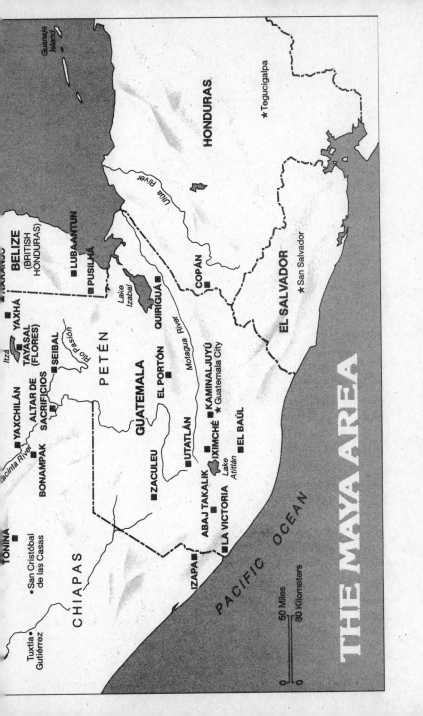

1 · DISCOVERY AND
CONQUEST: THE DEATH
OF A CIVILIZATION

When Spanish explorers first entered Mexico and Central America early in the sixteenth century, they revealed one of the greatest geographical mysteries of their age. Not only did they discover a vast new land—nameless and unmarked on existing charts—but they also opened the gateway to an astonishing panoply of indigenous, highly advanced peoples whose origins reached far back into antiquity.

From the outset of their explorations, the Spaniards found evidence of prosperous native kingdoms in the form of gold jewelry and exquisite works of art obtained in trade from Indians along Mexico's eastern coast. Eagerly the conquistadors flocked to these shores in the belief that here at last was the legendary El Dorado, which lured a generation of their countrymen onto the unknown Western Sea and ultimately led to the colonization of New Spain. For years they had searched in vain for the manifestations of this glorious illusion: the golden Temple of Doboyda, the jeweled sepulchers of Zenu, the elusive passage to Cathay and the Spice Islands, and a paradise rumored to exist in the Indies "where the sands sparkled with gems, and golden pebbles as large as birds' eggs were dragged in nets out of the rivers." Now it suddenly appeared as if these desperately sought dreams were about to materialize.

Driven by a restless spirit of adventure, inspired by religious zeal, hungry for the wealth and royal favors to be gained by conquering unclaimed frontiers, the Spaniards—the knights-errant of the Age of

Exploration—looked to these newly discovered lands with avid interest, unaware that their quest would signal the opening chapter in an historical event of extraordinary magnitude: the conquest of Mexico and Central America by a handful of intrepid Spanish soldiers in the face of overwhelming odds, unfamiliar terrain, and appalling hardships.

Nor did the Spaniards suspect that this conflict would result in the destruction of the last vestiges of the most brilliant civilization ever known in pre-Columbian America—that of the ancient Maya, whose long-forgotten cities shrouded in jungle embody an archaeological legacy that has held an almost obsessive fascination for scholars and laymen alike since the beginning of scientific exploration in the area during the mid-nineteenth century.

What the conquistadors encountered in Yucatán—then the heart of the Maya realm—was intriguing enough: populous cities filled with ornate palaces, temples raised on terraced pyramids, open courtyards, thriving markets, and paved stone roads. They were met by chieftains and priests bedecked in jaguar-skin skirts, bright feather capes, elaborate headdresses, and jewelry made of jade, gold, and shell. On the battlefield the Spaniards faced hordes of lavishly arrayed warriors outfitted with cotton armor, leather and tortoiseshell shields, plumed banners, lances, bows and arrows, and obsidian-tipped clubs. Astounded by these wondrous sights, the famous chronicler Bernal Díaz commented, ". . . we felt well content at having discovered such a country."

Unknown to the Spaniards, however, they were witnessing the final glimmer of far greater glories. At least two thousand years earlier, the Maya had emerged from shadowy origins to begin a steady climb toward what eventually became a civilization characterized by monumental architecture, superlative works of art, thriving trade networks, a system of writing and mathematics, a highly accurate calendar, a substantial body of astrological knowledge, and a powerful elite class who ruled over huge cities—all of which comprised one of the most original expressions of human ingenuity ever known.

On the map, the region occupied by the Maya comprises the southernmost section of a geographical zone known as Mesoamerica, which extends roughly from the drainages of the Sinaloa, Lerma, and Pánuco rivers in central Mexico southward into Honduras and El Salvador. First suggested in 1942 by the anthropologist Paul Kirchhoff, the term Mesoamerica defines those areas of Mexico and Central America that witnessed the development of advanced pre-Columbian civilizations such as the Olmec, Zapotec, Maya, Teotihuacáno, Toltec, Mixtec, and Aztec, all of which shared a number of interrelated cultural traits involving religious concepts, ritualism, architecture, arts and crafts, hieroglyphic writing, and calendrics.

Encompassing an expanse of approximately 125,000 square miles, the Maya realm consists of two distinct environments—lowlands and highlands—although it is usually subdivided by archaeologists into three sectors designated as the northern lowlands, southern lowlands, and highlands, or alternately as the Northern, Central, and Southern areas. Yet despite a sharp physical demarcation between the highlands and lowlands, these districts are characterized by an astonishing variety of terrain, vegetation, wildlife, and climate.

The southern border of the Maya area, along the Pacific littoral of Guatemala and El Salvador, is marked by mangrove swamps, lagoons, and flat alluvial plains some thirty to forty-five miles wide that run parallel to the coast. Beyond this point lies a chain of rugged mountains which extends from Chiapas in Mexico across Guatemala and into Central America and is dotted with volcanic cones, the highest being a 14,470-foot peak in Guatemala known as Tajumulco. Erosion and earthquakes have left these uplands deeply scarred, and the landscape is dissected by basins, rift valleys, steep gorges, and lakes fed by a network of rivers. Unlike the hot, humid coastal plains, the climate throughout the highlands is temperate, with average annual temperatures of between 60 and 80 degrees (Fahrenheit) and torrential rains that occur almost daily from May to December. Before the natural vegetation was decimated by centuries of human occupation and agriculture, much of this area was heavily forested—especially at higher elevations—and in a few remote sections there are still thick stands of evergreen and deciduous trees, including oak, pine, juniper, laurel, and cypress.

Toward the north the temperature rises, the vegetation becomes increasingly tropical, and the mountains yield to foothills and limestone formations which open almost imperceptibly onto an immense expanse of lowlands—the scene of the greatest triumphs of Maya civilization and, paradoxically, one of the least hospitable environments in the western hemisphere. Seldom exceeding seven hundred feet above sea level, this region constitutes a limestone plateau that covers the Petén district of northern Guatemala, Belize, western Honduras, the Yucatán Peninsula, and parts of eastern Chiapas and Tabasco. Enormous sections of this region are overgrown by dense rain forest consisting of mahogany, cedar, rubber trees, sapodilla, ceiba, breadnut *(ramón)*, wild fig, palms, ferns, and many other varieties of trees, shrubs, vines, and flowers. In the southern lowlands the terrain is punctuated by hills, steep ridges, and seasonal swamps or *bajos;* and a single range of metamorphic peaks—the Maya Mountains in southern Belize—rises to a maximum elevation of around three thousand feet. Four major river systems, supplied by numerous tributaries, drain this area, including the Usumacinta, Pasión, Motagua, and Belize rivers. A string of fourteen shallow lakes stretches across the center of the Petén, the largest of which is Lake Petén Itzá. Virtually all of the southern lowlands are plagued by heat, humidity, and heavy seasonal rains that vary from about 50 to 120 inches a year, although the rainfall becomes progressively less in the north, and semiarid conditions prevail near the coast of Yucatán. Average temperatures range from approximately 70 to 90 degrees during the rainy season (usually from May through October), but readings of 100 degrees or more are common in the dry months when there are no clouds to block the fierce tropical sun.

The northern lowlands encompass the upper portion of the Yucatán Peninsula, a thumb-shaped landmass projecting into the Gulf of Mexico. Within its boundaries are the Mexican states of Campeche, Yucatán, and Quintana Roo, though the entire peninsula is usually referred to collectively as Yucatán. Here the terrain becomes unrelentingly flat; its featureless vistas are broken only by a narrow string of hills called the Puuc (a Yucatecan word meaning ''hill''), which lie somewhat like an inverted V across northern Campeche and southwestern Yucatán. Because of its lower rainfall and thin, rocky soil, large sections of the Yucatán Peninsula cannot support a true rain forest, and its flora, although nearly impenetrable in places, consists primarily of low trees, thorny scrub, palmettos, and bushes. Lakes and rivers are almost nonexistent in this region due to the fact that its porous limestone surface (known as karst topography) does not retain moisture, and dependable sources of water are rare except where the limestone crust has collapsed into underground river systems, producing sinkholes or *cenotes* which are often quite deep.

So far as we know, the earliest recorded contact between Europeans and the Maya occurred during the last voyage made by Christopher Columbus to the New World in 1502. Near the island of Guanaja, off the northern coast of Honduras, his ships encountered a canoe carrying Indian traders who supposedly came from a province called *Maia* or *Maiam*, the name from which the word *Maya* was subsequently derived. It is not certain whether *Maia* referred to the Yucatán Peninsula or Honduras, and because Columbus sailed east after leaving Guanaja, he never visited the country described by his native informants.

Only vague references to *Maia* as reported by Columbus appeared in contemporary records, and the existence of the Maya did not become known to the outside world until 1517, when three ships commanded by Francisco Hernández de Córdova reached Cape Catoche on the northeastern tip of Yucatán after being blown off course by a storm. Weeks later the survivors of Córdova's expedition—almost dead from wounds, thirst, and starvation—arrived in Cuba with astonishing tales of mysterious cities discovered on Yucatán's coastline, and pitched battles waged against hordes of Maya warriors, one of which left Córdova himself mortally wounded. Most important, they brought back ornaments looted from Maya temples—necklaces, effigies, and diadems made of copper and low-grade gold!

However inferior the quality of the gold, the Spaniards' avarice was suddenly inflamed. Immediately the governor of Cuba, Diego Valásquez, organized another expedition under the command of his nephew, Juan de Grijalva. Setting out early in April of 1518, Grijalva's ships reconnoitered Yucatán's eastern coast between Cozumel Island and Ascensión Bay, then retraced Córdova's previous route around Cape Catoche, explored a large inlet now known as Laguna de Términos, and journeyed a few miles inland along the Río de Tabasco (later renamed Río de Grijalva), which empties into the Bay of Campeche. Near the mouth of this river the Spaniards encountered a group of Maya from whom they obtained a number of gold objects in trade. Here, too, they heard rumors of the fabled Aztec empire allegedly located toward the "direction of the sunset" in a region called *Méjico*. In an effort to verify these intriguing tales, Grijalva sailed up the Mexican coast past the Tonalá, Coatzacoalcos, and Jamapa rivers as far north as the present city of Veracruz. By then the accuracy of the reports could no longer be questioned: at the entrance of the Río Jamapa the explorers met Aztec emissaries, sent by their chieftain Montezuma, who brought large quantities of gold as a gift—a fatal mistake that was to cost Montezuma his empire and launch the Conquest of Mexico.

Lured by Grijalva's startling revelations, the illustrious conquistador Hernando Cortés marched into the heart of the Aztec realm in 1519 with soldiers, artillery, horses, and thousands of Indian allies—mostly Totonacs and Tlaxcalans, whose hatred of the Aztecs prompted them to join the Spaniards' cause—and trampled its glories to dust in one of history's most celebrated military campaigns. Within two years Cortés had defeated the Aztecs' once-feared armies, destroyed their magnificent capital of Tenochtitlán (rebuilt as Mexico City), and looted its treasuries of a fortune in gold, silver, and precious stones. Indeed, his stunning victory quickly opened the way for the tide of conquest and colonization to spread throughout the rest of Mexico and Central America, imposing upon their vanquished peoples a "new order" compounded of greed, exploitation, and the unyielding intolerance of the Spanish Inquisition.

With the collapse of the Aztec empire, vast sections of the Maya area soon began to fall under the Spaniards' rapacious yoke. In 1523 Cortés sent one of his captains, Pedro de Alvarado, with a force of approximately 420 soldiers reinforced by Indian auxiliaries, to conquer Guatemala and El Salvador, an assignment Alvarado carried out with relentless brutality. Early in 1524 an expedition led by Cristóbal de Olid was dispatched by Cortés to colonize Honduras, and although Olid was later killed in an ill-fated rebellion against Cortés, the pacification of Honduras was swiftly completed under Alvarado's direction. And in 1526 a wealthy adventurer named Francisco de Montejo received a royal decree authorizing him to undertake what would become the longest and most difficult campaign of the entire Conquest—the subjugation of Yucatán.

Montejo's first colony on Yucatán's eastern coast, established in the autumn of 1527, was promptly decimated by outbreaks of disease, threats of mutiny among his soldiers, and determined native resistance, thus forcing him to withdraw temporarily to Tabasco. Three years later, aided by his son, Francisco de Montejo the Younger, he invaded the peninsula from the direction of Campeche and attempted to found colonies in several different locations, including a garrison at the famous ruined city of Chichén Itzá. Eventually these settlements were also deserted because of unrelenting hardships, constant attacks by the Maya, and the growing disillusionment of his army, leaving the elder Montejo impoverished and bitterly disappointed by his failures.

Not until 1541 did Montejo the Younger, empowered by his aging father to carry on the venture, again return to Yucatán—this time with roughly 350 well-equipped soldiers augmented by a sizable force of Indian allies recruited among a group of Maya known as the Xiu, who had unexpectedly offered their support. A series of skillfully executed military expeditions were sent to subdue those provinces that refused to yield peacefully, and within less than a year, marked by bloody engagements against often superior native armies, Montejo succeeded in conquering the entire western half of the peninsula. Next he selected an ancient town called T'ho as the site of a permanent capital, and on January 6, 1542, he founded the "Very Noble and Loyal City of Mérida." Using this as a base of operations, Montejo gradually extended his campaign into the hostile districts to the north and east, and by the end of 1546 his troops had gained control over all of Yucatán.

Only one part of the Maya area still remained free of Spanish encroachment: the jungle-covered lowlands of northern Guatemala that now comprise the Department of Petén. Even though much of this forbidding wilderness was then uninhabited, some sections contained scattered groups of Maya, the largest of which was the Itzá, whose capital of Tayasal was situated on an island in Lake Petén Itzá. Yet despite its isolation, the rapid pace of colonial expansion on the Petén's borders eventually brought the full impact of the Conquest upon the Itzá with shattering force. In 1618 two Franciscan friars, Juan de Orbita and Bartolomé de Fuensalida, attempted unsuccessfully to introduce Christianity at Tayasal. Four years later another missionary named Diego Delgado was taken captive and sacrificed by the Itzá, and when subsequent efforts at peaceful conversion failed, the governor of Yucatán, Martín de Ursúa, resolved to subdue the Itzá by military action.

Early in March of 1697, Ursúa arrived at Lake Petén Itzá with an impressive array of infantry, cavalry, artillery, and Indian auxiliaries. After constructing a large galley from which Tayasal could be assaulted by water, he launched an attack that quickly turned into a massacre. With their infantry crowded aboard the ship, the Spaniards approached Tayasal under a protective barrage of musket fire. While an advance guard of soldiers swarmed onto the island and engaged its defenders in hand-to-hand combat, gunners on the boat continued firing at the terrified Indians with devastating effect. Hundreds were either killed outright or drowned as they sought to escape by swimming across the lake, and within a matter of hours the Itzá legions were hopelessly routed, enabling Ursúa and his victorious army to occupy the city.

With Tayasal's swift demise, the last stronghold of sustained Maya resistance was decisively crushed, and its survivors were inexorably consigned to the ominous destiny already inflicted upon the rest of their kinspeople. Marching behind the banner of "God, Glory, and Gold," the conquistadors—equipped with arquebuses, artillery, cavalry, metal armor, crossbows, and swords, none of which the Indians had seen before—accomplished their goals with unyielding determination. In their wake came hordes of colonists whose greed would wreak further havoc upon the Maya, reducing them to a life of persecution, servitude, and poverty. Even the remarkable legacy of their past, as evidenced by ruined cities and plundered works of art, rapidly faded into oblivion in the prolonged struggle for survival that now ensued.

From the beginning of Spanish supremacy in Mexico and Central America, the relegation of the Indians to various forms of slavery and the confiscation of their lands became an accepted practice. Initially the principal instrument for achieving these ends was the so-called *encomienda*. Under this quasi-feudal system the conquistadors were awarded land grants together with the services of natives who became vassals of the landowners. Indians thus conscripted were transplanted from their villages to the estates of the *encomenderos*, where, in addition to supplying labor for mining, construction projects, agriculture, and household duties, they were required to pay regular tributes in such products as cloth, cacao, game animals, fowl, cotton, beeswax, and salt. In theory, the granting of an *encomienda* imposed certain obligations on the landowner regarding the humane treatment of native workers. Yet these were frequently ignored or circumvented, and the conditions under which the Indians existed quickly became intolerable. Along with the burden of enforced labor and tributes, any expression of resistance or disloyalty toward the *encomenderos* brought severe punishment in the form of beatings, imprisonment, torture, or execution. Quite often, Indians guilty of "rebellious" acts were sold into outright bondage, and the exploitation of slaves grew into a profitable business, resulting in incredible tyranny and suffering.

Due largely to agitation for reform by certain members of the Dominican Order (led by the brilliant humanitarian Bartolomé de Las Casas), the "New Laws of the Indies" were enacted in 1542, aimed at abolishing both slavery and the *encomiendas*, neither of which was looked upon favorably by Spain's emperor, Charles V. But the outcry by colonists against these changes was so vehement that the New Laws were later modified, allowing many *encomiendas* to endure well into the eighteenth century. And despite the permanent outlawing of slavery, subtler forms of bondage survived in the Maya area until the late 1800s—namely "debt peonage," whereby laborers were indentured to the landowners in exchange for "loans" that they could seldom repay.

Even more serious than these abuses, however, was the introduction of European diseases against which the Maya had no natural immunity. Among the worst were smallpox, measles, and influenza; and many researchers believe malaria and hookworm, extremely prevalent in the region today, may originally have been brought to America by slaves from Africa, where both diseases were endemic. Entire towns were repeatedly decimated by epidemics—particularly of smallpox and measles—resulting in appalling fatalities throughout the area. So horrifying were the effects of European diseases that some authorities estimate the population of certain Maya groups was reduced by seventy-five to ninety percent in the century immediately after the Conquest.

Added to the other misfortunes suffered by the Maya was the systematic effort by the Spaniards to eradicate their culture. Many of their towns were forcibly abandoned and the inhabitants removed, either to settlements established by the *encomenderos* or to larger centers where the tasks of administrative control and conversion to Christianity could be more easily carried out. Native concepts of government and city planning were remodeled along European lines, and the colonists sought to impose their own social, political, and economic institutions, usually with exceedingly disruptive consequences.

Simultaneously, Franciscan and Dominican friars undertook the complete obliteration of Maya religious beliefs. Important temples, shrines, and altars were pulled down or smashed. Any attempt to worship idols was strictly forbidden. No one was permitted to wear ceremonial costumes, the enactment of pagan rituals was vigorously suppressed, and steps were taken to eliminate the influence of native priests. Instruction in the Catholic faith was mandatory, and those Indians who refused to accept conversion were subjected to harsh penalties.

Although some missionaries worked devotedly to protect the natives against religious and civil abuses (often evoking widespread hostility among the *encomenderos* by their actions), Christianity was frequently enforced by brutal methods. Various sixteenth-century accounts document the use of torture during the interrogation of Indians suspected of idolatry. Whipping, beating, mutilation, and scalding with boiling water were commonly employed in such cases, and chronicles written around 1563 by the *alcalde* of Mérida, Diego Quijada, describe other types of torture used by the friars: twisting ropes around the arms and legs with sticks, the use of pulleys to stretch the joints, scorching the flesh with wax tapers, and forcing water down a victim's throat to make his stomach swell, then standing on him until "water mixed with blood" flowed from his mouth, nose, and ears.

Such acts inevitably prompted the Maya to formulate desperate plots to overthrow their oppressors. Armed uprisings periodically erupted in various parts of the region, resulting in bloody massacres of colonists and the destruction of their towns, livestock, orchards, and crops. As late as 1847 the most successful of these rebellions—the famous War of the Castes—broke out in Yucatán, and before it was finally quelled large sections of the peninsula had been overrun by native armies, most of the haciendas in their path were burned, and the city of Mérida itself was seriously threatened. Yet none of these insurrections achieved anything more than momentary success. Each time, the Maya were unable to sustain their victories, and they invariably found themselves reduced to their previous status while their cultural heritage continued to fade into obscurity.

In Yucatán these objectives were initiated largely by one man, a religious fanatic whose curious complexity made him both a relentless enemy and a dedicated student of Maya culture. In 1549 a Franciscan friar named Diego de Landa arrived in Mérida to serve in the nearby monastery of Izamal. The spirit of the Inquisition burned brightly in the young cleric's determination to perform his duties, and he soon acquired a reputation as a missionary of extraordinary zeal. Wherever he traveled throughout Yucatán he instituted the swift destruction of all vestiges of the native religion; nor did he hesitate to apply the severe measures by which he believed pagans were "cleansed," frequently resorting to the most persuasive methods of torture.

Enraged by the Indians' stubborn refusal to renounce their deeply rooted beliefs, Landa continually sought more forceful ways of eradicating their heritage. Such an opportunity arose in the town of Maní, forty miles southeast of Mérida, where he discovered a repository of ancient hieroglyphic books. Here Landa committed an act of wanton destruction that robbed future scholars of what was undoubtedly one of the most important sources of information about the Maya to survive into historic times. He ordered the manuscripts confiscated and publicly burned.

On July 12, 1562, the disastrous auto-da-fé was carried out. Landa later wrote that because the books "contained nothing in which there was not to be seen superstitions and lies of the devil, we burned them all. . . ." In an instant an archaeological treasure of inestimable value lay smoldering in the embers of Landa's terrible deed.

The incident was particularly regrettable since there is considerable evidence that Maya literature had reached a remarkably high degree of development. Their books—or codices, as they are properly called— consisted of elongated strips of paper (approximately eight to nine inches wide and several yards long) made from the bark of the wild fig tree. These were then strengthened by the application of a natural gum substance and coated with white stucco. Onto this surface scribes laboriously drew figures and hieroglyphic symbols, coloring them with vegetable and mineral paints. Each strip of paper was folded back-to-back like a screen to form pages and may have been enclosed between wooden or leather covers, making a volume not unlike a modern book in outward appearance.

Only three Maya codices of unquestionable authenticity are presently known to exist. Apparently produced in Yucatán sometime between A.D. 1200 and 1450, they ultimately found their way to Europe, probably sent there as mementos by Spanish soldiers or colonists. The finest example, the Dresden Codex, was discovered in Vienna in 1739 and is now owned by the Sächsische Landesbibliothek in Dresden, Germany. Sections of two codices were found in Spain during the 1860s, but later examination showed them to be part of the same document now designated as the Codex Tro-Cortesianus, which is preserved in the Museo de América in Madrid. The third manuscript, the Codex Peresianus, is in the possession of the Bibliothèque Nationale in Paris where it accidentally came to light in 1860 in a box of discarded papers. Unfortunately, much of this codex is missing and the surviving pages are only partially legible due to their decayed condition.

Another codex, recently acquired by the Museo Nacional de Antropología in Mexico, was placed on display in 1971 at the Grolier Club in New York City as part of an exhibition entitled "Ancient Maya Calligraphy." According to Michael D. Coe, a noted archaeologist at Yale University and the show's organizer, this manuscript—an eleven-page fragment known as the Grolier Codex—was part of a funerary offering found in a cave either in Yucatán or Chiapas. Attached to the codex was a piece of unpainted paper that produced a radiocarbon date of A.D. 1230 (plus or minus a possible error of 130 years). Yet despite this fact, the eminent British epigrapher J. Eric S. Thompson denounced it as a fake. Working solely from photographs of the codex, Thompson discovered what he termed "glaring inaccuracies" in its iconography, and an article on his disclosures in the London *Times* suggested that the inscriptions might have been cleverly painted by forgers on blank sheets of ancient paper. Emphatically rejecting these charges, Coe maintains that the quality of the codex rules out any chance of fraud, but pending the outcome of further studies, the controversy over its authenticity remains unresolved.

Valuable though these codices are to archaeological research, they reveal nothing whatsoever about actual historical occurrences. Instead they deal entirely with astronomy, calendrics, divination, and ritualism. For example, the Dresden Codex contains data on the cycles of the planet Venus, tables for predicting lunar eclipses, and divinatory almanacs. Similarly, the Codex Tro-Cortesianus is concerned with ritualism and prophecy, and the Peresianus manuscript is largely devoted to ceremonies associated with various aspects of the calendar.

We can only speculate regarding other subjects the Maya treated in their codices, although several sixteenth-century Spanish chroniclers reported the existence of books involving genealogy, history, mythology, and science. What priceless records illuminating otherwise obscure facets of Maya civilization were destroyed in Landa's auto-da-fé will never be known. Quite possibly the books at Maní might have clarified a number of questions now confronting archaeologists. Surely the ravaged manuscripts would have been enormously helpful in deciphering Maya hieroglyphic writing, only a portion of which can presently be read. Equally frustrating is the fact that fragments of codices have been excavated in tombs, raising the tantalizing possibility that hieroglyphic books may frequently have been included among funerary offerings. Although centuries of exposure to moisture make it unlikely that readable specimens could have survived under such conditions, several badly decayed pieces of codices were found at the sites of Uaxactún, Altun Ha, and Guaytan, and a nearly complete specimen was unearthed at El Mirador in Chiapas, but unfortunately its pages were so tightly cemented by the effects of water that it was impossible to separate them.

Other indications of Maya literary achievements have come down to us via historical sources. After the Conquest, missionaries began teaching the Indians to read and write the Spanish alphabet and use it in translating their own languages. Oddly enough, it was necessary to invent only two new alphabetical symbols in order to represent all the sounds present in the Maya tongues. One of these is a *sh* phoneme designated by a Portuguese *x* and pronounced as in Uxmal (oosh-mal); the other is a *tz* sound first indicated by an inverted *c* (ɔ) and now written as *dz* in words like Dzibilchaltún (tzi-bil-chal-tun). Such instruction was originally undertaken to facilitate the propagation of Christianity, but inevitably it was used by the Maya to compile narratives intended to preserve their rapidly passing heritage.

Several of these documents have survived to convey in eloquent language the recollections of anonymous authors concerning history, folklore, and traditions. From the Guatemalan highlands came a manuscript known as the *Popol Vuh*, a fragmentary record of the myths, cosmology, and traditions of the Quiché Maya. Apart from its ethnohistoric significance, the *Popol Vuh* is actually a long epic poem of extraordinary literary merit; and although the original manuscript— probably written during the sixteenth century in Utatlán, the capital city of the Quiché—subsequently disappeared, a copy of an early translation was found in the mid-1800s. Another work discovered in Guatemala, the *Annals of the Càkchiquels,* contains similar information about the Cakchiquel tribe and deals in considerable detail with their history up through the period of the Conquest. And an important collection of native chronicles from Yucatán was assembled in the *Books of Chilam Balam*, named after an order of ''Jaguar Priests'' renowned for their abilities as prophets. Sections of about fourteen of these manuscripts have turned up so far, each bearing the name of the town where it was written, and while they pertain mainly to folklore, calendrics, astrology, and medicine, three of them recount historical incidents.

Some scholars believe that portions of the *Books of Chilam Balam* were translated directly from hieroglyphic codices—an intriguing possibility in view of archaeological research that has verified certain details relating to specific cities, ruling families, and political alliances mentioned in these works. Indeed, if the historical information in the *Books of Chilam Balam* was actually based on hieroglyphic texts (as opposed to oral traditions), we can appreciate even more fully the potential loss to science inflicted by Landa's burning of the codices at Maní. Assuming they could be deciphered, it is reasonable to suppose that these books might have shed light on a broad spectrum of factual events. No doubt other collections of codices also existed at the time of the Conquest which were subsequently lost or destroyed; one such group of documents was reportedly in the possession of the Itzá at Tayasal as late as 1697, but no one knows what became of them after that city's downfall.

In spite of the tragic vandalism wrought by Landa's inquisitorial fervor, his career unexpectedly resulted in a scholarly contribution of unique importance. To prepare himself for his ecclesiastical labors he had plunged into a thorough study of Maya culture shortly after his arrival in Yucatán. He soon became fluent in the Yucatecan language and spent much of his time with members of Maya ruling families—especially the Xiu and Cocom, who were formerly among the region's most powerful dynasties—questioning them about every aspect of native life. Even during his wide-ranging crusades to remote sections of the peninsula, he diligently gathered information from local inhabitants whenever the opportunity arose.

About 1566 he began writing a treatise on the Maya based upon his earlier studies. Landa may have undertaken the project as a guide for younger missionaries or in the hope of lessening official criticism of his brutal treatment of the Indians and the auto-da-fé at Maní. Indeed, in 1563 he had been recalled to Spain to account for his actions before the Council of the Indies, only to return triumphantly ten years later after being elected Bishop of Yucatán. Whatever his purpose in writing the work, Landa's manuscript, entitled *Relación de las Cosas de Yucatán*, is the most extensive ethnographic account of the area to emerge from the colonial period and has therefore been of immense value to archaeologists in reconstructing various facets of Maya civilization.

Unfortunately, the original draft of the *Relación* was eventually lost, and it was not until 1863 that a French antiquarian, Abbé Charles Étienne Brasseur de Bourbourg, discovered a copy in the library of the Academia de Historia in Madrid. Some sections of the text were missing, but enough remained intact to provide detailed descriptions of ceremonies, religious beliefs, arts, social customs, warfare, and a wealth of other information. Of particular interest are Landa's notes on Maya hieroglyphic writing and calendrics, and he had even attempted to devise an "alphabet" for use in reading the inscriptions. Essentially it consisted of drawings representing figures or objects, which, when pronounced in Yucatec, sounded similar to the characters of the Spanish alphabet; for instance, one of the signs for *a* illustrated by Landa is the head of a turtle, and the Yucatecan word for turtle is *ac*. It was a literal phonetic approach that was later dismissed by most scholars as useless in understanding the complexities of the hieroglyphs. Yet a careful reevaluation of Landa's alphabet in recent years has shown that although his methods reflect serious misconceptions concerning the structure of Maya writing, he nevertheless provided—perhaps unwittingly—certain clues which have helped epigraphers establish the fact

Landa's alphabet.

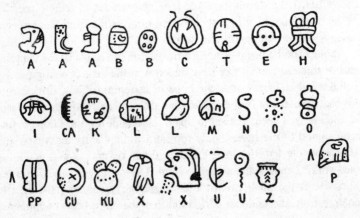

16

that the glyphs are partly phonetic. Moreover, Landa's contribution to our knowledge of the calendrical glyphs proved to be so significant that the *Relación* has often been called the nearest thing to a Rosetta Stone (the celebrated key to the decipherment of Egyptian hieroglyphics) ever to come out of the Maya area.

Although Landa's *Relación* constitutes our most exhaustive early source pertaining to Maya culture, it is by no means the only such document in existence. Valuable ethnological data are found in a number of accounts written by churchmen, native chroniclers, and historians during the colonial era. Francisco Ximénez, a Dominican friar who spent years among the Quiché, Cakchiquel, and Tzutuhil tribes in the Guatemalan highlands, published several books dealing with native history and customs. Eyewitness reports of the Itzá at Tayasal are preserved in the journals of the Franciscan monk Andrés de Avendaño, as well as in the historical works of Juan de Villaguitierre Soto-Mayor. Important material on the Maya of Yucatán is contained in the writings of Gaspar Antonio Chi (a member of the Xiu family who probably served as one of Landa's informants), Cervantes de Salazar, Bernardo de Lizana, and Diego López de Cogolludo, whose *Historia de Yucatán* (1688) is among the most useful sources. References to the Maya also appear in various general histories of Mexico and Central America, including those by Las Casas, Oviedo, Gómara, Torquemada, Clavijero, and the famous chronicler of the Conquest, Bernal Díaz del Castillo.

Especially notable was the work of Antonio de Ciudad Real, a Franciscan friar who came to Yucatán in 1573. This remarkable scholar-missionary quickly developed a keen interest in Maya culture and learned to speak Yucatec so fluently that Cogolludo called him "the greatest master of the [native tongue] this country has produced." Aside from his linguistic studies, Ciudad Real traveled extensively in Mexico and Central America, writing on various aspects of aboriginal life; and his most prodigious undertaking was a dictionary of the Yucatecan language with Spanish translations known as the *Gran diccionario o calepino de la lengua maya de Yucatán*, a project that reportedly required forty years to complete and filled six volumes of more than two hundred pages each.

Some time later the manuscript of this monumental work disappeared without a trace, but in the 1860s Brasseur de Bourbourg purchased a dictionary matching the description of Ciudad Real's *Calepino* for four pesos in a secondhand bookshop in Mexico City. It had apparently been written in a monastery at Motul, near Mérida, where Ciudad Real is known to have resided for several years, and examination by the Yucatecan linguist and epigrapher Juan Martínez Hernández established that this document—known today as the Motul Dictionary—is almost certainly a part of Ciudad Real's long-missing *Calepino*. Now a priceless possession of the John Carter Brown Library in Providence, Rhode Island, it ranks among the most important aids to Maya research ever discovered.

Except for the efforts of these authors, we would know practically nothing about the Maya as they existed in the years before prolonged European contact radically altered their culture. Such matters held little interest for the fortune-hungry colonists who overran the country after the Conquest; their primary concerns were land, cheap labor, and the expanding economic frontiers of a newly won empire. Few of them had any concern for the past achievements of pagan "devil worshippers." Nor could the Maya themselves hope to preserve more than desultory fragments of their legacy. By then most of their cities already lay in ruins or had recently been deserted, leaving them to the ravages of time and the all-pervasive jungle. With the passing of the ruling classes and native priesthood, such esoteric knowledge as astronomy, calendrics, hieroglyphic writing, and mathematics soon faded from memory. Innumerable examples of Maya art and architecture were deliberately destroyed by the Spaniards, and the suppression of the religious beliefs that had inspired these creations extinguished any further artistic expression. Worst of all, the obliteration of their civilization was so thorough, and so swiftly were alien values and concepts substituted in its place, that there was no possibility that future generations could ever resurrect it.

Yet the Maya had declined not only because of the onslaught of European invaders, although this was certainly the decisive factor. There is considerable evidence that their culture was plagued by internal problems long before the Spaniards' arrival. For almost a century prior to the Conquest, Yucatán was the scene of civil unrest, internecine warfare, and social upheaval. Earlier attempts at centralized government had broken down, and the entire peninsula was split into sixteen independent provinces ruled by chieftains who constantly fought among themselves. In Guatemala the two strongest nations—the Quiché and Cakchiquel—had likewise joined with their respective allies in a prolonged struggle for control of the highlands. Everywhere militarism supplanted the creative endeavors of past centuries, and there was a marked disintegration in art, architecture, and intellectual pursuits. Uprisings, intrigue, and political assassinations had beset nearly all of the Maya area, touching off smoldering enmities that the Spaniards quickly exploited to their own advantage.

Like acts of punishment from the gods, a series of natural catastrophes overtook the Maya in the midst of these tribulations. Native chronicles record a severe hurricane that laid waste to vast portions of Yucatán sometime around 1464. Sixteen years later a devastating pestilence swept through the area, and in 1514 an epidemic (probably of smallpox introduced from Spanish colonies in Panama) broke out, causing its victims to suffer "great pestules which rotted their bodies with a terrible stench." According to another account, swarms of locusts ravaged Yucatán for five years until "nothing green was left, and they experienced such a famine that people fell dead on the roads."

From the *Books of Chilam Balam* a cryptic chant warned the Maya of portents heralding the end of their age:

> *Eat, eat, thou hast bread;*
> *Drink, drink, thou hast water;*
> *On that day, dust possesses the earth,*
> *On that day, a blight is on the face of the earth,*
> *On that day, a cloud arises,*
> *On that day, a mountain rises,*
> *On that day, a strong man seizes the land,*
> *On that day, things fall to ruin,*

> *On that day, the tender leaf is destroyed,*
> *On that day, the dying eyes are closed,*
> *On that day, three signs are on the tree,*
> *On that day, three generations hang there,*
> *On that day, the battle flag is raised,*
> *And they are scattered afar in the forests.*

History's eternal drama had again been enacted. Maya civilization—one of the most remarkable expressions of higher attainments in pre-Columbian America—was destroyed, utterly obliterated from the stage of human affairs. Everything the Maya had accomplished lay buried in their ruined cities, enshrouded in the primeval jungle out of which they were spawned centuries before. For the surviving Maya only two paths of survival lay open: a pallid existence of servitude under foreign overlords, or the alternative which claimed those who sought to escape from oppression by fleeing to remote areas, to live like outcasts "scattered afar in the forests."

It now remained for men possessed of insatiable curiosity about the past to reclaim the Maya from permanent obscurity, men of fewer worldly ambitions than their Spanish predecessors—explorers, historians, and archaeologists to whom the quest for knowledge was as enticing as the lure of gold.

2 · JOHN LLOYD STEPHENS:
THE CITIES COME TO LIGHT

In 1836 a meeting occurred in London which was to have a profound effect upon the rediscovery of Maya civilization. John Lloyd Stephens, an American lawyer with a predilection for travel and antiquities, encountered the English artist and architect Frederick Catherwood. Although they met by accident, the course of their lives had been conspicuously similar, for both men had traveled extensively and were deeply immersed in Greco-Roman, Egyptian, and Near Eastern archaeology.

Stephens was born in Shrewsbury, New Jersey, in 1805, the son of a moderately wealthy merchant named Benjamin Stephens. He spent his childhood in New York City, where his family moved in 1806, and after graduating from Columbia University he entered Tapping Reeve's Law School in Litchfield, Connecticut. Eventually he joined his father's mercantile company, opened a law office on Wall Street, and became involved in politics, but these pursuits did not satisfy his adventurous nature and he periodically abandoned them in order to travel.

While on an extended trip in 1835, he toured France, Italy, and Greece, visited Constantinople, and journeyed into Russia, Poland, and Austria. The next year he sailed up the Nile from Cairo to Aswan, ventured across the Sinai Peninsula to Mount Sinai and Aqaba, explored the ruined city of Petra in Arabia, and traveled to Jerusalem, the Dead Sea, Nazareth, and Beirut. At the conclusion of these journeys, Stephens published two highly successful books—*Incidents of Travel in Egypt, Arabia Petraea, and the Holy Land* (1837) and *Incidents of Travel in Greece, Turkey, Russia, and Poland* (1838)—which firmly established his reputation as a travel writer of exceptional ability.

Frederick Catherwood had long been a serious student of archaeology. After spending his youth in the London suburb of Hoxton, where he was born in 1799, he worked as an architect's apprentice, studied drawing and painting, and exhibited at the Royal Academy. He later went to Italy, Sicily, and Greece to study classical architecture and sculpture, and from there he traveled widely in Egypt, making scale drawings of archaeological monuments at Memphis, Abydos, Karnak, Deir el-Bahri, Luxor, and Thebes. In 1823 Catherwood was engaged as an architectural consultant by Mehemet Ali to supervise the restoration of Cairo's mosques, and the following year he set off on a journey through Sinai, Arabia, and the Holy Land, during which he drew a detailed plan of the Mosque of Omar in Jerusalem and sketched the ruins of Jarash, Baalbek, and Palmyra.

This experience left Catherwood unusually adept at rendering skillful reproductions of sculpture, architecture, and inscriptions. Unlike the works of so many artist-travelers of the period who indulged in romantic fantasies, his drawings reflected the unerring pen and critical eye of an accomplished draftsman and scholar, and he often employed a camera lucida to ensure the accuracy of minute details. The fact that Stephens was guided by the same integrity in his literary observations made their meeting a fortunate one in view of future events. Both men were destined to play singularly important roles in resurrecting Maya civilization from obscurity.

Soon after returning from his Near Eastern tour in 1836, Stephens read an account written by an officer in the Spanish army—a Captain Antonio del Río—describing a ruined city known as Palenque, located in the rain forest of Chiapas in southern Mexico. Working with a crew of Indian laborers, del Río had partially excavated some of its buildings in 1787, but the report of his findings vanished into an archive in Madrid until 1822, when an English translation was published in London. Entitled *Description of the Ruins of an Ancient City* and illustrated with engravings by a German artist and soldier of fortune,

Jean-Frédéric Waldeck, it was this work that first awakened Stephens' interest in Maya archaeology.

Several years later a friend showed Stephens a portfolio containing Waldeck's drawings of ruins in Yucatán. Waldeck—who among his many exploits is said to have studied painting under Jacques Louis David, served with Napoleon's army in Italy and Egypt, traveled extensively in Africa, and sailed with the notorious Lord Cochrane during Chile's war of independence against Spain—had only recently returned from a lengthy sojourn in Mexico. In 1838 he published a volume entitled *Voyage Pittoresque et Archéologique dans la Province d'Yucatán,* its pages filled with engravings of Maya sculpture, architecture, and inscriptions executed in a style reminiscent of Piranesi and embellished by Waldeck's vivid imagination. Figures of richly attired lords appeared in unmistakably Phoenician dress, shattered buildings were reconstructed to resemble Egyptian and Assyrian temples, and he even depicted certain sculptured heads found among the ruins as those of elephants. Nonetheless, the exotic images of rulers and gods, ornate monuments, and intricate decorative motifs adorning structures of seemingly Herculean proportions excited Stephens' imagination.

His interest was further heightened by a series of books known as *Antiquities of Mexico,* the work of an eccentric Irish nobleman named Edward King, the Viscount of Kingsborough. While studying an Aztec codex in the Bodleian Library at Oxford in 1814, Lord Kingsborough had succumbed to the lure of Mexican and Central American archaeology, and thereafter it became an ill-fated obsession. For years he persistently sought everything on the subject available in European museums and archives, and between 1831 and 1848 the results of his labors appeared in nine enormous folio volumes printed on handmade paper and illustrated with etchings and lithographs of pre-Columbian sculpture, architecture, and codices. Out of the jumbled text—written in Latin, Greek, Hebrew, Sanskrit, and English—emerged the author's firm conviction that the American Indians were descendants of the biblical Lost Tribes of Israel. But Kingsborough's admirable attempt to prove this theory eventually brought about his untimely demise. He died in a debtor's prison, unable to pay the staggering expense of his publications.

Other reports of ruins in Mexico and Central America soon came to Stephens' attention: a volume entitled *Antiquités Mexicaines* by a retired captain of dragoons named Guillermo Dupaix, who made three expeditions in the early 1800s to survey archaeological sites in central and southern Mexico; an article by a Yucatecan diplomat, Lorenzo de Zavala, containing a description of the ruins of Uxmal in Yucatán; the writings of the renowned German naturalist and explorer Alexander von Humboldt, whose famous treatise on Mexico, *Vues des Cordillères et Monuments des Peuples Indigènes de l'Amérique*, appeared in France in 1814; and an entry in the *Proceedings of the American Antiquarian Society* by Juan Galindo, an Irish-born soldier, adventurer, and civil servant then residing in Guatemala, which described a vast ruined city known as Copán, hidden in the wilderness of western Honduras. Finally Stephens' curiosity was aroused beyond resistance, and in the spring of 1839 he announced his intention to visit Central America in an effort to conduct what he termed "an unbiased investigation" of these mysterious ruins.

Not surprisingly, his plan touched off a flurry of controversy. The public's imagination, already excited by sensational archaeological discoveries in Italy, Greece, the Near East, and Egypt, was captivated by Stephens' intriguing quest. But professional historians were openly skeptical of its merits. Most scholars viewed the American Indians as having never risen above a condition of barest savagery, and the suggestion that civilizations of the highest order had once flourished in the western hemisphere was unacceptable in academic circles. At that time few systematic excavations had been carried out anywhere in America, and prevailing theories concerning its antiquities were largely based upon studies of widely scattered museum collections or pure speculation. Many important ethnohistoric documents, such as Landa's *Relación*, still lay undiscovered in various libraries, and the eyewitness accounts of sixteenth-century Spanish explorers, who first observed the splendid achievements of the Aztecs, Maya, and Incas before their destruction, were either ignored or discounted. It was generally agreed that the conquistadors had been blinded by grandiose illusions; their descriptions of sprawling cities, lavish temples and palaces, superb works of art, and treasures of gold, silver, and precious stones were viewed as exaggerations or outright fantasies.

The attitude of most scholars was aptly expressed by the Scottish historian William Robertson when he wrote in his widely read *History of America* (1777): "America was not peopled by any nation of the ancient continent, which had made considerable progress in civilization. The inhabitants of the New World were in a state of society so extremely rude as to be unacquainted with those arts which are the first essays of human ingenuity in its advance towards improvement. Even the most celebrated nations of America were strangers to many of those simple inventions which were almost coeval with society in other parts of the world, and were known in the earliest periods of civil life with which we have acquaintance."

Robertson further declared that "neither the Mexicans nor Peruvians [were] entitled to rank with those nations which merit the name civilized." Regarding the magnificent Aztec and Maya cities that had so astounded early chroniclers, he insisted they were "more fit to be the habitation of men just emerging from barbarity than the residence of a polished people. . . . Nor does the fabric of their temples and other public edifices appear to have been such as entitled them to the high praise bestowed upon them by many Spanish authors. . . . Such structures convey no high idea of progress in art and ingenuity; and one can hardly conceive that [buildings] more crude and simple could have occurred to a nation in its first efforts towards erecting any great work. . . ."

In view of this sentiment, Stephens was acutely aware that in the event his search proved successful he would need evidence to support his discoveries. No one was better qualified to provide such material than his friend Frederick Catherwood, whose superb drawings of Egyptian, Greek, and Roman antiquities had achieved considerable recognition. Eager for an opportunity to explore new areas, Catherwood (who had recently arrived in New York from England, joined an architectural firm, and opened an exhibition of huge panoramas depicting scenes from his earlier travels) promptly accepted Stephens' offer to accompany him. As their first objective, they decided to seek the ancient city of Copán in Honduras.

On the eve of their departure, Stephens was awarded the post of United States ambassador to Central America, a position for which he had applied upon the sudden death of the former minister. His appointment was especially fortunate, since the countries Stephens intended to visit were locked in the midst of violent internal disturbances. Rebellious armies were fighting for political control of Central America's fledgling republics. Opposing factions within the contending forces were battling among themselves; attempts to preserve law and order had broken down, and the countryside teemed with marauding soldiers, bandits, and smugglers. All things considered, the situation was hardly encouraging to travelers entering upon a purely scholarly quest, though Stephens believed his diplomatic passport would afford some degree of immunity from these dangers.

In October of 1839 the explorers embarked by ship for Belize in British Honduras. From there they boarded a steamer that sailed due south to Punta Gorda, then up the Río Dulce to Lake Izabal, a short distance inland from the northeastern coast of Guatemala. At a small village situated on the southern edge of the lake, they hired guides and pack mules for the overland journey across a rugged barrier known as Mico Mountain into the war-torn interior of Guatemala.

Slowly they ascended the mountain's treacherous slopes toward what they hoped would be the ruins of Copán. Once engulfed by the tangled rain forest blanketing their route, Stephens had sufficient reason to question the wisdom of his undertaking. With each mile it became increasingly difficult to imagine that a civilization had ever flourished in such hostile surroundings, and they proceeded, as Stephens recalled, "with the hope rather than the expectation of finding wonders."

Of the hazards that befell them from the outset of their journey, Stephens wrote: "The ascent began precipitously and by an extraordinary passage, a narrow gulley worn by the tracks of mules and the washing of mountain torrents. It was so deep that the sides were higher than our heads, and so narrow that we could barely pass through without touching them. Our whole caravan moved singly through this muddly defile. The muleteers scattered among them and on the bank above, extricating the mules as they stuck fast, raising them as they fell, arranging their cargoes, cursing, shouting, and lashing them on; if one stopped, all behind were blocked up, unable to turn. Any sudden start pressed us against the sides of the gulley, and there was no small danger of getting a leg crushed. Emerging from this defile, we came again to deep mudholes and projecting roots of trees, which added to the difficulty of a steep ascent. . . . The woods were of impenetrable thickness and we could see nothing but the detestable path before us. . . . We were dragged through mudholes, squeezed in gulleys, knocked against trees, and tumbled over roots. Every step required care and great physical exertion, and . . . I felt that our inglorious epitaph might well read: 'tossed over the head of a mule, brained by the trunk of a mahogany tree, and buried in the mud of Mico Mountain.'"

Eventually they emerged into thickly forested highlands, crossed the Río Motagua, and ascended a volcanic plateau near Guatemala's eastern border. But scarcely had the physical rigors of their journey eased when they encountered political dangers. Upon entering the village of Camotán, a few miles from their destination, they were suddenly "arrested" by a band of soldiers, Indians, and mestizos—"ragged and ferocious-looking fellows," wrote Stephens, "armed with staves of office, swords, clubs, muskets, and machetes. . . ." When the officer in charge of the group examined Stephens' diplomatic passport, he angrily declared it invalid and ordered them held in confinement during a precarious night of negotiations. Stephens' refusal to surrender his passport, even with "two assassin scoundrels," as he described them, pointing muskets at his chest, almost brought the expedition to a disastrous end. But the matter was finally resolved as mysteriously as it began, and the next morning they were released without explanation. Hastily they departed Camotán, crossed into Honduras, and proceeded to a remote Indian settlement bearing the name of Copán, a disappointing place, which, Stephens reported, "consisted of half a dozen miserable huts thatched with corn."

Here again the appearance of outsiders was an unwelcome event. No one knew anything about ruins such as Stephens described, but all agreed that the one person who might be of assistance was Don Gregorio, a suspicious, ill-tempered tyrant who was the self-styled *patrón* of the village. Don Gregorio received them with cold indifference. Neither gestures of friendship nor offers of money could alter his menacing disposition, but he eventually consented to help in the hope of ridding himself of unwanted visitors. He knew of an Indian who could lead them to the ruins, and they were allowed to stay overnight at his hacienda until the necessary arrangements were completed.

Early the next day Stephens and Catherwood, accompanied by their newly acquired guide, set off by mule into the fathomless jungle. In places the underbrush was so dense they were forced to travel on foot along a path cleared with machetes. Soon they reached the edge of a stream called the Río Copán, and on the opposite bank a stone wall roughly a hundred feet high and partially overgrown with trees was clearly visible. Quickly they forded the river and climbed a weathered stairway leading to a terrace from which vestiges of other structures were barely discernible in the surrounding forest. When the explorers descended into its shadowy depths, they found themselves in the midst of wonders exceeding their wildest expectations.

Scattered about were gigantic sculptured monoliths and altars, some standing erect, others fallen over or broken, their surfaces richly carved with masks, animals, human figures, and inscriptions. Huge pyramid-shaped structures reached up through the trees, scarcely visible under a thick mantle of rubble and vegetation. Elsewhere were the remains of stairways, platforms, buildings, and walls, all shattered by the roots of trees and vines growing between the fissured stones. Grotesque heads of jaguars, serpents, and mythical creatures had fallen from their façades—images of unknown gods in whose veneration the once-magnificent temples had been erected. Obviously Copán was formerly the scene of extraordinary artistic and intellectual achievements, and wherever Stephens and Catherwood looked they saw miracles frozen in its crumbled monuments. As a traveler who had visited the site years before remarked: "The genii who attended on King Solomon seem to have been the artists."

"Who were the people who built this city?" Stephens wrote. "America, say historians, was peopled by savages, but savages never reared these structures, savages never carved these stones. . . . Architecture, sculpture, and painting, all the arts which embellish life, had flourished in this overgrown forest; orators, warriors, and statesmen, beauty, ambition, and glory had lived and passed away, and none knew that such things had been or could tell of their past existence. . . .

"The city was desolate. . . . It lay before us like a shattered bark in the midst of the ocean, her masts gone, her name effaced, her crew perished, and none to tell whence she came, to whom she belonged, how long on her voyage, or what caused her destruction—her lost people to be traced only by some fancied resemblance in the construction of the vessel, and, perhaps, never to be known at all. . . . All was mystery, dark, impenetrable mystery. . . ."

After setting up quarters in a native hut near the site, Stephens recruited a small group of Indian workmen from the village, and soon the task of reclaiming Copán from its jungle grave was under way. But hardly had explorations begun when a serious problem of diplomacy arose, touched off by the growing resentment of Don Gregorio. Aside from his instinctive dislike of outsiders, he was angered that some of his laborers were being lured away by the high wages Stephens offered them to work at the ruins. Viewing this as an open challenge to his authority, Don Gregorio denounced Stephens and Catherwood as disruptive, suspicious, and politically dangerous; and to prove these charges he submitted the testimony of two Indians from Camotán who claimed that Stephens' party had "escaped" from imprisonment and were chased to the borders of Honduras by a detachment of soldiers under orders to kill them.

Stephens was finally able to quiet the villagers' apprehensions by exhibiting his diplomatic passport, letters of recommendation, and a note that had arrived unexpectedly from the district's military commander—a General Cascara—expressing regrets over their false arrest at Camotán. Still, they found themselves in a precarious position; they were strangers in a remote country torn by civil unrest and subject to the caprices of irresponsible politicos. Should anyone seriously question their right to continue the exploration of Copán, they would be without legal recourse. Realizing the gravity of the situation, Stephens sought a means of ensuring the completion of their project. He resolved to purchase the ruins!

The land on which they were located was owned by one Don José María Acevedo, a respected member of the village whose wife the explorers had previously treated for a severe attack of rheumatism. Eager to discuss the transaction, Stephens visited Don José's home. He emphatically denied the rumors being spread by Don Gregorio, assured him of his good intentions, and explained the reasons for his interest in the ruined city. "In short," he wrote, "in plain English, I asked him, 'What will you take for the ruins?' I think he was not more surprised than if I had asked to buy his poor old wife. . . ."

After several days of deliberation, Don José consented to sell. To him the land was useless: almost six thousand acres of rain forest littered with meaningless carved stones and mounds of rubble. And the price he was offered—fifty dollars—was irresistible. Despite last-minute delays caused by Don Gregorio's violent objections, the sale was finally completed amid a pompous display of deeds, official credentials, and witnesses. Stephens was well pleased with the arrangement; the sensation of owning an ancient city in the wilds of Honduras had an undeniable enchantment about it. Under the circumstances it was also a practical necessity, and he now resumed his archaeological quest with renewed confidence.

Equipped with machetes, measuring tapes, and a compass, Stephens and his Indian workmen undertook the tasks of investigating new sections of the site, surveying and mapping structures, and clearing vegetation from monuments. Meanwhile Catherwood, often ankle deep in mud and severely hampered by rain, inadequate light, and swarms of mosquitoes, painstakingly drew each important discovery.

"It is impossible to describe the interest with which I explored these ruins," recalled Stephens. "The ground was entirely new; there were no guidebooks or guides; the whole was virgin soil. We could not see ten yards before us, and never knew what we should stumble upon next. At one time we stopped to cut away branches and vines, which concealed the face of a monument . . . a sculptured corner of which protruded from the earth. I leaned over with breathless anxiety while the Indians worked, and an eye, an ear, a foot, or a hand was disentombed; and when the machete rang against the chiseled stone, I pushed the Indians away and cleared out the loose earth with my hands. The beauty of the sculpture, the solemn stillness of the woods disturbed only by the scrambling of monkeys and the chattering of parrots, the desolation of the city, and the mystery that hung over it, all created an interest higher, if possible, than I had ever felt among the ruins of the Old World.''

Gradually the outlines of Copán's ground plan began to emerge from the wilderness. Roughly oriented along a north-south axis, the city was located on the west bank of the Río Copán and consisted of a huge acropolis, five adjoining plazas, and several outlying districts. The principal group of buildings was situated atop the acropolis, which covered approximately twelve acres and reached 125 feet at its highest point. Near the center of this artificial mound a massive pyramid rose up in a series of terraces to a flat summit. Immediately west of this structure was a rectangular courtyard surrounded by smaller pyramids, temples, and platforms. To the east lay another plaza enclosed by terraces, stairways, and buildings heavily ornamented with sculptured friezes, including a temple (unknown at the time of Stephens' visit) with a doorway constructed in the form of a stylized serpent's mouth.

Adjacent to the northeast corner of the acropolis stood one of the most spectacular achievements of Copán's builders—the Temple of the Hieroglyphic Stairway, a terraced pyramid ascended by a flight of stairs thirty feet wide, sixty-five feet high, and consisting of sixty-three steps flanked by decorative ramps. Every stone used to construct the risers was carved with hieroglyphs, and the entire stairway was composed of almost 2,500 individual glyphs, the longest single inscription ever found in the Maya area.

Next to the Hieroglyphic Stairway was a ball court made up of an I-shaped stone floor bordered on two sides by slanting walls attached to platforms crowned with temples. North of this complex the city opened into a broad courtyard—the Great Plaza—containing a number of stelae and altars richly carved in high relief with human figures, mythical creatures, religious symbols, and hieroglyphs. Stephens correctly assumed that these remarkable "idols" were originally erected to commemorate historical events or the passing of certain time inter-

31

vals. "In workmanship," he noted, "[they are] equal to the finest Egyptian sculpture. Indeed, it would be impossible, with the best instruments of modern times, to cut stone more perfectly."

For almost two weeks Stephens and Catherwood labored to redeem Copán's secrets from the forest. Scarcely an hour passed without revealing some new cause for speculation, and Stephens' brain fairly reeled with the mysteries surrounding the ruins. "In regard to the age of this desolate city," he wrote, "I shall not at present offer any conjecture. Some idea might perhaps be formed from the accumulations of earth and the gigantic trees growing on top of the ruined structures, but it would be uncertain and unsatisfactory. Nor shall I at this moment offer any conjecture in regard to the people who built it; or to the time when or the means by which it was depopulated . . . or as to whether it fell by the sword, or famine, or pestilence. The trees which shroud it may have sprung from the blood of its slaughtered inhabitants; they may have perished howling with hunger; or pestilence, like the cholera, may have piled its streets with the dead and driven forever the feeble remnants from their homes. . . . One thing I believe: its history is graven on its monuments. No Champollion has yet brought to them the energies of his inquiring mind. Who shall read them?

> *Chaos of ruins! who shall trace the void,*
> *O'er the dim fragments cast a lunar light,*
> *And say, 'here was or is,' where all is doubly night?"*

Since they had stayed at Copán longer than expected, it was decided that Stephens would travel to Guatemala City to fulfill certain diplomatic obligations while Catherwood continued working at the site. Specifically, Stephens' instructions directed him to present his credentials to representatives of Central America's federal government, close the United States legation in Guatemala City, and secure the ratification of a trade agreement. But in view of the civil turmoil then ravaging the area, it proved to be a frustrating mission. Stephens' efforts to locate anything resembling a unified government ultimately carried him from Guatemala to El Salvador, Nicaragua, and Costa Rica without success, and nowhere was he able to find any individual or group empowered to negotiate treaties. "Under the circumstances," he reported, ". . . I made a formal return to the authorities in Washington, in effect, 'after diligent search, no government found.'" Not that Stephens was unduly disturbed by this turn of events. His interest in politics had long since yielded to archaeology, and he pursued his official duties in the knowledge that once they were accomplished he would be free to resume his explorations. He was now intent upon seeking the city of Palenque in Chiapas.

During Stephens' absence Catherwood had discovered another ruin of major importance. Known as Quiriguá, it was located thirty miles north of Copán, near the Río Motagua. Quiriguá's structures covered a relatively small area, but Catherwood was able to discern the unmistakable outlines of pyramids, stairways, and platforms, together with stone sculpture decorated with zoomorphs, human figures, and hieroglyphs.

On the basis of Catherwood's observations, Stephens concluded that Copán and Quiriguá exhibited similar characteristics and had probably been erected by the same people. "Of one thing there is no doubt," he wrote in reference to Quiriguá, "a city once stood there, its name lost, its history unknown. Except for a notice taken from Mr. Catherwood's notes and inserted . . . in a Guatemalan paper which found its way also to the [United States] and Europe, no account of its existence has ever before been published. . . . Every traveler from Izabal to Guatemala has passed within three hours of it; we ourselves had done the same; and yet, there it lay, like the rock-built city of Edom, unvisited, unsought, and utterly unknown."

By April of 1840 the explorers were launched upon their quest for Palenque. Setting out from Guatemala City with an entourage of Indian carriers, they journeyed westward via Antigua, Lake Atitlán, and Quetzaltenango into southern Mexico. Entering Chiapas at the town of Comitán, they endured ten days of severe hardships caused by drenching rains, extremely hazardous trails, and oppressive heat before reaching Santo Domingo del Palenque—a remote village from which the ruined city of Palenque (the Spanish word for "palisade") a few miles to the west took its name. When they finally stumbled into Santo Domingo's muddy streets, their only thought was to recover from what

Stephens described as their "shattered condition" brought on by illness, hunger, and exhaustion.

But the idea of deserted temples, palaces, and monuments lying about in the overgrown forest soon revived their determination. And when they were led to Palenque's ruins they could scarcely contain their elation. Upon approaching the site, Stephens recalled: "We spurred up a sharp ascent of [stones], so steep the mules could barely climb it, to a terrace which, like the whole road, was so covered with trees it was impossible to make out the form. . . . We stopped at the foot of a second [terrace] when our Indians cried out *El Palacio* (The Palace), and through openings in the trees we saw the front of a large building richly ornamented with stuccoed figures on the pilasters, curious and elegant, with trees growing close against it, their branches entering the doors; in style and effect it was unique, extraordinary, and mournfully beautiful. We tied our mules . . . ascended a flight of steps forced apart and thrown down by trees, and entered the palace. For a few moments we ranged along the corridor and into the courtyard, and after the first gaze of eager curiosity was over, went back to the entrance. Standing in the doorway, we fired a *feu-de-joie* of four rounds each, using up the last charge of our firearms. But for this way of giving vent to our satisfaction we should have made the roof of the old palace ring with a hurrah.''

Situated on a high artificial terrace, this imposing building—now called the Great Palace—was a massive labyrinth of vaulted rooms, narrow corridors, and subterranean chambers arranged around four inner courtyards. Near its center a square tower suggestive of an Oriental pagoda rose to a height of fifty feet above the ground level. Sculpture, bas-reliefs, and hieroglyphic inscriptions of exceptional quality embellished the palace's façades, walls, and plazas, and many of these decorations had originally been painted with brilliant colors, traces of which were still visible. The building's outer pilasters were adorned with a series of exquisite stucco reliefs representing life-sized "portraits" of ruling lords or priests bedecked in elaborate costumes. Some of them stood in rigid solemnity, holding plumed staffs and flanked by seated attendants. Others were frozen in courtly attitudes, with one foot rising slightly from the ground, their bodies bent gently forward, clasping ritual scepters in their outstretched hands.

Near the southwest corner of the Great Palace, a terraced pyramid sixty-five feet high lay buried under a thick mantle of vegetation. With Indians wielding machetes ahead of them, Stephens and Catherwood struggled up its crumbled stairway until they reached a temple whose lavish ornamentation left them speechless. Leading into its interior were five doorways divided by pilasters decorated with stucco reliefs and panels of hieroglyphs. Its upper façade reflected a maze of sculptured designs, and crowning the roof were the remains of an openwork crest or "comb" made of stucco and cut stone. "No description and no drawing can give the moral sublimity of the spectacle," commented Stephens on first viewing this superb structure—the Temple of the Inscriptions.

Inside the building a corridor opened into three narrow vaulted chambers divided by partitions. Set in the interior walls were three limestone tablets covered with hieroglyphs finely carved in low relief. Two of these panels, flanking the entrance to the central chamber, measured eight by thirteen feet and contained 240 individual glyphs; the third tablet, embedded in the central chamber's rear wall, was considerably smaller—slightly over three feet wide—but because of its location within the temple's inner recesses its inscriptions were almost perfectly preserved.

Everywhere lay more evidence of Palenque's former grandeur: stairways, plazas, fragments of sculpture, overgrown temples, and an underground aqueduct designed to channel a small stream—the Río Otolum—through the center of the city. East of the Great Palace stood a group of structures now bearing such descriptive names as the Temple of the Sun, Temple of the Cross, Temple of the Beau Relief, and Temple of the Foliated Cross, all of them ornamented with sculptured reliefs of unusual refinement. Enclosing the city's northern boundary was another complex of courtyards, platforms, and temples dominated by a lofty terraced pyramid supporting a building known as the Temple of the Count, the roof of which was originally decorated with a gigantic stucco mask long since destroyed by decay.

As he had done at Copán, Stephens wandered through Palenque's ruins in utter astonishment. "Here were the remains," he wrote, "of a cultivated, polished, and peculiar people who had passed through all the stages incident to the rise and fall of nations, had reached their golden age, and had perished, entirely unknown. The links connecting them with the human family were severed and lost; these were the only memorials of their footsteps upon earth. We lived in the ruined palace of their kings; we went to their desolate temples and fallen altars; and wherever we moved we saw evidence of their taste, their skill in arts, their wealth and power. In the midst of desolation and ruin we looked back to the past, cleared away the gloomy forest, and fancied every building perfect, with its terraces and pyramids, its sculptured and painted ornaments, grand, lofty, and imposing. . . . We called back into life the strange people who gazed at us in sadness from the walls; pictured them, in fanciful costumes and adorned with plumes of feathers, ascending the terraces of the palace and the steps leading to the temple. . . . In the romance of the world's history, nothing ever impressed me more forcibly than the spectacle of this once great and lovely city, overturned, desolate, and lost; discovered by accident, overgrown with trees, it did not even have a name to distinguish it. Apart from everything else, it was a mourning witness to the world's mutations."

After a month at the site, further exploration was made increasingly difficult by the onset of the rainy season. Every morning swollen black clouds rode in on restless winds and broke upon the forest with drenching fury. The walls of buildings dripped with moisture, and droves of mosquitoes swarmed in their darkened vaults. For several weeks Catherwood had suffered intermittent attacks of malaria; rarely did anyone sleep longer than three or four hours a night, and then it was with "twinging apprehensions of the snakes and reptiles, lizards and scorpions which infested the ruins."

By June, Stephens and Catherwood were forced to leave Palenque. Journeying north across palmetto-studded savannas to the Usumacinta River, they proceeded by boat through Chiapas and the crocodile-infested swamps of Tabasco and Campeche to a point where the Usumacinta's waters empty into the Gulf of Campeche. From the island of

Carmen at the mouth of Laguna de Términos they boarded a ship bound for Yucatán with the intention of examining the ancient city of Uxmal near Mérida.

Once again the sight that confronted them defied all expectations. Standing in the midst of Uxmal's ruins was a remarkable building called the Palace of the Governors. Elevated on a high terraced platform, this structure was 320 feet long, 40 feet wide, and contained 24 vaulted chambers. Its façade was decorated with thousands of carved stones carefully set into an intricate mosaic of geometric designs, stylized masks, and human faces. It is often described as the most beautiful example of Maya architecture in existence, and Stephens spoke without exaggeration when he remarked: "There is no rudeness or barbarity in its design or proportions; on the contrary, the whole wears an air of symmetry and grandeur. If it stood this day on its grand artificial terrace in Hyde Park or the Garden of the Tuileries, it would form a new order . . . not unworthy to stand side by side with the remains of Egyptian, Grecian, and Roman art."

Adjacent to the Palace of the Governors was a large cluster of mounds, pyramids, and platforms, their details obliterated by debris and underbrush. Several hundred yards to the north stood a group of four rectangular buildings enclosing a wide courtyard. Known as the Nunnery Quadrangle, each of these structures, which contained double rows of cell-like rooms, was richly ornamented with geometric mosaics, serpents, and masks. East of this complex a truncated pyramid rose to a height of eighty-four feet, with two steeply inclined stairways leading to a magnificent temple—the House of the Magician—at its summit. Visible in every direction were other mounds, ruined buildings, and outcroppings of walls, and there could be no doubt that Uxmal had once been a city of major importance.

But the exploration of Uxmal was short-lived. While sketching among the ruins, Catherwood, now experiencing the symptoms of acute malaria, collapsed and was carried in delirium to a nearby hacienda.

On July 31, 1840, the explorers arrived back in New York, where they quickly began preparing the results of their expedition for publication. Stephens' two-volume account entitled *Incidents of Travel in*

Central America, Chiapas, and Yucatan, illustrated with Catherwood's meticulous engravings, appeared in June of 1841. Its impact was phenomenal!

Historians read with dismay his vivid descriptions of the long-ignored ruins. Raging academic debates erupted over hastily propounded theories concerning their origin. Scholars reexamined the narratives of the Conquest and the accounts of early travelers, searching for new clues and interpretations; the images in Catherwood's drawings were compared with classical, Near Eastern, and Oriental antiquities in an attempt to define possible analogies; and occultists seized upon Stephens' discoveries as "proof" of their belief in lost continents and vanished races.

Amid this storm of controversy the ever-curious Stephens and Catherwood, accompanied by a physician and naturalist from Boston, Dr. Samuel Cabot, Jr., embarked upon a second expedition in October of 1841—this time bound for Yucatán.

Six weeks were required to complete their unfinished survey of Uxmal. Next they spent three months investigating a number of other ruins, exploring the Wells of Bolonchén (where the Maya had drawn water from a vast system of underground cisterns), and examining sections of ancient stone roads that once traversed the area. March of 1842 found them camped at Chichén Itzá, the most celebrated of Yucatán's archaeological sites. For eighteen days they wandered awestruck through acres of impressive buildings now familiar to thousands of travelers who visit Chichén Itzá every year—among them the Temple of the Warriors, El Castillo, the Ball Court, the Temple of the Jaguars, the Observatory, and Las Monjas, some of which, Stephens declared, "may be regarded as the most important [ruins] we have met with in our entire explorations. . . ."

Early in April they sailed to Cozumel Island and explored the nearby city of Tulúm, a walled complex of pyramids, temples, and palaces located atop a windswept cliff on the coast of Quintana Roo. En route back to Mérida they stopped to inspect the huge mounds of rubble marking the ruins of Dzilám, Izamal, and Aké, the last sites visited by the explorers whose union had been responsible for uncovering so many archaeological wonders. After seven months in the field, Catherwood's health was again failing, and Stephens, fortified with new evidence, was eager to plunge into the waiting caldron of academic debate. On May 18, 1842, having "now bid farewell to ruins," as Stephens regretfully noted, they departed from the port of Sisal, bound for New York.

Immediately after returning, Stephens began writing another book, *Incidents of Travel in Yucatan,* which was published early in 1843. In its preface he described the work as a record of "the most extensive journey ever made by a stranger to [Yucatán], and . . . an account of visits to forty-four ruined cities in which remains or vestiges of ancient populations were found. . . . For a brief space the stillness that reigned around them was broken, and they were again left to solitude and silence. Time and the elements are hastening them to utter destruction. In a few generations, great edifices, their façades covered with sculptured ornaments, already cracked and yawning, must fall and become mere shapeless mounds. It has been the fortune of the author to step between them and the entire destruction to which they are destined; and it is his hope to snatch from oblivion the perishing but still gigantic memorials of a mysterious people."

In retrospect, John Lloyd Stephens had succeeded admirably in focusing public attention on the splendors of Maya civilization. His explorations opened the way for scholars to begin systematically probing the area, and his perceptive books on the subject—long ago acclaimed as classics—have remained in print and are still widely read. Quite rightly, Stephens has been called "the father of Maya archaeology," and he ranks with that select group of gifted amateurs such as Schliemann, Botta, Rawlinson, and Layard, who contributed so enormously to our knowledge of the ancient world.

3 · MYTHS AND THEORY: THE BIRTH OF A SCIENCE

By the mid-1840s the existence of ruins of advanced civilizations in Mexico and Central America could no longer be seriously challenged. But when questions arose concerning the identity of their builders, most antiquarians ruled out any suggestion of an indigenous development, looking instead to Europe, Asia, the Near East, and Africa as possible sources of influence.

The unexpected revelation of the scope and achievements of these pre-Columbian civilizations added new intensity to the already heated controversy surrounding the origins of the American Indians. In a flood of articles, popular books, and scientific papers, innumerable theories were advanced to demonstrate that the Indians were descended from such widely diversified ancestry as the Assyrians, Hittites, Phoenicians, Scythians, Chinese, Hindus, Tartars, Norsemen, Welsh, Irish, and a host of other peoples, all of whom had allegedly reached America at some unknown time in the past.

Various sixteenth-century Spanish historians concluded that the Indians were descendants of the Lost Tribes of Israel, who they believed had sailed across the Atlantic after their expulsion from Samaria by the Assyrians about 721 B.C. (as related in the Old Testament). In later years this hypothesis was expounded by William Penn, Cotton Mather, Roger Williams, and many other prominent figures, and the appearance in the 1830s of Lord Kingsborough's impressive folios, *Antiquities of Mexico*, lent an air of scholarly credence to this so-called "Jewish Theory." It received additional impetus from the Mormon

Church—founded in 1830—whose *Book of Mormon* incorporates the idea of Israelite migrations to America. Even today the New World Archaeological Foundation, organized and financed by the Mormons, is sponsoring a series of excavations which the Church hopes will uncover evidence to support its teachings.

With the upsurge of interest in Egypt during the nineteenth century, a number of students advocated the view that various pre-Columbian cultures originally stemmed from the Nile Valley. Great significance was attributed to certain traits associated with Egyptian antiquities which also occurred in the Western Hemisphere; for example, pyramids, temples, hieroglyphic writing, elaborate tombs, bas-relief sculpture, and sun worship were common to both regions. Mummies wrapped in woven shrouds had been excavated in Peru and Bolivia, and some of the figures depicted in Maya sculpture were vaguely suggestive of elephants. To many observers these apparent analogies constituted positive proof of former contacts between Egypt and America, either by means of ships or long-vanished land connections.

Numerous authors championed this theory with reckless abandon. Among its leading exponents was Augustus Le Plongeon, an eccentric French adventurer, self-styled physician, and amateur archaeologist who traveled extensively in Yucatán and conducted haphazard excavations at Chichén Itzá. In two wildly imaginative books, *Queen Moo and the Egyptian Sphinx* and *Sacred Mysteries Among the Maya and the Quichés: Their Relation to the Mysteries of Egypt, Greece, Chaldea, and India,* Le Plongeon compiled a staggering amount of spurious information to support his belief in direct links between Yucatán and Egypt. Not content to let the matter rest there, he endowed the Maya with incredible technological advances (including electricity and telegraphic communications!), and even insisted that they had established colonies in the Nile Valley, Mesopotamia, and India more than 11,000 years ago.

Another prominent writer on this subject was G. Elliot Smith, an Australian anatomist who became interested in Egyptology while teaching at the Cairo Medical School. Eventually Smith formulated a theory, detailed in a lengthy work entitled *Human History,* which held that the basic attributes of civilization—namely agriculture, urbanization, architecture, writing, art, and the use of metals—had originated in the Nile Valley and subsequently spread to Europe, Asia, and America. Smith quickly found an enthusiastic disciple in the person of William J. Perry, a professor of comparative religion at the University of Manchester, whose widely read book, *The Children of the Sun*, outlined the routes by which civilized attainments had supposedly been diffused from Egypt to other parts of the world. According to the conclusions reached by Smith and Perry, these influences were transmitted to America via Southeast Asia and achieved their maximum expression in the emergence of Maya civilization.

Naturally a dilemma of such protean aspects—one involving unaccounted-for races and vanished civilizations—also encouraged the popular occult belief that the Indians were survivors of "lost continents" long since submerged beneath the sea. Exactly which of these mysterious lands they had allegedly come from was a matter of sharp disagreement, but there were three persistent choices: Atlantis, Lemuria, and Mu.

Unquestionably the most famous was Atlantis. Originally described by the Greek philosopher Plato in his dialogues *Timaeus* and *Critias*, this imaginary paradise was located in the Atlantic just west of the Strait of Gibraltar, and had once been the center of a vast empire whose power extended into Europe and Asia. Dominating the island was a magnificent city filled with splendid temples, villas, and gardens, and the surrounding countryside abounded with game animals, wild fruit, herbs, and spices, all of which, wrote Plato, "that sacred island lying beneath the sun brought forth . . . in infinite abundance." Supposedly the Atlanteans had enjoyed an untroubled existence "as long as the divine nature lasted in them, they were obedient to the laws, and well affectioned toward the gods." But as invariably happens when humans achieve an idyllic state, they slowly fell victim to corruption, jealousy, and greed, thus causing the angry gods to plunge the island into the ocean, never to be heard from again—or so Plato thought.

He had created Atlantis to prove a philosophical point, yet his tale continued to hold an almost mystical fascination for countless writers, antiquarians, and occultists. Such intellectuals as Voltaire, Montaigne, and Buffon debated the possibility of the legendary continent's existence; and the renowned scientist-philosopher Sir Francis Bacon also succumbed to its lure, drawing upon Plato's ideas to set forth his own Utopian concepts in an essay entitled *New Atlantis* (1627). Even Brasseur de Bourbourg—the scholar responsible for discovering Landa's *Relación*, the Motul Dictionary, a section of the Madrid (Tro-Cortesianus) Codex, and several other important manuscripts pertaining to pre-Columbian archaeology—published a curious work in 1868, *Quatre Lettres sur le Mexique*, in which he offered a rash of outlandish theories seeking to prove that Atlantis had been the "mother culture" of all ancient civilizations, including those of Mexico and Central America. (Using Landa's hieroglyphic "alphabet" to supposedly translate the Madrid Codex, Brasseur claimed that it contained detailed references to Atlantis, but his assertions were demolished when it was later discovered that, apart from the obvious flaws in Landa's notations, Brasseur had read the entire codex backwards.) And in 1882 a lawyer from Minnesota named Ignatius Donnelly released what became the most celebrated book ever written on the subject, *Atlantis: The Antediluvian World*. Not only did Donnelly view Plato's narrative as historical fact rather than allegorical fancy, he envisioned Atlantis as the Garden of Eden, the scene of mankind's transition from savagery to civilization, and the place from which advanced culture spread to Europe, Egypt, the Orient, and America. Strangely enough, the fascination with Atlantis has endured unabated to the present day; it still figures prominently in the teachings of various occult groups, and there have been repeated attempts in recent years to locate the fabled island by means of sophisticated scientific technology.

Another vanished land was believed to have existed in the Indian Ocean. First suggested in the mid-nineteenth century by an English zoologist named Philip Sclater to explain the geographical distribution of lemurs, this continent—known as Lemuria—was later embellished by the vivid imagination of the noted theosophist Helena P. Blavatsky. According to her famous treatise, *The Secret Doctrine*, Lemuria was inhabited by creatures of the most bizarre description: egg-laying, hermaphroditic giants who gave rise to several "root races" from which various branches of mankind had evolved, including the American Indians.

Equally fantastic was the continent of Mu, allegedly located somewhere in the area of the Pacific bordered by Easter Island, Hawaii, the Ladrones, and Fiji. Numerous writers have offered varying accounts of Mu (some identify Mu and Lemuria as the same island), but its principal advocate was James Churchward, who purportedly discovered a record of Mu's history inscribed on a set of stone tablets acquired in India from a Hindu priest. In a series of books entitled *The Lost Continent of Mu*, *The Children of Mu*, and *Sacred Symbols of Mu*, Churchward conjured up an astonishing picture of a tropical paradise inhabited simultaneously by dinosaurs, an assortment of modern animals and birds, and exactly 64 million humans whose technical prowess enabled them to develop a highly advanced civilization more than fifty thousand years ago. Unfortunately, however, Mu sank into oblivion amid earthquakes and a fiery holocaust when the gas chambers supporting the island unexpectedly collapsed, though by then colonists from Mu had already settled in Europe, Asia, and America.

For years the debate over the origin of the Indians raged on, seemingly without hope of resolution. New theories, usually predicated on extremely tenuous evidence, constantly appeared in print, and endless analogies were drawn between pre-Columbian cultures and various Indo-European civilizations. The existence in Mexico and Central America of terraced pyramids (similar to Sumerian ziggurats), calendrical systems, mathematics, and sculptured figures with beards or negroid features implied to many observers a connection with such peoples as the Assyrians, Phoenicians, Hittites, Babylonians, or Carthaginians. Other students viewed certain motifs in Mesoamerican art—lotus blossoms, tree-of-life designs, scrolls, dragonlike creatures, and sun disks—as conclusive evidence that massive migrations had reached America from India, Southeast Asia, China, or Japan. Inscriptions on a stone found in 1872 near Paraíba, Brazil, were pronounced to be a Canaanite text. Burial mounds in the Mississippi Valley yielded tablets inscribed with markings variously interpreted as Arabic, Chinese, Hebraic, Greek, Celtic, Sumerian, and Gaelic; and several monoliths supposedly bearing a Viking script turned up along the eastern coast of the United States. But regardless of how much these arguments differed in specific details, they all served the same basic purpose: to prove that America's aboriginal cultures were either founded or strongly influenced by immigrants from distant lands, a concept that is still being expounded today.*

As early as 1840, John Lloyd Stephens stated in his book *Incidents of Travel in Central America, Chiapas, and Yucatan,* that the ruins he had explored were those of an *indigenous* civilization, which developed apart from any outside influences. He categorically ruled out the principal sources of foreign inspiration from which Maya culture might have sprung. "I set out with the proposition that they are not Cyclopean," he wrote, "and do not resemble the works of Greek or Roman; there is nothing in Europe like them. . . ." So far as Asia was concerned, Stephens found little evidence for serious comparisons. He saw no similarity between Maya buildings and those of ancient China or Japan, and he emphasized the complete absence in Mexico and Central America of the artificially excavated caves and rock chambers typical of Buddhist and Hindu temples.

Stephens then challenged the premises on which Maya and Egyptian architecture were so often equated, particularly the occurrence of pyra-

---

*Although modern archaeologists have traditionally rejected the idea of contacts between the ancient civilizations of the Old World and America, they have recently begun to reexamine this problem in the light of new evidence—especially a number of remarkably parallel culture traits which appear to indicate that certain pre-Columbian peoples may have experienced limited contacts with groups from Europe, the Near East, and Asia. For a detailed discussion of this question, see the following publications: Carroll L. Riley, J. Charles Kelley, Campbell W. Pennington, and Robert L. Rands, editors, *Man Across the Sea* (Austin: University of Texas Press, 1971); Cyrus H. Gordon, *Before Columbus* (New York: Crown Publishers, 1971); Gordon F. Ekholm, "Transpacific Contacts," in *Prehistoric Man in the New World,* edited by Jesse D. Jennings and Edward Norbeck (Chicago: University of Chicago Press, 1964); David H. Kelley, "Eurasian Evidence and the Mayan Calendar Correlation Problem," in *Mesoamerican Archaeology: New Approaches,* edited by Norman Hammond (Austin: University of Texas Press, 1974); Emilio Estrada and Betty J. Meggers, "A Complex of Traits of Probable Transpacific Origin on the Coast of Ecuador," *American Anthropologist,* Vol. 63 (1961); Robert Heine-Geldern, "The Problem of Transpacific Influences," in *Handbook of Middle American Indians,* Vol. 4, edited by Gordon F. Ekholm and Gordon R. Willey (Austin: University of Texas Press, 1966).

mids in both regions. "The pyramidal form," he observed, "is one which suggests itself to human intelligence in every country as the simplest and surest mode of erecting a high structure upon a solid foundation. It cannot be regarded as a ground for assigning a common origin to all people among whom structures of that character are found unless the similarity is preserved in its most striking features." Egyptian pyramids, he pointed out, were characteristically uniform in design and intended solely as burial places; by contrast, those in America varied greatly in form and were constructed primarily to support temples or shrines on their summits.

With regard to other types of structures, Stephens noted that massive columns, "a distinguishing feature of Egyptian architecture," were absent in Maya ruins. Nor did they exhibit the *dromos* (avenue of approach), the *pronaos* (porch or vestibule), or the *adytum* (inner sanctum) usually found in Egyptian temples. He cited marked differences in comparative methods of construction and decorative embellishment, and the relatively small stones used by the Maya were, in Stephens' words, "scarcely worthy of being laid in the walls of an Egyptian temple." Furthermore, he conceded only the most superficial resemblances between the sculpture of the two areas. "If there be any at all," he declared, ". . . it is only that the figures are in profile, and this is equally true of all good sculpture in bas-relief."

Exploding as they did in the midst of overwhelming opinion to the contrary, Stephens' speculations were as daring as they were prophetic. In refuting the assumption that Maya civilization stemmed from Indo-European sources of inspiration, he had advanced a revolutionary hypothesis now generally accepted by archaeologists. "The works of these people," he insisted, "are different from the works of any other known people; they are of a new order, and entirely and absolutely anomalous: they stand alone."

Elsewhere Stephens wrote:

> Unless I am wrong, we have a conclusion far more interesting and wonderful than that of connecting the builders of these cities with the Egyptians or any other people. It is the spectacle of a people skilled in architecture, sculpture, and drawing, and beyond doubt in other more perishable arts . . .

not derived from the Old World, but originating and growing up here, without models or masters, having a distinct, separate, independent existence: like the plants and fruits of the soil, indigenous.

I am inclined to think that there are not sufficient grounds for the belief in the great antiquity . . . ascribed to these ruins; that they are not the work of a people who have passed away and whose history has become unknown. Opposed as is my idea to all previous speculations, I am inclined to think that they were constructed by the races who occupied the country at the time of the invasion by the Spaniards, or of some not very distant progenitors.

It perhaps destroys much of the interest that hangs over these ruins to assign to them a modern date; but we live in an age whose spirit is to discard phantasms and arrive at truth, and the interest lost in one particular is supplied in another scarcely inferior; for, the nearer we can bring the builders of these cities to our own times, the greater is our chance of knowing all. Throughout the country the convents are rich in manuscripts and documents written by the early fathers, caciques, and Indians, who very soon acquired the knowledge of Spanish and the art of writing. These have never been examined with the slightest reference to this subject; and I cannot help thinking that some precious memorial is now mouldering in the library of a neighboring convent, which would determine the history of some of these ruined cities; moreover, I cannot help believing that the tablets of hieroglyphs will yet be read. No strong curiosity has hitherto been directed to them. . . . For centuries the hieroglyphics of Egypt were inscrutable, and, though not perhaps in our day, I feel persuaded that a key surer than that of the Rosetta Stone will be discovered. And if only three centuries have elapsed since any one of these unknown cities was inhabited, the race of the inhabitants is not extinct. Their descendants are still in the land, scattered, perhaps, and retired, like our own Indians, into wildernesses which have never yet been penetrated by a white man. . . .

In 1883 a former officer in the British foreign service, Alfred P. Maudslay, embarked on a campaign of wide-ranging explorations that signaled the birth of Maya research as a science. Educated at Cambridge, where he studied engineering, he had later accepted a post as a colonial administrator in the south Pacific. In 1881 he visited the ruins of Copán and Quiriguá in Guatemala while on vacation, and although he had read Stephens' descriptions of these sites, he was overwhelmed by their grandeur and mystique, declaring that they were "more important . . . than any account I had heard of them led me to expect." Two years later Maudslay abandoned his diplomatic career and returned to Guatemala determined to pursue his newly awakened interest in archaeology. As it turned out, he quickly emerged as a meticulous investigator whose tireless efforts profoundly influenced the future of Maya studies.

During the next eleven years Maudslay not only explored Copán and Quiriguá but also carried out expeditions to Tikal, Palenque, Uaxactún, and Chichén Itzá. Aided by Indian assistants and an impressive array of equipment, he surveyed structures, made plaster casts of monuments, and compiled an extraordinary photographic record of buildings, sculpture, and inscriptions. Eventually these data were incorporated into Maudslay's five-volume contribution to an exhaustive work on the natural history of the area entitled *Biologia Centrali-Americana*, published in London between 1889 and 1902. With its lucid text, accurate architectural plans, and superb illustrations (including precise drawings of sculpture and hieroglyphs), this study set a standard of scholarship seldom equaled in the annals of archaeology, and even today it remains an indispensable reference.

About the time Maudslay appeared on the scene, various scientific institutions were becoming involved in Maya research. In 1884 the Peabody Museum of Archaeology and Ethnology at Harvard University engaged an explorer named Teobert Maler to survey archaeological sites in remote sections of the lowlands—primarily Tikal, Altar de Sacrificios, Seibal, Piedras Negras, Cancuén, Yaxhá, Naranjo, and Cobá. Solitary and temperamental by nature, Maler was an intrepid if decidedly eccentric Austrian who originally came to Mexico in 1864 as a soldier in Maximilian's army and subsequently developed a consuming interest in antiquities. Unlike Maudslay, he traveled rapidly and with minimal equipment, accompanied only by Indian guides who often deserted him because of his disdain for physical comforts. In addition to being a skilled engineer, draftsman, and photographer, Maler possessed a keen eye for details, and six of his reports published in the early 1900s as *Memoirs* of the Peabody Museum belatedly earned him a reputation as a highly competent scholar, although at the time his efforts were largely ignored. Unfortunately, however, Maler's erroneous suspicion that the museum was reaping huge profits from his reports caused him to terminate his explorations, and he retired to Mérida, where he died in 1917 in virtual obscurity.

By 1892 the Peabody Museum had begun digging at Copán (the first large-scale excavation of a Maya site) and it has since carried out fieldwork at a number of other ruins, including, most recently, Barton Raime, Altar de Sacrificios, and Seibal. In 1914 the Carnegie Institution of Washington initiated a program of research that led to major excavations at such important sites as Uaxactún, Tulúm, Kaminaljuyú, Chichén Itzá, and Mayapán. Significant work has also been sponsored by the British Museum, the Field Museum of Natural History in Chicago, the Middle American Research Institute at Tulane University, the Instituto Nacional de Antropología e Historia in Mexico, and the Royal Ontario Museum. And in 1956 the University of Pennsylvania, which had previously dug at Piedras Negras in Guatemala, launched one of the most ambitious projects ever undertaken in the region: a fourteen-year campaign of excavation and restoration at the immense site of Tikal, an endeavor that was to have a tremendous impact on the future of Maya archaeology.

With the advent of systematic excavations, the silent realm of earth which had enveloped the ruins for centuries was finally penetrated. Gradually it became possible to trace stylistic developments in art and architecture, to define chronological sequences, and to classify the enormous quantities of pottery recovered by archaeologists, which provided a highly sensitive indicator of cultural change, outside influences, and technological advances. Simultaneously, naturalists studied the region's geology, climate, flora, and fauna to determine the effects of environment on the evolution of Maya civilization, while ethnologists and linguists worked among contemporary Maya peoples, examining their culture for possible links with the past. Equally important was the evaluation of ethnohistoric documents in the form of early Spanish chronicles, colonial records, and native manuscripts, especially where associations could be made between these sources and specific archaeological questions.

One of the principal tasks facing scholars was the decipherment of Maya hieroglyphic writing and the correlation of their calendar with our own. In addition to the three authenticated codices—the Dresden, Tro-Cortesianus, and Peresianus—explorations have revealed a bewildering profusion of hieroglyphic texts inscribed on ceramics, monuments, and ornaments, as well as on the walls, lintels, doorjambs, columns, and stairways of buildings. Obviously, no comprehensive insight into Maya civilization could be achieved without determining the content of these inscriptions, but this has proved extremely difficult. Epigraphers quickly recognized that the system of writing used by the Maya was both unique in pre-Columbian America and totally unrelated to Indo-European scripts, leaving them with no precedents to follow in deciphering it. Only through painstaking efforts on the part of many students using a variety of approaches has any progress been made toward this end—and that has been disappointingly slow.

Although Landa failed in his attempt to formulate an alphabet for reading the inscriptions, his *Relación* contained drawings of the hieroglyphs representing the days and months of the calendar, their Yucatec names, and information on the divisions of the 365-day solar year. He had further noted that the Maya recorded twenty-year periods called *katuns,* and sketched a diagram to show how they were calculated. In making these observations, Landa provided the cornerstone on which future efforts to interpret the hieroglyphs rested, but this material remained unknown until Brasseur de Bourbourg discovered the manuscript of the *Relación* in 1863.

Not long thereafter, a number of scholars began to challenge the problem of glyphic decipherment. In 1876 a Frenchman, León de Rosnay, succeeded in identifying the glyphs representing the four cardinal directions, and six years later an American epigrapher named Cyrus Thomas established the sequence in which the glyphs were intended to be read. But it was Ernst Förstemann, a German philologist and librarian to the Elector of Saxony, whose studies of Maya writing loom as the outstanding achievements of this period. Working with the codices (particularly the Dresden manuscript) and inscriptions on stone monuments, Förstemann made a series of singularly important discoveries. Among other things, he explained the vigesimal system used in Maya mathematics, identified two symbols for zero, and deciphered the month signs illustrated in the Dresden Codex, together with its complicated tables for computing Venus cycles and predicting lunar eclipses. Moreover, Förstemann was able to unravel the intricacies of the Maya calendar—including the fact that all dates were calculated from a starting point equivalent to 3114 B.C.—thereby allowing him to correctly read the calendrical inscriptions on seven monuments at Copán.

In 1897 a newspaper editor in California, Joseph T. Goodman, published a work entitled *The Archaic Maya Inscriptions*. Although profoundly influenced by Förstemann, whose ideas he freely incorporated without acknowledging their source, Goodman deciphered what are known as "head-variant" glyphs representing the numbers 0 to 19, and his treatise became a widely used reference, especially its insightful data on calendrics. Indeed, Goodman's most important achievement occurred in 1905, when he arrived at a correlation of the Maya and Christian calendars which is still in general use today with only minor revisions: the Goodman-Martínez-Thompson correlation (see pages 55–56). By 1904 a German epigrapher, Paul Schellhas, had identified the deities shown in the Maya codices and matched them with glyphs denoting their names. Another of Schellhas' countrymen, a renowned scholar named Eduard Seler, who was noted for the versatility of his research, deciphered numerous hieroglyphs, including those for the colors red, yellow, blue-green, black, and white.

Important contributions were also made by J. E. Teeple, Daniel Brinton, William Gates, Charles P. Bowditch, and Hermann Beyer, all of whom were responsible for major advances in theoretical studies and the reading of individual glyphs. And in recent years two of the leading figures in Maya epigraphy were the late Sylvanus G. Morley—one of the most influential Mayanists of the twentieth century and the author of the classic works *The Inscriptions at Copán* and *The Inscriptions of the Petén*—and the English archaeologist J. Eric Thompson, whose prolific writings prior to his death in 1975 added greatly to our knowledge of the glyphs. In fact, Thompson's exhaustive study, *Maya*

Hieroglyphic Writing: An Introduction (1950), remained the only comprehensive reference on the subject until the publication in 1976 of David H. Kelley's updated summary, *Deciphering the Maya Script*.

During the past three decades the study of Maya hieroglyphs has entered an intensive new phase. In 1952 a Russian linguist, Yuri Knorozov, began reporting on the results of his efforts to apply computer technology to the problems of decipherment. Using a revolutionary approach, he translated various glyphs by analyzing elements that in his opinion represented consonant-vowel patterns and offered a key to reading the inscriptions phonetically. Although Knorozov's conclusions were flawed and touched off a heated controversy (J. Eric Thompson was among his severest critics), they awakened a renewed interest in the question of phoneticism in Maya writing, an idea that began with the discovery of Landa's alphabet and was championed by several early scholars. By about 1900, however, this view was almost completely rejected in favor of the belief—strongly advocated by Morley and Thompson—that the glyphs were ideographic in nature and conveyed only ritualistic and calendrical information, with no historical content. But in light of overwhelming evidence to the contrary, these conjectures have now been disproved. Major discoveries in the late 1950s by Tatiana Proskouriakoff and Heinrich Berlin (discussed in Chapter 7) demonstrated conclusively that the Maya frequently recorded historical data in their inscriptions; and despite the inaccuracies in Landa's alphabet and Knorozov's methods, epigraphers have established beyond any doubt that the glyphs are partly phonetic in structure.

Along with other innovative approaches, of which Knorozov's work is one example, a massive effort is being made to assemble a comprehensive source of information as a basis for future research. To accomplish this goal, a far-reaching program—the Maya Hieroglyphic Inscription Study—was launched in 1968 under the direction of a Scottish explorer-scholar named Ian Graham. Organized by the Peabody Museum at Harvard University, this venture, which is expected to require years to complete, is aimed at compiling an exhaustive inventory of inscribed monuments, an objective that has taken on a sense of urgency because of increasing activity by looters who are plundering unguarded archaeological sites in their quest for valuable art. Working in widely scattered sections of the lowlands, Graham and his colleagues have already collected a wealth of material, including drawings and photographs of many previously unknown or endangered monuments, and the data from this project will eventually fill an estimated fifty-volume publication entitled the *Corpus of Maya Hieroglyphic Inscriptions*.

Given these developments, plus the steadily accelerating pace of current research, there is reason to be cautiously optimistic that Maya writing may someday be fully deciphered. By a combination of persistent study and dramatic breakthroughs, encouraging strides toward this objective have already been made. Most of the glyphs pertaining to calendrics, astronomical data, and mathematics can now be easily read, along with certain historical and ritualistic inscriptions. Scholars are rapidly gaining new insight into the grammatical structure of the hieroglyphs; and the relationship between iconography—the scenes depicted in codices and works of art—and the explanatory texts that often accompany them is becoming increasingly clear.

Yet there are still frustrating obstacles to overcome. The meaning of numerous inscriptions remains obscure, and tentative readings of others have not been adequately verified. Epigraphers do not agree on the function of many glyphic components, or know to what extent the symbols are ideographic, logographic, or phonetic, although there is no question that the glyphs contain a mixture of these elements. Nor can they fully explain the relationship of ancient inscriptions to the various Maya languages spoken today, which include a variety of dialects divided into several major subgroups—all having presumably evolved from a Proto-Maya root whose origins are uncertain.

Such difficulties result from structural complexities inherent in the hieroglyphs themselves. Each glyph is composed of a combination of symbols, including a main or central element together with variable affixes. The latter serve to modify the meaning of the central element, and they appear as prefixes attached above or to the left of the central element, as postfixes occurring below it or to the right, or as infixes incorporated into the central element itself. In most cases the central element represents an ideogram or logogram, while the affixes act as grammatical or phonetic modifiers, though this is not always the case. Glyphic components are frequently quite abstract and difficult to recognize, and there are a distressingly large number of possible combinations of central elements and affixes. In his *Catalogue of Maya Hieroglyphs* (1962), J. Eric Thompson listed 356 main signs, 370 affixes, and 136 miscellaneous signs, and elsewhere he noted an example of a particular central element that occurred with eighty separate arrangements of affixes.

Many glyphs had two distinct forms that were interchangeable: a "normal" form, represented by abstract or symbolic signs, and a "head-variant" form, derived from the heads of deities, humans, animals, and mythological creatures. Apparently the choice of a specific glyph form, its dimensions and stylistic traits, or the exact position of affixes in relation to main elements was largely determined by aesthetic considerations. Marked differences existed between the type of glyphs seen in the codices and those inscribed on sculpture and ceramics, and there is considerable evidence that the hieroglyphs underwent some degree of evolution in the sense that new glyphs frequently appeared and older ones either changed in design or ceased to be used. Inscriptions were usually organized into double rows or columns (called glyph groups) that were intended to be read from left to right and top to bottom, but this order could vary somewhat depending upon the length of a particular text, the shape of the monument on which it was carved, or its position in relation to iconographic elements such as human figures, deities, or religious symbols.

Despite slow progress in hieroglyphic decipherment, efforts to correlate the Maya and Gregorian calendars have been considerably more successful. Early attempts to solve this question rested primarily upon cross-checking native dates as recorded in post-Conquest documents for which we have precise Gregorian equivalents. For instance, the *Books of Chilam Balam* contain information on the twenty-year *katun* period coinciding with the founding of Mérida by the Spaniards on January 6, 1542. In his *Relación,* Landa cited a date in an ancient system called the Calendar Round that probably corresponds to July 16, 1553, and several other chronicles give indications of the *katuns* in which important events of the Conquest took place. Working backward from these historically known occurrences, it was theoretically possible to arrive at an accurate correlation of Maya and Gregorian dates.

But the matter was not that simple. By the sixteenth century the so-called Long Count calendar formerly used by the Maya (see Chapter 5), which recorded a series of continuous time segments beginning from a fixed starting point in the past (3114 B.C.), had been replaced by an abbreviated system known as the Short Count or *u kahlay katunob* (literally "count of the *katuns*"). With this method, only repeating cycles of thirteen *katuns* were computed, and since a *katun* was actually composed of 19.71 years (due to the fact that a 360-day year was employed in these calculations), the *u kahlay katunob* consisted of 13 × 19.71 years, or the equivalent of 256¼ years in the Gregorian calendar. Unfortunately, Short Count dates tell us nothing except the day on which a particular *katun* ended, and the knowledge of exactly where each *katun* fitted into the overall scheme of Long Count chronology—information clearly understood by the Maya—has since been lost. In effect, these *katun* cycles appear to "float" in time; they are accurate within isolated spans of 256¼ years, while giving no indication of their relation to longer periods—as if, for instance, we knew the years and decades referred to by specific dates, but not the centuries or millennia. Hence numerous uncertainties surrounding the correct order of the *katuns* mentioned in post-Conquest sources have made the problem of correlation exceedingly complex.

Of the various methods proposed for equating the Maya and Gregorian calendars, two have been most commonly used in recent years. One was the previously mentioned correlation introduced by Joseph T. Goodman in 1905, which was later modified by Juan Martínez Hernández and J. Eric Thompson. An alternative system was devised by the late Herbert J. Spinden, a specialist in Maya art who subsequently turned his attention to hieroglyphic writing and calendrics. According to Spinden's calculations, all dates in the Maya calendar are 260 years earlier than those of the Goodman-Martínez-Thompson chronology, and the relative accuracy of these correlations was the subject of a prolonged controversy.

A major breakthrough in resolving this debate resulted from the use of radiocarbon dating, a technique developed in 1947 by a physicist at the University of Chicago named Willard F. Libby. This method of determining the age of organic matter is based on the fact that the atmosphere contains among its other elements a radioactive substance designated as carbon 14. It is formed by the action of cosmic radiation upon nitrogen, and it accumulates within most living organisms in direct proportion to the quantity of carbon 14 in the atmosphere. Immediately after death this balance is interrupted, and the carbon 14 retained in the organism gradually disintegrates at a fixed rate. By comparing the amount of radioactive carbon in remains such as bone, wood, and vegetable fiber, the span of time from the date of death until these materials are unearthed can be calculated with reasonable accuracy.

Applying this technology, scientists at the University of Pennsylvania examined a series of wood samples taken from door lintels found in the ruins of Tikal, all of which bore carved date inscriptions. Even with the margin of error normally occurring in carbon-14 analysis, the tests convincingly supported the Gregorian dates assigned to these inscriptions using the Goodman-Martínez-Thompson system. As a result, the GMT correlation (as it is often referred to in technical literature) has since gained almost universal acceptance among Mayanists, and is therefore used as the basis for the dates in this book.

While calendrical data are extremely important in reconstructing the development of Maya civilization, it is by no means the only such guide available to archaeologists. Valuable insight is obtained through the careful study of ceramics, stylistic changes in art and architecture, and various social, religious, and economic factors. By utilizing such information along with radiocarbon dating, stratigraphy (the study of the sequence in which archaeological remains are deposited in the earth), calendrical inscriptions, and ethnohistoric documents, it has been possible to define the successive stages of Maya history and the approximate dates at which they occurred. Allowing for some degree of regional differentiation, since cultures rarely evolve uniformly over large geographical areas, this basic chronology and the generally accepted terminology applied to its periods can be outlined as follows:

PALEO-INDIAN		15,000?– 7000 B.C.
ARCHAIC		7000 – 2000?
PRECLASSIC (*Also called Formative*)	Early	2000 – 1000
	Middle	1000 – 300
	Late	300 – A.D. 250
CLASSIC	Early	250 – 550
	Late	550 – 800
TERMINAL CLASSIC		800 – 1000
POSTCLASSIC	Early	1000 – 1250
	Late	1250 – THE SPANISH CONQUEST

Regardless of everything scientists have learned about the Maya so far, we constantly encounter unanswered questions. No one has satisfactorily explained where or when Maya civilization originated, or how it evolved in an environment so hostile to human habitation. We have almost no reliable information on the origin of their calendar, hieroglyphic writing, and mathematical system; nor do we understand countless details pertaining to sociopolitical organization, religion, economic structure, and everyday life. Even the shattering catastrophe leading to the sudden abandonment of their greatest cities during the ninth century A.D.—one of the most baffling archaeological mysteries ever uncovered—is still deeply shrouded in conjecture.

In view of unresolved problems of such magnitude, any synthesis of Maya history must necessarily draw to some extent upon tentative conclusions. Obviously the existing literature, scientific and popular alike, contains errors and omissions that are unavoidable given the current state of research. It is hoped that these gaps in our knowledge will ultimately be closed by future discoveries, for this, after all, is the *raison d'être* of archaeology.

4 · THE SEARCH FOR ORIGINS

Archaeologists now agree that humans first entered America from Asia via the Bering Strait during the geological epoch known as the Pleistocene or Ice Age. Exactly when the earliest such migrations occurred is uncertain. We have conclusive proof that people were roaming the New World at least by 10,000 B.C., but most authorities believe their arrival may date back twenty to forty thousand years. Equipped with flint-tipped spears, crude stone implements, animal-skin clothing, and a knowledge of fire-making, these ancient hunters—the direct ancestors of the American Indians—slowly spread throughout most of this hemisphere, living in caves or rock shelters and subsisting on the meat of now-extinct animals. Numerous sites where they had slaughtered camels, mastodons, bison, mammoths, and sloths have been unearthed in western Canada, the United States, South America, and at several localities in Mexico, especially in the vicinity of Mexico City near the villages of Tequixquiac, Santa Isabel Iztapán, and Tepexpán.

Yet little is known about this stage of human occupation in the Maya area. Only scattered evidence of early hunters has turned up thus far, mainly at sites in the Guatemalan highlands, Belize, and Yucatán. Among the most notable discoveries was a flint projectile point from San Rafael near Guatemala City. It is strikingly similar to a widely distributed type designated as Clovis fluted points (first discovered in 1936 outside Clovis, New Mexico) dating from eight to ten thousand years ago, but because it was found on the surface its precise archaeological context is unknown. At a location in western Guatemala—Los Tapiales—archaeologists excavated stone implements, including the base of a Clovis point, left by hunters who inhabited the area possibly as far back as eleven thousand years; and at Loltún Cave in Yucatán the bones of extinct Pleistocene fauna were unearthed in association with several spear points.

Around 7000 B.C. a significant transition occurred that ushered in an era known archaeologically as the Archaic period (ca. 7000–2000 B.C.). By then the roving bands of nomadic hunters or "Paleo-Indians," as scientists have labeled them, seem to have virtually disappeared, due partly to the extinction of various species of animals on which they relied for food. Gradually they were supplanted by semi-sedentary groups who inhabited caves, overhanging cliffs, and crude shelters made of poles covered with hides and brush. Like their predecessors, these people killed whatever game animals were available, but their economy became increasingly dependent on gathering wild nuts, seeds, and berries—and ultimately on the cultivation of plants.

Archaic-period sites are widely distributed in the Americas, especially in the southwestern United States and central Mexico, where their contents are unusually well preserved because of arid climatic conditions. Artifacts from these horizons reveal a steady progression from a simple hunting and gathering life-style to the rise of agrarian societies, a change evidenced by the presence of more technically advanced items such as milling stones, weaving tools, ritualistic objects, ornaments, and basketry. Archaic sites have also produced the oldest examples of plant domestication found anywhere in the western hemisphere. Excavations by Richard S. MacNeish in the Tehuacán Valley, southeast of Mexico City, established that maize (corn), squash, beans, chili peppers, avocados, pumpkins, and amaranth were being cultivated in that area by 3500 B.C., though some of these plants were probably introduced two or three thousand years earlier. Additional evidence of incipient agriculture has been uncovered elsewhere in Mexico, and there is no question that the trend toward an agriculture-based economy spread throughout Mesoamerica in the period from roughly 5000 to 2000 B.C.

Archaic sites are relatively common in the Maya area, but those found so far have yielded only sparse information. A rock shelter known as Santa Marta, situated near Tuxtla Gutiérrez in western Chiapas, contained artifacts similar to materials excavated in the Tehuacán Valley, and radiocarbon dates place them in the same general time frame—7000 to 3000 B.C. Another site belonging to the Archaic period is El Chayal, a large obsidian quarry and workshop southeast of Guatemala City. Explorations in the Quiché Basin in western Guatemala have revealed stone implements at over a hundred locations, and although the age of these sites has not been accurately determined, it is estimated that they were first occupied no later than 8000 B.C. Since 1979 a number of campsites left by Archaic hunting-gathering peoples have been discovered along the coast of eastern and northern Belize; in fact, these sites, tentatively dated at 9000 to 2000 B.C., have produced an extensive inventory of stone projectile points, blades, choppers, scrapers, adzes, milling stones, pestles, and net-sinkers, suggesting that their inhabitants exploited a wide variety of animal, marine, and plant resources.

Exactly when this hunting-gathering existence gave way to settled village life in the Maya area is not certain, but present evidence indicates that it occurred sometime after 5000 B.C. Undoubtedly the advent of agriculture and pottery-making marked the beginning of this transition, but we cannot determine how or when these innovations occurred. Nor do we know the identity of the earliest Maya—whether they were direct descendants of their Archaic predecessors or a different people who entered the area at a later date. Linguistic studies involving two techniques for estimating the age of languages, glottochronology and lexicostatistics, suggest that Proto-Mayan (the tongue from which all Maya languages evolved) originally appeared in the highlands of western Guatemala about 2500 B.C., but certain variable factors inherent in this research have triggered a considerable amount of controversy as to its accuracy.

To date, the earliest archaeological remains of permanent villages in the Maya area come from excavations in northern Belize by a joint British Museum–Cambridge University expedition under the direction of Norman Hammond. Working at a site known as Cuello, Hammond and his colleagues uncovered implements, human burials, and fire pits, together with house platforms constructed of earth and stone coated with lime plaster. A series of carbon-14 dates show that Cuello was occupied between 2500 and 2000 B.C. Even more unexpected was the discovery of well-made pottery in these deposits, including jars, bowls, and plates decorated with simple incised designs. Designated as the Swasey Ceramic Complex (named after the lowest horizon or Swasey phase at Cuello), these wares constitute the oldest pottery found anywhere in the Maya region. In addition, the presence of grinding stones and kernels of maize associated with Swasey material from Cuello indicates that agriculture was being practiced there by at least 2000 B.C.

Especially significant was the fact that the Swasey Complex lay beneath the ruins of more recent Classic-period structures at Cuello, proving conclusively that the Swasey phase—which marks the beginning of the Preclassic or Formative period (2000 B.C. to A.D. 250)—was directly antecedent to the rise of Maya civilization in this area. Moreover, permanent settlements were springing up elsewhere in the region at approximately the same time, and by 1000 B.C. nearly all of the Maya realm was inhabited by village dwellers whose culture was rapidly becoming more complex.

We know that these Preclassic villages already exhibited traits which remained largely unchanged throughout Maya history. Essentially they consisted of loosely knit clusters of single-room habitations intended to accommodate small family groups. Usually such dwellings were built of a framework of poles lashed together by vines and plastered with mud, though stone, reeds, or other materials may sometimes have been used. Their roofs were high-pitched and made of thatched palm leaves or grass, and most units stood on low mounds to ensure adequate drainage. Set apart from the domestic houses were special structures designed for ceremonial purposes. The earliest buildings of this type were simple earthen platforms and terraced, flat-topped pyramids, which often supported temples or shrines similar in appearance and construction to the peasants' huts. Gradually this religious architecture became more elaborate, incorporating masonry, sculptural embellishments, and stairways; and important temples were arranged around open courtyards to form ceremonial precincts within the core of each settlement.

Agriculture and foraging constituted the principal economic basis of Early Preclassic culture. Maize, beans, squash, manioc, and a variety of other crops were cultivated in fields on the outskirts of villages. Abundant supplies of wild fruits, nuts, and seeds were available in most areas, and meat was obtained by hunting deer, peccaries, tapirs, monkeys, turkeys, iguanas, and other game animals. Groups living near the ocean supplemented their diet with crustaceans, sea turtles, and fish, probably caught in nets woven of henequen fibers and weighted with pottery disks or stones.

Artifacts unearthed in the oldest Preclassic sites reflect levels of technology comparable to those of Neolithic cultures in Europe and Asia. Among these objects is an assortment of stone implements that includes scrapers, knives, spear points, choppers, drills, and milling stones called *metates* and *manos*. Ornaments such as beads, earplugs, and pendants fashioned out of stone, pottery, or shell are commonly found, together with tiny clay figurines representing animals, birds, and humans, especially female forms, which presumably had some connection with fertility cults. Few examples of more fragile articles have survived, but Preclassic peoples undoubtedly utilized antler, bone, and wood to make awls, needles, weaving tools, looms, simple furniture, and other specialized items. Animal hide was used for sandals, and cotton and henequen fiber (also called sisal) supplied raw material for cloth, baskets, matting, bags, and nets.

It has not been determined when or by what means pottery was introduced among the Maya, but large quantities of sherds and whole vessels are recovered in Preclassic sites. As previously mentioned, the Swasey wares being produced at Cuello in Belize by 2000 B.C. were surprisingly sophisticated in view of their age. Another ancient ceramic sequence, the Barra Complex, originated between 1700 and 1500 B.C. in southern Guatemala and Chiapas; and a comparable pottery tradition, the Ocós Complex from the Pacific coast of Guatemala, dates back to around 1500 B.C. By approximately 900 B.C., ceramics associated with a culture known as Xe (pronounced "shay") appeared at Seibal and Altar de Sacrificios on the Pasión River, and throughout the lowlands a type of pottery known as Mamom is widely distributed in Middle Preclassic horizons dating from 800 to 300 B.C.

Generally, these Mamom wares consisted of rounded jars called *tecomates*, cylindrical vases, bowls, and shallow, flat-bottomed plates with slightly flaring sides, though in the Guatemalan highlands effigy vessels, tripod jars, and incense burners were quite common. One particularly notable expression of early ceramic art, the famous Las Charcas ware made at Kaminaljuyú near Guatemala City during the Middle Preclassic period, was characterized by exquisite bowls embellished with monkeys, grotesque masks, and abstract elements superbly painted in red on a white background. Otherwise, most Early and Middle Preclassic pottery was rather prosaic, and except for certain varieties decorated with incised geometric designs, appliqué, or simple painted motifs, it usally had plain surfaces ranging from white, cream, and gray to red, orange, buff, brown, and black.

As Preclassic communities grew in size and complexity, a number of new sociopolitical elements began to appear. With expanding populations, greater craft specialization, and the development of extensive trade networks, differences in wealth and social status became more pronounced, leading to the emergence of so-called "ranked societies" or chiefdoms dominated by hereditary rulers. Increasing emphasis on religious concepts and ritualism—stemming from a desire to deify nature and thereby control environmental forces on which survival depended—probably gave rise to a powerful priesthood, though we cannot be sure whether the ruling elite and priests were separate entities. As a result of these factors, the villages themselves underwent a gradual metamorphosis from small agrarian settlements to thriving centers of religious, political, and economic activity, a transition that ultimately led to the construction of huge complexes of temples, palaces, and courtyards. Exactly how and when these fundamental changes occurred is not well understood. Until recently our clearest picture of these events came from Middle and Late Preclassic horizons in the highlands, but excavations in lowland sites are beginning to reveal a comparable body of information pertaining to that region.

Nowhere are these occurrences better exemplified than by what is called the Miraflores phase at Kaminaljuyú, the period from about 300

B.C. to A.D. 150 that witnessed the transformation of this site from a relatively small village into an imposing center whose influence dominated the highlands for centuries. Today most of Kaminaljuyú's ruins lie underneath the outskirts of Guatemala City, but investigations conducted intermittently since 1935 have revealed more than one hundred pyramids and platforms erected during the Miraflores phase. Originally intended to support temples on their summits, these mounds ranged up to sixty-five feet in height and consisted of several superimposed structures built in successive stages over long periods of time. Some of them contained elaborate tombs—rectangular shafts cut into the tops of pyramids and roofed with heavy wooden beams, fiber matting, and reeds—in which important persons believed to have been rulers or priests were buried.

Judging by the wealth of objects unearthed in these graves, there can be no question that by Late Preclassic times the elite classes already enjoyed a highly exalted social position. The bodies were carefully wrapped in cotton shrouds, covered with red cinnabar, and placed fully extended on wooden litters before being lowered into the tombs. Sometimes adults and children (possibly servants or relatives of the deceased), who appear to have been sacrificial victims, were interred with the corpses, and the chambers were filled with funerary offerings of remarkable beauty. Two spectacular tombs concealed in a structure at Kaminaljuyú known as Mound E-III-3 yielded ornaments of jade, shell, and stone, translucent bowls carved of marble and chlorite schist, obsidian flakes, iron pyrite plaques, a mosaic mask made from albite, tiny soapstone bottles, effigies, a stone sculpture representing a mushroom rising from the back of a crouched jaguar, and approximately 455 pottery vessels (some shattered beyond repair), including a jar in the form of a seated human decorated with polychrome stucco applied to its surface.

Levels of cultural development approximating the Miraflores phase at Kaminaljuyú have also been found in the lowlands. Here our initial information concerning this period came to light in 1926 when archaeologists from the Carnegie Institution began excavating the important site of Uaxactún in the Petén district of Guatemala. Among the buildings selected for exploration was a cluster of twelve mounds in the city's eastern sector designated as Group E, and the seventh structure in this complex unexpectedly provided a discovery of major significance. Outwardly this pyramid was typical of other Classic-period ruins at Uaxactún. Its exterior was severely damaged by decay, but since it was the custom of Maya builders to frequently modify or enlarge their religious edifices, a considerably older pyramid in a nearly perfect state of preservation was revealed underneath the outer shell. This exceptional structure—known as E-VII-sub—stood twenty-seven feet in height and was made of earth and rubble covered with a veneer of gleaming white stucco. Its terraced sides were ascended by stairways and adorned with ponderous, highly stylized masks representing jaguars and serpents; altogether eighteen of these curious masks decorated the pyramid, all skillfully modeled in stucco and measuring about six feet high by eight feet wide.

E-VII-sub is one of the finest examples of early religious architecture ever uncovered in the lowlands. It was probably constructed in the first or second century A.D. and was associated with a type of pottery called Chicanel, which is characteristic of Late Preclassic culture throughout the lowlands. Equally important, the discovery of E-VII-sub and Chicanel ceramics *underlying* Classic buildings demonstrated not only the existence of populous settlements in the lowlands during the Preclassic period, but also that these centers had eventually expanded into the great cities which flourished there between A.D. 250 and 800.

Further confirmation of this has since emerged at the huge site of Tikal, twelve miles south of Uaxactún. Excavations by the University of Pennsylvania have shown that Tikal was already occupied by 600 B.C., with an accelerated emphasis in Late Preclassic times on ceremonialism, ruling hierarchies, architecture, and art. Digging below the city's North Acropolis (one of the most incredible achievements of Maya engineering), scientists unearthed the remains of numerous temples and platforms dating from this era, along with large quantities of Chicanel ceramics. Some of these structures were surprisingly refined, and one outstanding example—a terraced pyramid-temple erected about 50 B.C.—was constructed of masonry and ornamented with heavy apron moldings, two massive stucco masks, and a complex sculptured frieze adorning its façade, which was originally painted red, pink, black, and cream.

Splendid tombs were found in conjunction with these buildings. Usually situated beneath plaza floors or concealed in temple platforms, they consisted of rectangular crypts built of cut stone and often roofed with crude corbeled vaulted ceilings, a feature that later became a hallmark of Classic architecture. As was the case at Kaminaljuyú, such graves were intended for persons of high status, and they contained lavish mortuary offerings: jade and shell ornaments, figurines, masks, ceramics, stingray spines (highly prized for ceremonial bloodletting), obsidian blades, and gourds covered with painted stucco. Several of these tombs also revealed badly decayed polychrome frescoes depicting humans wearing ornate headdresses and costumes; and in 1983 a group of Late Preclassic structures was discovered at Tikal on which superbly executed murals showing elite figures and mythological scenes were used to decorate exterior walls.

Impressive examples of Late Preclassic activity have turned up elsewhere in the lowlands. For instance, excavators found that a site in northern Belize known as Cerros had already grown into an important maritime trading center by A.D. 100, and among its buildings were extraordinary stucco-plastered pyramids adorned with large painted masks. At the nearby city of Lamanai a massive structure erected sometime between 150 B.C. and A.D. 200 proved to be a hundred-foot-high pyramid with multiple terraces, three stairways, and a wide supporting platform—a building equal to the finest Classic-period architecture. Similar remains have been uncovered at various places in the Yucatán Peninsula, particularly at the sprawling city of Dzibilchaltún near Mérida, where an expedition from Tulane University and the National Geographic Society excavated scores of Late Preclassic structures ranging from domestic houses to aggregations of platforms, pyramids, and courtyards.

In 1978 a team of archaeologists began exploring the site of El Mirador, located in the Petén near the northern border of Guatemala. Almost immediately they found evidence that by Late Preclassic times El Mirador had burgeoned into a thriving center of political, economic, and religious activity, with a well-established elite class, a stratified society, and spectacular public buildings. By about 150 B.C. the city had reached enormous proportions (even larger perhaps than Tikal at its zenith during the eighth century A.D.); its central core consisted of two major architectural complexes—the East and West Groups—which included temples, palaces, residences, platforms, acropolises, and causeways. The West Group was bounded on the south and east by a masonry wall with parapets, and several narrow gates afforded controlled access to this section of the city. Within the East Group lies the so-called Danta Complex, a series of gigantic platforms and pyramids that Bruce Dahlin, the director of the El Mirador Project, has described as "the largest single architectural achievement yet known anywhere in the entire Maya realm."

The profusion of Late Preclassic remains in the lowlands attests not only to expanding populations, a vigorous economy, and steady advances in art, architecture, and technology, but also to a high degree of sociopolitical organization, as well as managerial control by the ruling elite over natural resources and labor. Obviously, many details surrounding the rise of Maya culture are still obscure, though it is clear that the basic traits which characterized Maya civilization during the Classic period were deeply rooted in Preclassic traditions. Foremost among these were massive religious architecture, a complex pantheon coupled with formalized rituals, hereditary dynasties, hieroglyphic writing, calendrics, a high degree of sophistication in sculpture and ceramics, and the widespread practice of erecting dated stelae to commemorate important historic and ritualistic events or to mark the passing of specific time intervals.

Scholars are not certain how or when the Maya acquired the calendar and hieroglyphic writing, though in recent years some fascinating clues bearing on this question have surfaced. At first these inventions were believed to have been devised independently by the Maya, presumably in the lowlands where they reached their highest levels of development. But most archaeologists have now concluded that they probably originated among a shadowy people called the Olmec, who inhabited Tabasco and southern Veracruz at a remote date.

Olmec culture is known mainly from three important ruins: La Venta, Tres Zapotes, and San Lorenzo. By roughly 1200 B.C. at least two of these sites, San Lorenzo and La Venta, were already flourishing settlements complete with pyramids, temple platforms, and stone sculpture. Another intriguing fact about the Olmec is that although their origin remains a mystery, their influence was extremely widespread. Unmistakable Olmec traits are found in archaeological sites extending from the Valley of Mexico to El Salvador, and some authorities view the Olmec as a kind of "mother culture" that played a vital role in stimulating the rise of civilization throughout the area.

Olmec craftsmen were exceptionally adept at cutting and polishing materials such as jade, serpentine, quartz, and steatite, and they had mastered the art of carving basalt, which was used for altars, stelae, and colossal human heads, some of which weigh up to eighteen tons. Olmec sculpture, noted for its vigor, originality, and emphasis on realism, is unique in Mexico and Central America, and students consider it the first major art style to have evolved anywhere in the region. It centered on full-figure and bas-relief depictions of fat, "baby-faced" humans, often displaying pronounced negroid or Oriental features as well as anthropomorphized monsters or werejaguars with flat noses, flamelike brows, fangs, and snarling, downturned mouths.

Apparently the Olmec also possessed the earliest calendar and hieroglyphic writing in Mesoamerica. In 1939, Matthew W. Sterling, excavating at Tres Zapotes under the sponsorship of the Smithsonian Institution and the National Geographic Society, dug up a broken monument known as Stela C. One side was carved with a relief mask representing a typical Olmec werejaguar, but to the astonishment of Sterling and his colleagues, its backside contained a date inscription employing the same bar-and-dot numerals and Long Count calendrical system used by the Maya. It recorded a year equal to 31 B.C.—one of the oldest surely dated objects ever found in the area.

Now another curious fact suddenly assumed new significance. In 1902 a small jade effigy of a duck-billed figure, the Tuxtla Statuette, was unearthed near San Andrés Tuxtla in Veracruz, only fifteen miles east of Tres Zapotes. Generally conceded to be of Olmec workmanship, this piece had puzzled archaeologists because it was carved with a Long Count date equivalent to A.D. 162. Since the inscriptions on both the Tuxtla Statuette and Stela C from Tres Zapotes were considerably older than any known Maya dates, speculation arose that it was perhaps the Olmec who actually invented hieroglyphic writing and the calendar. Added support was given to this idea by the discovery of Olmec artifacts—figurines, pendants, celts, and plaques—inscribed with glyphic symbols that suggest early forms of Maya hieroglyphs. Furthermore, the existence of extremely ancient hieroglyphic texts associated with Olmec influences has been established at the famous Zapotec ruins of Monte Albán in Oaxaca and at Chiapa de Corzo in central Chiapas, where a section of a stela probably dating from 36 B.C. was excavated.

An expedition from the University of Pennsylvania led by Robert J. Sharer uncovered a badly effaced monument at the site of El Portón in the Salama Valley of central Guatemala. Nothing remained of its original carvings except eleven figures believed to represent glyphic elements, but several of these are strikingly similar to certain Olmec motifs. Other early dates and inscriptions associated with Olmec traits have been found in Guatemala. Included among these are a number of carved stones at Abaj Takalik, a site located on the Pacific slopes south of Quezaltenango, which has also yielded several stelae executed in a style clearly related to Classic Maya sculpture and inscribed with dates ranging from the first or second century before Christ to A.D. 126. Another monument, designated as the Herrera Stela from El Baúl, approximately fifty miles southeast of Abaj Takalik, exhibited a partially eroded Long Count inscription tentatively dated at A.D. 36. Excavators working at Kaminaljuyú stumbled upon a portion of a magnificent Late Preclassic relief carving—Stela 10—depicting an anthropomorphized jaguar and two lavishly costumed humans interspersed with bar-and-dot numbers and hieroglyphs, which appear to represent an antecedent of Maya script.

In the case of the monuments from El Baúl, Kaminaljuyú, and some of those at Abaj Takalik, the scenes they depict reflect elements derived from an important center called Izapa, situated in southeastern Chiapas near the Guatemalan border. Izapan art is distinguished by its superbly executed, if somewhat florid, bas-relief sculpture, usually portraying mythological creatures, richly attired chieftains, and gods. Inherent in these works are a number of Olmec-inspired characteristics, and many archaeologists envision Izapa as a major entrepôt through which Olmec influences were infused into Maya culture during the Late Preclassic era. This argument is strengthened by the early appearance at Izapa of several features subsequently adopted by the Maya, especially images of a "Long-Lipped God" who probably became the rain deity Chac, and various stylistic conventions incorporated into Early Classic sculpture. Furthermore, there is scattered evidence that Olmec traits penetrated the lowlands by other means during the Middle and Late Preclassic periods, although as yet the extent and significance of this Olmec presence is unclear.

Whatever the facts surrounding the origin of Maya calendrics and hieroglyphic writing, these innovations reached their highest development in the lowlands between A.D. 300 and 800, especially in the Petén and adjacent regions. Thus far the oldest Maya inscription found anywhere in the lowlands was carved on Stela 29 at Tikal, which bears a Long Count date corresponding to July 6, A.D. 292. By this time the Maya had attained a remarkably high level of advancement in many fields of endeavor, and the stage was set for the extraordinary achievements that marked the florescence of Classic civilization.

In spite of the obvious environmental advantages offered by the highlands—its temperate climate, fertile soil, and abundant natural resources—this region remained curiously outside the mainstream of Classic Maya culture. As J. Eric Thompson pointed out, sculpture, architecture, and ceramics never approached the levels of excellence in the highlands that they did elsewhere, and the corbeled vault, one of the most fundamental concepts of Maya engineering, was restricted to several sites near the periphery of lowland influence. Even the auspicious beginnings in hieroglyphic writing and calendrics evidenced by the monuments at Abaj Takalik, El Baúl, and Kaminaljuyú mysteriously disappeared from the area sometime before A.D. 300, and no inscriptions from the Classic period have occurred in any highland sites. Equally strange was the sudden abandonment of Long Count dates and the stela cult in this region by the end of the Late Preclassic era, both having previously played an important role in the development of its early cultures.

Archaeologists believe these puzzling circumstances are partly attributable to intruders from Teotihuacán, the great urban center near Mexico City so famous for its lavish palaces, long avenues of temples, and the Pyramids of the Sun and Moon. Large numbers of immigrants from Teotihuacán began infiltrating the highlands around A.D. 400, heralded perhaps by military invasion or a massive colonization which resulted in Kaminaljuyú's loss of political and economic independence. Over the next two centuries the city was practically rebuilt in Teotihuacán's architectural style. Much of the pottery from Classic-period tombs at Kaminaljuyú was either imported directly from Teotihuacán or copied by local craftsmen, who produced vessels decorated with images of Teotihuacán's gods and human figures wearing the typical dress of its elite classes. Unquestionably, Kaminaljuyú, together with vast sections of the surrounding territory, fell under the domination of Mexican rulers, sociopolitical institutions, and religious beliefs, and although certain Maya traditions continued to survive, and extensive trade was carried on with lowland cities, life in this region was radically altered by these foreign contacts.

By the fifth century A.D. strong Mexican influences had appeared in the lowlands, particularly at Tikal, where Early Classic monuments and ceramics reflect the unmistakable imprint of Teotihuacán's artistic conventions. A powerful ruler at Tikal known as Curl Nose (ca. A.D. 378–426)—whose name is taken from his identifying glyph—may even have been a member of Kaminaljuyú's royalty who married into Tikal's ruling family. The funerary offerings unearthed in his tomb closely resemble Teotihuacán-period burials at Kaminaljuyú, and a depiction on Stela 31 at Tikal of his successor (and presumed son), Stormy Sky, exhibits a number of pronounced Mexican traits, including two attendants bedecked in the typical military regalia worn by Teotihuacán's warriors.

A second factor that apparently contributed to the decline of Early Classic Maya culture in the highlands was a natural disaster of catastrophic proportions. Sometime around A.D. 200 to 250 an enormous volcano called Ilopango erupted in central El Salvador. As a result, thick layers of ash rendered the area within a sixty-mile radius of Ilopango virtually uninhabitable for almost two hundred years, a calamity that presaged a serious economic crisis with far-reaching consequences. The prosperity of Kaminaljuyú, Izapa, Abaj Takalik, Chalchuapa (in El Salvador), and other highland centers had depended on extensive trade networks that stretched from southern Mexico into El Salvador. These commercial ties were suddenly disrupted, and while some areas seem to have been only slightly affected by this up-heaval, many settlements were abandoned, some experienced drastic shifts in population density, and others—especially Kaminaljuyú—suffered a prolonged economic decline. Very likely the newly emerging lowland cities benefited from these chaotic circumstances to the south by seizing the opportunity to expand their own trade networks, and it is probable that the eruption of Ilopango drove large numbers of refugees from central El Salvador into the southeastern sector of the lowlands, thereby accelerating the growth of its centers.

Regardless of many unanswered questions concerning the ascendancy of Early Classic culture in the lowlands, it was here that Maya civilization reached the peak of its development. One can hardly imagine a more unfavorable setting for this extraordinary upsurge in terms of climate, relatively poor soils, and the constant encroachment of vegetation. Yet in these inhospitable surroundings the artistic and intellectual ingenuity of the Maya achieved its maximum expression. Here architects designed and built cities on a truly heroic scale. Such pursuits as astronomy, calendrics, hieroglyphic writing, and mathematics opened new scientific and philosophical vistas. Stone sculpture gave expression to a wide range of aesthetic concepts; and skilled artisans produced ceramics, murals, ornaments, and textiles of exceptional refinement. Increasing populations encouraged the rapid spread of established traditions, restless building, and the founding of new settlements until the countryside was dotted with villages and cities.

Despite regional variations in certain aspects of Maya culture—particularly art and architecture—the fundamental precepts of cosmology, ritualism, iconography, hieroglyphics, and calendrics remained essentially alike throughout the lowlands, a fact suggesting a high degree of orthodoxy and singleminded devotion to deeply rooted spiritual ideals. Everywhere the nature of Maya society displayed a similar uniformity: a rigid class structure dominated by powerful priests and nobles in whom all authority resided. Leading the way before masses of illiterate peasants, these elite groups established the tenets around which the daily existence of the people revolved. Under their direction, life for the commoners was an endless round dedicated to cultivating the soil, public service necessary to construct, maintain, and enlarge the cities, and adoration of the gods through strict observance of rituals, offerings, and sacrifices. In the beginning the peasants were content to subject themselves to this powerful elite. Willingly they upheld the mandates of rulers who they believed were divinely chosen to guide their destinies. Ample reward was to be found in the Golden Age that their ingenuity had ushered into reality and that now burst upon them with intoxicating brilliance.

Above everything else the Maya accomplished during the Classic period, their ingenuity was most pronounced in the fields of astronomy and calendrics. As such pursuits were closely connected to religion, they expended enormous effort to achieve mastery in these realms of knowledge. No other people in history were so obsessed with the passing of time, and they labored tirelessly to understand its mysteries and control its awesome influences. Ultimately these endeavors led them to evolve a calendrical lore extending millions of years into the past and encompassing a profoundly complex philosophy.

To the Maya, time was never a purely abstract means of arranging events into an orderly sequence. It was envisioned as a supernatural phenomenon involving omnipotent forces of creation and destruction, with all of its aspects directly influenced by gods who were believed to be either benevolent or evil. Such deities were associated with specific numbers and took forms by which they could be portrayed in hieroglyphic inscriptions. Each division of the Maya calendar—whether days, months, years, or larger segments—was conceived as a "burden" carried on the backs of these divine guardians of time; at the conclusion of their allotted cycles the burdens were assumed by whatever god represented the next appropriate number. To translate this principle into our calendrical system, one must imagine, for example, that at midnight on October 31 the god of number thirty-one unloads his burden—the month of October. Immediately the god of number one picks up the month of November, carries it on his back for twenty-four hours, then releases it to the god of number two, who the next day gives it to the god of number three, and so forth. The same procedure would also apply to the years, decades, centuries, and millennia, all of them moving through eternity on the backs of various gods responsible for their proper numerical sequence. If a malevolent deity happened to acquire the burden of a particular cycle, grievous consequences could be expected until it was relinquished to a more favorable bearer. Whether or not a certain month or year held promise of good or bad fortune was a matter predetermined by the temperament of the god on whose back it was transported. Moreover, the Maya viewed time as cyclical rather than linear, and events associated with specific calendrical cycles in the past were considered likely to repeat themselves when those cycles recurred—a belief that fostered a strong emphasis on divination and astrology.

It was a curious concept of time, and one that explains in part the power of the ruling elite and priesthood over the populace, who must surely have considered survival impossible without learned mediators to interpret the gods' irascible tendencies. Only persons with specialized esoteric knowledge stood between the continuation of life and catastrophes brought about by misjudging divine inclinations. Having recognized the attributes of the gods and plotted their restless paths across the highways of time and space, they alone could determine when beneficial and harmful deities ruled a specific period, or, as was frequently the case, when the number of benevolent gods outweighed the less sympathetic ones. Thus this obsession with time was tantamount to a grand-scale quest for lucky and unlucky periods in the hope that, once forewarned of future prospects, one could then prophesy the outcome of events.

Altogether the Maya observed three distinct year measurements: the 260-day sacred year or *tzolkin,* the *tun* or 360-day year, and the *haab* or vague year, which was composed of 365 days divided into 18 months of 20 days each, with the addition of an extra 5-day month known as the *Uayeb*. Ordinarily the vague year (often referred to as the "civil year") was used in secular affairs, the *tzolkin* determined certain matters pertaining to ceremonials and prophecy, and the *tun* was employed in computing Long Count dates.

Great ritualistic importance was placed on the so-called Calendar Round, or the meshing of the vague year with the *tzolkin*. To accomplish this it was necessary to synchronize the days and months of the 365-day vague year with repeating sequences of 20 days and the numbers from 1 to 13, which comprised the 260-day *tzolkin*. A total of 18,980 possible combinations of days, months, and numbers were involved in these permutations, and the Calendar Round—the interval required for a particular date to return to its original position—occurred only once every 52 years. Actually, the Calendar Round was not an exclusively Maya innovation. It was widely used throughout Mesoamerica both for recording time and as a divinatory almanac, and though its origin is unknown, there is evidence of its appearance among the Zapotecs at Monte Albán in the fifth century B.C.

Unquestionably the outstanding achievement of Maya calendrics was the Long Count—also called the Initial Series. Generally considered to be the most accurate calendar ever devised in the ancient world, it was surprisingly complex in structure and consisted of recurring cycles of nine interrelated periods, which made it possible to keep track of enormous time spans in somewhat the same way as we compute months, decades, centuries, and millennia. The basic unit of the Long Count was the day or *kin*. Since there is no evidence that it was divided into anything comparable to hours, minutes, or seconds, we must assume a day was the smallest segment of time recorded by the Maya. Beginning with the *kin*, the sequence of Long Count intervals was as follows:

20 *kins*	=	1 *uinal* (20 days)
18 *uinals*	=	1 *tun* (360 days)
20 *tuns*	=	1 *katun* (7,200 days)
20 *katuns*	=	1 *baktun* (144,000 days)
20 *baktuns*	=	1 *pictun* (2,880,000 days)
20 *pictuns*	=	1 *calabtun* (57,600,000 days)
20 *calabtuns*	=	1 *kinchiltun* (1,152,000,000 days)
20 *kinchiltuns*	=	1 *alautun* (23,040,000,000 days)

Each of these cycles revolved independently, expanding from *tuns* to *alautuns* by multiples of twenty. Virtually every Long Count inscription included only the first five divisions, or *kins* through *baktuns*, plus the position of the Calendar Round on which the date terminated. Hieroglyphs representing these periods were inscribed in double rows of vertical columns descending in order from *baktuns* at the top to *kins* at the bottom. Numeral coefficients accompanying the glyphs indicated the number of times each cycle had occurred since the beginning of Maya chronology. Hence a typical date as written by archaeologists would read 8.14.10.13.15 7 *Ahau* 3 *Xul*, or 8 elapsed *baktuns*, 14 *katuns*, 10 *tuns*, 13 *uinals*, and 15 *kins*, together with a Calendar Round position equal to the day 7 *Ahau* of the *tzolkin* and the third day of the month *Xul* in the *haab* or vague year—in this case a date corresponding to April 9, A.D. 328. In addition, Long Count inscriptions were usually augmented by what is known as a Supplementary Series, which included glyphs denoting such information as the length of the lunar month, the phase of the moon, and the patron deities associated with the specific date involved.

One of the initial challenges faced by epigraphers was to determine the starting point of the Maya calendar. This question was resolved in 1887 with Ernst Förstemann's discovery that every Long Count inscription was calculated from a base of 13.0.0.0.0. 4 *Ahau* 8 *Cumku*, or 3114 B.C. It is referred to as the ''zero date'' of Long Count computations, and its function is analogous to the birth of Christ in the Gregorian calendar. Because this date occurred more than three millennia before the earliest known Maya inscription on Stela 29 at Tikal, it undoubtedly represents a hypothetical rather than an actual historical event. Sylvanus Morley suggested that the Maya might have considered 13.0.0.0.0. 4 *Ahau* 8 *Cumku* the day of the world's creation, or its origin may be rooted in some mythological event.

While unraveling the complexities of the calendar, scholars quickly became aware of the exceptional skills possessed by Maya astronomers. Using fixed lines of sight, crossed sticks, or buildings aligned so as to provide observation points, they had meticulously plotted the movements of the sun, the moon, and Venus. There is some evidence they might also have probed Mars, Jupiter, Mercury, and Saturn; and they undertook intensive studies of lunar eclipses, enabling them to accurately predict these phenomena. They were acutely aware that seemingly minute discrepancies in certain computations would eventually lead to irreconcilable flaws, and as a result of cautious observations their margin of error was remarkably slight. For example, their measurement of the length of the tropical year was 365.2420 days as compared with our present figure of 365.2422; and they calculated the average synodical revolution of Venus at 584 days, whereas its actual span is 583.92. Although there is no evidence that adjustments were made to allow for fractional increases in the duration of the solar year (which we eliminate by the addition of leap years), they succeeded in correcting discrepancies in the length of lunar cycles. Moreover, the Maya appear to have envisioned time in infinite terms: examples of calendrical inscriptions have been uncovered reaching back 90,000,000 and 400,000,000 years.

Achievements of this magnitude would obviously have been impossible without a system of mathematics. As was the case with many other hieroglyphs, the Maya employed two means of representing numbers: head-variant symbols and the more commonly used bar-and-dot notations in which a bar had the value of five and a dot signified one. With this method numbers from one to nineteen were written as follows:

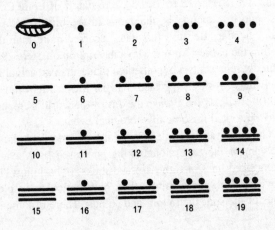

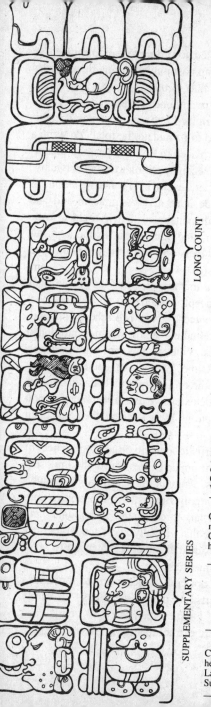

How a Long Count or Initial Series date is read; an inscription from Stela E at Quiriguá, which records the date 9.17.0.0.0. 13 *Ahau* 18 *Cumku*, or January 22, A.D. 771. (Redrawn from *The Ancient Maya*, Fourth Edition, by Sylvanus G. Morley and George W. Brainerd; revised by Robert J. Sharer, with the permission of Stanford University Press. Copyright 1947, 1956, and 1983 by the Board of Trustees of Leland Stanford Junior University.)

LONG COUNT

LONG COUNT INTRODUCING GLYPH
Grotesque head in center is the only variable element of this sign. This is the name glyph of the deity who is patron of the month (here *Cumku*) in which the Long Count terminal date falls.

9 *baktuns* (9 × 144,000 days = 1,296,000 days)

17 *katuns* (17 × 7,200 days = 122,400 days)

0 *tuns* (0 × 360 days = 0 days)

0 *uinals* (0 × 20 days = 0 days)

0 *kins* (0 × 1 day = 0 days)

13 *Ahau* (day reached by counting forward above total of days from starting point of Maya Era)

GLYPH G9
Name glyph of the deity who is patron of the Ninth Day in the nine-day series (The Nine Gods of the Lower World)

GLYPH F
Meaning unknown

GLYPHS E AND D
Glyphs denoting the moon age of the Long Count terminal date, here "new moon"

GLYPH C
Glyph denoting position of current lunar month in lunar half-year period, here the second position

GLYPH X3
Meaning unknown

GLYPH B
Meaning unknown

SUPPLEMENTARY SERIES

GLYPH A9
Current lunar month, here 29 days in length. Last glyph of the Supplementary Series

18 *Cumku* (month reached by counting forward above total of days from starting point of Maya Era). Last glyph of the Long Count

Numbers above nineteen were noted according to their placement in vertical columns, with each ascending position increasing by multiples of twenty, or a sequence of 1, 20, 400, 8,000, 160,000, 3,200,000, and 64,000,000. A numeral placed in any one of these positions automatically increased in value as determined by its corresponding multiple, and the column was then added to formulate the total. To write a number such as 827, two dots were placed in the third position, denoting two units of 400, one dot in the second position to indicate twenty, and a bar and two dots (the number seven) in the first position. A vigesimal system of this type made it relatively simple to add and subtract, and recent studies have demonstrated that it could also be adapted to multiplication, division, and square-root extractions, although to what extent the Maya understood these more complicated procedures is unknown.

Another notable feature of Maya mathematics was the principle of the zero. In fact, this abstract concept, essential to all but the most rudimentary calculations, was invented by only two other peoples in history—the Babylonians and the Hindus—and it was not introduced into Europe until the Middle Ages. Whether the zero's invention in Mesoamerica can be attributed to Olmec or Maya ingenuity is closely tied to the uncertainty surrounding the origin of the calendar and hieroglyphic writing. Yet the Maya made extensive use of its potential, and it was represented in their inscriptions by a stylized shell, an open hand, or a head-variant glyph.

Along with intellectual and artistic pursuits, the florescence of Classic-period culture reached its ultimate expression in the imposing cities that dominated the lowlands. And contrary to the once-popular notion that these cities were essentially ritualistic in function (a concept that originally prompted scholars to call them ''ceremonial centers''), there is mounting evidence that virtually all of the larger sites contained religious, civic, and residential buildings intended to serve the needs of truly urbanized communities.

Even though Maya cities were not laid out according to formalized plans, they all included characteristic types of structures—primarily open plazas, terraced pyramids, temples, palaces, ball courts, and shrines. Often these buildings were extraordinarily impressive in size,

design, and external decoration, and Maya architects utilized various techniques to impart an overwhelming sense of grandeur to their creations. Nearly always they enhanced important temples and palaces by elevating them on pyramids, platforms, or acropolises. Widespread use was made of tall, crestlike appendages called roof combs, usually of openwork design, which adorned the rooftops and further accentuated the illusion of height. Great effort was expended in decorating the roof combs and upper façades of many buildings, and both were frequently ornamented with sculpture or friezes executed in cut stone or stucco. Traces of polychrome paint have been found on the remains of some of these embellishments, indicating that they were originally coated with bright colors.

In the Río Bec area of southern Quintana Roo and Campeche, the use of elaborate ornamentation reached its apogee, with emphasis on pseudopyramids attached to the fronts of temples to create the effect of towers, together with façades graced by huge stylized masks surrounded by a wealth of intricate sculptural detail. Immediately to the north, in the Chenes district of Campeche, another group of ruins shows similar kinds of architectural flamboyance, especially in the use of gigantic masks and restless design elements. And in the vicinity of the Puuc Hills in northern Campeche and southwestern Yucatán, this florid decorative tradition attained a remarkable degree of refinement at such sites as Uxmal, Kabáh, Sayil, and Labná, where the façades of buildings exhibit a veritable maze of geometric forms, false columns, serpents, human figures, and masks representing the rain god Chac.

In contrast to the external splendor achieved by Maya architects, the interiors of buildings were curiously uninspired. Usually the temples consisted of several small rooms, sometimes with shrines or antechambers concealed within them; and typical palaces contained a number of tiny, cell-like compartments divided by partitions. Generally these rooms were narrow and damp, with few windows and no chimneys (some had small openings intended as ventilating ducts), and the principal source of light and air was provided by doorways. Occasionally the walls were decorated with murals, hieroglyphic inscriptions, or graffiti, but for the most part interior rooms were plastered with white stucco and left unadorned.

Archaeologists disagree sharply as to the exact function of temples and palaces, especially the latter, which are sometimes quite complex in design, with a maze of interior rooms, corridors, partitions, and courtyards. In some cases it is difficult to distinguish between the two categories of buildings, and there is reason to suspect that ritual and civil activities may have taken place in temples and palaces alike. Undoubtedly, however, certain important temples were exclusively ceremonial in nature, and the presence in many palaces of benches, occasional windows, and ringlike devices or niches for hanging coverings over doorways strongly suggests that they served as elite residences. Other such buildings might also have been used for administrative purposes, dormitories for young men studying to be priests, or retreats for the hierarchy during rituals.

In every major city there was a ball court in which a popular game known as *pok-a-tok* was played, and many of the larger centers had several such courts (see Chapter 8). As a rule they were shaped like a capital I, with a flat playing surface about 100 to 150 feet long and 25 to 50 feet wide, flanked on two sides by either sloping or vertical walls. Elaborate rituals accompanied these contests, and the courts were often associated with temples where appropriate ceremonies were enacted in conjunction with the games. Quite possibly these temples also served as viewing stands for the elite classes, while ordinary spectators watched the matches from atop the enclosing walls.

Numerous cities contained sweat baths—rooms fitted with stone benches, drainage troughs, and hearths for boiling water to make steam. In some sites there are groups of buildings that were arranged to serve as astronomical observatories; these consisted of a pyramid oriented due east, opposite which stood three temples positioned to give observers on the pyramid's stairway lines of sight for viewing the sunrise in order to determine equinoxes and solstices. Among other types of structures found in Maya cities are artificial reservoirs designed to store rainwater, and underground bottle-shaped pits called *chultuns* used as cisterns, storage places, and burial vaults. Elaborate drainage systems for carrying off excess water from buildings and courtyards were common, and aqueducts and bridges have been uncovered at several sites.

1 Diego de Landa (1524–79), third Bishop of Yucatán, relentless destroyer of Maya culture and author of the *Relación de las Cosas de Yucatán*.

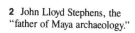

2 John Lloyd Stephens, the "father of Maya archaeology."

3 The Acropolis, Copán, Honduras, as it looked about A.D. 750.

4 Stela H, Copán, as drawn by Frederick Catherwood.

5 Stela F, Copán. John Lloyd Stephens observed that these extraordinary monuments were equal in workmanship "to the finest Egyptian sculpture."

6 Rear view of Stela A, Copán, showing hieroglyphic inscriptions.

7 Stela A, Copán.

8 The Hieroglyphic Stairway, Copán. Each of the more than 2,500 stones used to construct the risers was carved with glyphs, making this the longest single inscription found to date in the Maya area.

9 The Ball Court, Copán. Courts such as this were used for the popular game of *pok-a-tok*. Although these structures varied in specific details from one site to the next, their basic design included a rectangular or I-shaped playing surface, sloping or vertical walls fitted with stone markers or rings, and adjoining temples where rituals associated with the game were enacted.

10 A trachyte head from the façade of Temple 22, Copán. This sensitive sculpture, believed to represent the maize god, embodies the Maya concept of youthful beauty. Height, 14³⁄₈ inches.

11 Stela F, Quiriguá, Guatemala. Although it was a relatively small center, Quiriguá is famous for its enormous monuments, including the tallest-known stelae in the Maya region. This example, more than 30 feet high, is adorned with a portrait of Cauac Sky, an important ruler who was inaugurated in A.D. 724.

12 Altar P, Quiriguá. A massive zoomorph depicting a two-headed monster encircling an elite figure, it bears a dedicatory date corresponding to A.D. 795.

13 Structure K-5 3d, Piedras Negras, Guatemala. This thatched-roof building, erected on a terraced platform, illustrates a Late Preclassic prototype of the more elaborate Classic-period temples and palaces. Despite the fact that Maya builders had not yet discovered the corbeled arch, a number of Late Preclassic structures were remarkable for their size and decorative embellishments.

14 *Below:* A fuchsite statuette, Uaxactún, Guatemala. Excavated from an Early Classic cache, this remarkable figurine exhibits unmistakable Olmec traits and was undoubtedly an heirloom piece carved during the Late Preclassic period and subsequently used as an offering. Its babylike features are characteristic of Olmec figures, as are the rectangular eyes, which were originally inlaid. Height, 10 inches.

15 *Above:* A two-part ceramic effigy censer in the form of a seated human figure and decorated with incised lines filled with white pigment, Uaxactún. Early Classic. Height, 9 inches.

16 A section of Uaxactún, as it looked during the Classic period.

17 *Left:* Stela 11, Kaminaljuyú, Guatemala. A superbly carved granite stela showing a dignitary wearing the mask of a long-nosed god. Although it was excavated at Kaminaljuyú, in the Guatemalan highlands, its style is strongly influenced by conventions derived from the site of Izapa, near the Pacific coast of Chiapas. Indeed, the Izapan style—largely an outgrowth of earlier Olmec traditions—penetrated the highlands during the Late Preclassic period and exerted a significant influence on the development of Early Classic sculpture in the lowlands. This stela dates from 300 B.C. to A.D. 150. Height, 74½ inches.

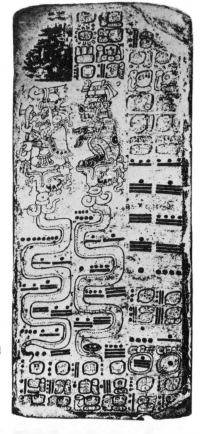

18 *Right:* A page from the Dresden Codex, the finest of the three authenticated Maya codices. When unfolded, this document is 11 feet long and consists of 39 leaves. Its text deals primarily with divination and astronomy, including tables for predicting lunar eclipses.

19 Alfred P. Maudslay, seated on Stela A, Copán. Maudslay's explorations during the late nineteenth century were vitally important in the development of scientific archaeology in the Maya area, and his photographs of buildings and monuments are among the finest ever taken.

20 Temple III, Tikal, Guatemala. One of five towering pyramid-temples erected at this enormous site during the Classic period, Temple III was the last to be constructed, probably toward the end of the eighth century.

21 A group of stelae and circular altars in front of a pyramid known as Complex Q, Tikal.

22 *Left:* Stela 31, Tikal. A portrait of the ruler Stormy Sky, who rose to power at Tikal about A.D. 426. The stela was buried in a temple constructed above his tomb. On both sides of the stela (not visible here) Stormy Sky is flanked by two attendants dressed in the military regalia associated with warriors from the powerful city of Teotihuacán, near Mexico City, which extended its influence into the Maya region at the beginning of the Classic period.

23 *Right:* Jade mosaic mask from Burial 160, Tikal. This exceptional lifesize mask was part of the funerary offerings uncovered in the grave of a nobleman buried sometime around A.D. 527. The eyes and mouth are inlaid with shell and pyrite.

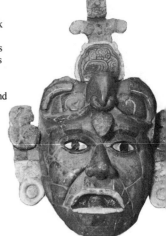

24 The Great Plaza at Tikal, showing Temple I *(center)*, a section of the North Acropolis *(left)*, and clusters of stelae and altars.

25 *Left:* A polychrome two-part ceramic censer, Tikal. From the tomb of a ruler who was buried in the North Acropolis—with nine other individuals, a headless crocodile, and numerous birds—this magnificent Early Classic effigy probably represents the Old Fire God, an ancient Mesoamerican deity, who holds a severed head in his hands. Height, 14¼ inches.

26 *Right:* Jade mosaic jar, Tikal. The lid of this masterpiece of Maya lapidary art, recovered from the tomb of a ruler who died in A.D. 758, may be an actual portrait of the deceased lord. Height, 7½ inches.

27 Polychrome vase from Burial 116, Tikal. In a richly furnished tomb beneath Temple I in the Great Plaza, archaeologists unearthed the grave of a lord known as Ah Cacau, who was inaugurated in A.D. 682. His body had been laid to rest in a vaulted sepulcher along with 16 pounds of jade ornaments, 22 ceramic vessels, carved bones, and other offertory items. Among the finest of the painted ceramics was this vase, which shows a man, possibly Ah Cacau himself, seated on a throne and gesturing toward an attendant. Cylindrical vessels of this type, decorated with court scenes or mythological tableaux, are commonly found in Classic-period tombs. Height, 12 inches.

28 Vessel with a bird-effigy knob on the lid, Tikal. A superb example of Early Classic ceramic art, this bowl was covered with a thin layer of stucco and painted. The design on the lid depicts the rain god, with ringed eyes and fangs, wearing a headdress in the form of a bird. Diameter, 10¾ inches.

29 A structure known as the "Lost World" pyramid, Tikal. This building is part of an architectural complex that contained a series of tombs filled with some of the most exceptional ceramics ever produced by the Maya.

30 Two polychrome lidded bowls from a tomb located in the "Lost World" complex at Tikal. *Left:* Turtle flange bowl with a waterbird lid. Diameter, 6½ inches. *Below:* Tetrapod bowl with a lid in the form of a turkey. Diameter, 8⅞ inches.

31 Polychrome cylindrical vase, Tikal. This striking masterpiece, recovered in pieces from a trench dug by looters, shows a small, limp jaguar being handed by a seated figure to an enthroned lord (on the other side of the vessel). Height, 5³/₁₆ inches.

32 A vase depicting a god holding a necklace of jade beads and emerging from a gastropod shell. A hieroglyphic text encircles the rim of the vessel. The provenience of this vessel is unknown, but it was made during the Late Classic period, probably in the eighth century A.D. Height, 6³/₈ inches.

33 A lidded ceramic cache urn of unknown provenience. This magnificent urn, embellished with appliquéd masks, was designed to hold a ceremonial offering. Early Classic. Height, 18³/₄ inches.

34 *Below:* Polychrome vase from Guatemala, possibly Alta Verapaz. The scene on this vessel shows a god in the form of an anthropomorphic fox. Late Classic. Height, 7¼ inches.

35 *Above:* An "eccentric" flint in the form of a human wearing an elaborate headdress. It was probably used as a scepter, but eccentric flints were frequently included in offertory caches. Late Classic. Height, 13⅝ inches.

36 Polychrome tripod plate depicting a dancer, Petén, Guatemala. Late Classic. Diameter, 13¼ inches.

37 Late Classic polychrome vases, Petén, Guatemala. *Below:* A seated dignitary gesturing with an outstretched hand. *Right:* A figure in a pose suggesting dancing.

38 The Great Palace, Palenque, Chiapas.

39 Stucco decoration on a pilaster of the Great Palace at Palenque, showing two elite figures who appear to be grasping a serpent. Late Classic.

40 Detail of two sculptured figures in the East Court of the Great Palace. *Above:* The profile head of a male with the characteristic Maya nose, flattened forehead, and downturned lower lip. *Right:* A man with one arm across his chest and his hand resting on the opposite shoulder—a gesture of submission.

41 Alfred Maudslay's expedition working in the West Court of the Great Palace in 1891.

42 Temple of the Cross, Palenque. The height of this relatively small structure has been enhanced by an openwork roof comb.

43 Temple of the Inscriptions, Palenque.

44 *Right:* Lord Pacal's sarcophagus in the burial chamber discovered by Alberto Ruz in the Temple of the Inscriptions. *Opposite page:* Detail of the relief sculpture on the sarcophagus lid. Lord Pacal is seen reclining on a throne that represents the god Itzamná. Above Pacal there rises a tree-of-life motif and a celestial two-headed serpent. Pacal ruled Palenque from A.D. 615 until his death in 683 at the age of eighty.

42 Temple of the Cross, Palenque. The height of this relatively small structure has been enhanced by an openwork roof comb.

43 Temple of the Inscriptions, Palenque.

44 *Right:* Lord Pacal's sarcophagus in the burial chamber discovered by Alberto Ruz in the Temple of the Inscriptions. *Opposite page:* Detail of the relief sculpture on the sarcophagus lid. Lord Pacal is seen reclining on a throne that represents the god Itzamná. Above Pacal there rises a tree-of-life motif and a celestial two-headed serpent. Pacal ruled Palenque from A.D. 615 until his death in 683 at the age of eighty.

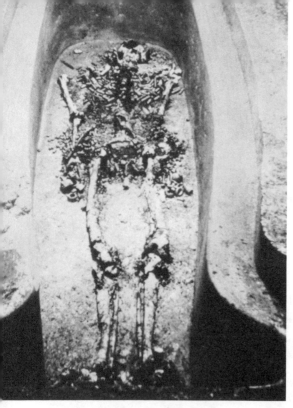

45 *Above:* Interior of the sarcophagus in the Temple of the Inscriptions, containing the skeleton of Lord Pacal surrounded by jade ornaments.

46 *Right:* Jade mosaic funerary mask found in the tomb of the ruler Pacal. Made from 200 pieces of jade—with mother-of-pearl and obsidian eyes—this remarkable creation was placed over the face of the corpse and may have been intended as an actual portrait of the deceased lord. Height, 9½ inches.

47 Two stucco heads from the burial vault of Lord Pacal, among the finest stucco sculptures ever recovered in the Maya area. *Left:* A male, originally thought to be a youthful maize god but now believed to be Pacal. Height, 15½ inches. *Below:* The portrait of a woman who may be Lady Ahpo Hel, Pacal's sister. Height, 11 inches.

48 *Right:* Oval limestone tablet from the Great Palace, Palenque. The figure seated on a two-headed jaguar throne is Pacal; a woman—probably his mother, Lady Zac Kuk—is handing him a "drum major" headdress, a symbol of royal authority. Scholars believe this scene may depict the inauguration of Pacal as ruler of Palenque in A.D. 615.

49 The Acropolis, Piedras Negras, Guatemala, as it looked during the Late Classic period.

50 A polychrome ceramic incensario, adorned with the heads of four deities and arranged in a column, Palenque-style, Chiapas. Late Classic. Height, 35¾ inches.

51 Lintel 26, Yaxchilán, Chiapas. This relief sculpture, originally set into the doorway of a building, shows two dignitaries conversing; one holds a jaguar head, possibly a votive offering. A hieroglyphic inscription above the figures records a date corresponding to A.D. 726.

52 Lintel 53, Yaxchilán. The richly attired figure on the right was an important eighth-century ruler of Yaxchilán, known by his name glyph as Shield-Jaguar. He holds the traditional symbol of royal authority, a manikin scepter in the form of a small image representing a patron deity. The young woman facing him may be his bride, although the exact meaning of this scene is uncertain. Height, 64¼ inches.

53 Lintel 29, Yaxchilán. A woman heavily adorned with jade kneels before the ruler Shield-Jaguar. She performs a blood sacrifice by pulling thorns attached to a cord through her tongue; she has placed a bowl filled with bark paper in front of her to catch the blood. A date on this monument corresponds to A.D. 709.

54 Late Classic polychrome vases depicting court scenes, probably from the northern Petén, Guatemala. *Near right:* A lord seated on an elaborate throne conversing with three other figures (not visible), who may be retainers or visitors. Height, 8⅞ inches. *Far right:* A standing dignitary arrayed in a lavish costume and headdress and holding a staff. Height, 8¾ inches.

55 A polychrome plate of unknown provenience. The central figure is performing self-penance by drawing blood—indicated by the black spots—from his hand and arm. At his back is a hairpin-like design that may represent a tool used to perforate the skin; examples of objects such as this have been excavated from several sites. Late Classic. Diameter, 14¾ inches.

56 A Late Classic vase from the northern Petén or southern Campeche. It shows a seated lord who is staring at his reflection in an obsidian mirror that is held by an attendant (out of sight on the left). Height, 4⁹/₁₆ inches.

57 Stela 1, Bonampak, Chiapas. An elaborately attired lord wears a cape, a headdress with tassels and plumes, and jade earflares, necklaces, and wristbands. Around his waist is a wide belt made of jade beads and shells. Now broken into several pieces, this monument was originally more than 15 feet high. Because the stela was lying upside down when discovered, the image is reversed.

58 Scenes from murals discovered in a temple at Bonampak. *Above:* Captives taken in battle are arraigned before the victorious lords. *Below:* A group of musicians play turtle-shell carapaces, a drum, and rattles.

Maya engineers excelled in the building of roads and causeways. Known by the Yucatec word *sacbeob* (''white roads''), they were constructed of large stones overlaid by rubble and surfaced with a smooth layer of cement. Usually they were raised about two to four feet above ground level (sometimes up to eight feet where the roadways crossed swamps) and varied in width from approximately twelve to thirty-two feet. *Sacbeob* frequently connected important buildings or complexes, forming avenues through the heart of the city's ceremonial precincts. Many centers were linked to outlying districts by a network of roads extending for miles into the countryside, and the longest *sacbe* yet discovered stretches from Cobá in Quintana Roo westward to Yaxuná in Yucatán, a distance of slightly more than sixty-two miles.

Obviously the expenditure of labor required to erect the cities was enormous. Trees and underbrush were first cleared from prospective sites, and if necessary the land was leveled to permit the construction of foundations. Tons of stone had to be quarried and transported either by hand or on log rollers before it was cut, shaped, and set into place by masons. Limestone supplied the predominant source of building material throughout most of the lowlands, except at a few locations; at Quiriguá, for example, rhyolite and sandstone were used, and Copán's structures are made of trachyte. One site situated on Tabasco's coastal plains—Comalcalco—was built entirely of fired clay bricks, and several lowland centers made use of dolomite and slate. Wood from sapodilla and mahogany trees was utilized for lintels over doorways, crossbeams to reinforce vaults, and joists under masonry roofs; stucco, mortar, and concrete could easily be obtained by burning limestone until it was reduced to powder and then mixing it with water, gravel, or a sandlike substance called *sascab*.

In erecting substructures such as pyramids, acropolises, and platforms, the customary method was to build up the central core using rubble and earth, then secure it with masonry retaining walls. By contrast, the temples and palaces, with their interior space and vaulted rooms, presented complex problems involving balance and stress; and the use of corbeled arches in place of the true arch (which the Maya never perfected) required unusually thick walls to support the cantilevered blocks that formed the vaults. Initially these difficulties were resolved by means of large stones that extended through the entire width of the building's walls and sustained the weight of the super-structure. But by about A.D. 600 walls composed of smaller stones set in concrete and faced with a thin veneer of cut masonry were intro-duced, an innovation that increased structural stability and afforded greater flexibility of design—though because the older technique con-tinued to be employed, it is not uncommon to find a single building incorporating both types of walls. Nor did the Maya ever completely abandon the use of wooden poles, wattle and daub, and thatch for certain religious structures. Even in Classic and Postclassic sites there are platforms and pyramids with postholes on their summits, indicating that perishable buildings of this kind, doubtlessly patterned after Pre-classic prototypes, were occasionally constructed.

In general, Maya cities appear to have grown more by accretion than by deliberate design, though the grouping of temples and palaces around an open plaza is a characteristic feature of lowland centers. Originally, the most important of these complexes occupied a central or dominant position within the core of the city, but as many sites expanded, new clusters of public buildings sprang up at considerable distances from the city's epicenter. Regional variation in architectural styles was also common throughout the lowlands, and Maya builders frequently experimented with innovative approaches involving meth-ods of construction and aesthetic concepts. Nor did they hesitate to destroy or renovate older structures once their original function had been served. In fact, this practice was a major element in the evolution of Maya architecture; individual buildings or entire complexes were constantly torn down, modified, or enlarged to meet changing social, religious, and economic needs.

We do not know whether architects worked from plans or sketches, or what units of measurement might have been used in their designs; but the size and complexity of many buildings make it difficult to be-lieve they were erected without preliminary drawings as a guide. Other technical aids available to Maya builders were extremely limited by modern standards, particularly since they had no metal tools, no draft animals, and no wheeled vehicles to haul materials. (Oddly enough, toys in the form of ceramic animals mounted on wheels with axles have been excavated in Mexico, but there is no evidence that the wheel ever had practical applications in Mesoamerica.) Instead, the Maya relied solely on human energy, fiber rope to help lift heavy objects, log rollers for moving stone, plumb bobs used to align walls, and stone implements, including axes, celts, hammerstones, chisels, and drills. As most buildings are oriented to the cardinal directions, usually facing a few degrees east of north, there has been some speculation that a magnetic device was used to determine alignments, though it is more likely that they were made by astronomical observations.

Yet regardless of these mechanical limitations, the magnificence of Maya architecture almost defies the imagination. One needs only to view the spectacular ruins of Tikal, Copán, Palenque, Uxmal, Chichén Itzá, or dozens of lesser-known cities to appreciate the phenomenal impact of their structures, or to sense the dedication of the artisans and peasants who labored so diligently to execute such grandiose conceptions.

Like the architects, Maya artists and craftsmen also worked without the benefit of sophisticated tools. Sculptors cut and shaped their materials—whether it was the much-favored limestone or other media such as trachyte, sandstone, basalt, or wood—with nothing more than stone chisels, hammerstones, and possibly wooden mallets. The carving and polishing of jade, shell, and bone, along with the production of featherwork, mosaics, and inlays, were accomplished with equally primitive instruments; and weaving was done on simple backstrap looms, using needles and battens of wood or bone. Even the potter's wheel, introduced in the Old World more than four thousand years ago, was never invented in Mesoamerica, though a crude device called a *kabal*, a wooden turntable rotated between the potter's feet, was used for shaping ceramics in colonial Yucatán and may have been known in that region prior to the Conquest. Nevertheless, the Maya created a unique artistic tradition displaying originality, vigor, and remarkable aesthetic refinement, an art whose ingenuity was unexcelled in pre-Columbian America.

Ever since the Late Preclassic era, Maya artisans were primarily concerned with religious and hierarchic themes. Even so, within this prescribed framework highly innovative approaches evolved, and many cities developed easily recognizable styles and specializations. Amid the rigid and often abstract symbolism inherent in much of their iconography, the Maya also succeeded in conveying perspective and a sense of movement while depicting, with a startling degree of realism, such activities as rituals, human sacrifice, warfare, and scenes from daily life. Even in the most formalized works, with their mystic symbolism, strangely aloof figures, and aura of impersonality, there is a tremendous sense of vitality.

The conventionalized aspects of Maya art were most pronounced in sculpture. Undoubtedly this is attributable to its use in embellishing temples and religious monuments, particularly those commemorating events of ritualistic or historical significance. Inspired by the sacrosanct nature of these creations, sculptors produced powerful images of deities, mythological creatures, and animals in supernatural contexts. Equally important were numerous depictions of elegant human figures representing ruling lords. Invariably these regal personages are portrayed in a manner contrived to accentuate their lofty status: attired in elaborate costumes and jewelry, holding emblems of authority, attended by retainers, receiving tributes, presiding over captives or slaves, seated on thronelike daises, or being carried in litters. Generally they are shown in profile or with their bodies slightly angled toward the viewer; sometimes they face straight forward with only the head in profile and the feet turned out. Great attention was lavished on details of clothing, headdresses, and ornaments, which are often so ornate as to virtually obscure the figure itself, and because the remaining space within the composition was frequently covered with hieroglyphs or decorative elements, the total effect resulted in a visual opulence reminiscent of Oriental art.

Large-scale monuments were usually carried out in bas-relief, but the Maya were also adept at working in the round. Among the best examples of full-figure modeling are small ceramic effigies noted for their elegant style and execution. Made either by hand or in molds (occasionally both techniques were combined) and fired in kilns, these took the form of animals, supernatural creatures, or humans in the guise of elite men and women, warriors, ball players, musicians, or dancers. Some of the most sophisticated types come from the island of Jaina off the coast of Campeche, where they were placed in richly appointed tombs as funerary offerings. Jaina figurines often portray unusual subjects including dwarfs, hunchbacks, aged persons with wrinkled faces and toothless jaws, and erotic scenes of men caressing young girls; but the finest pieces represent elite dignitaries whose aristocratic features, magnificent costumes, and imperious hauteur suggest the same lofty positions they assume in stone sculpture.

Another supreme triumph of Maya art is reflected in the so-called Tzakol and Tepeu ceramics made in the Petén and neighboring regions during the Early and Late Classic periods respectively. Each of these styles is characterized by a variety of shapes—primarily jars, bowls, plates, and vases—and exhibits absolute mastery over such decorative techniques as incising, appliqué, modeling, and painting, all applied with consummate sensitivity and skill, Aesthetically, Tzakol and Tepeu vessels rank among the most beautiful pottery made anywhere in the ancient world, especially the Tepeu wares produced between about A.D. 600 and 800, which were frequently placed in elite tombs as offerings; and some of the finest of these vessels are cylindrical vases adorned with superb figurative paintings executed in a wide range of colors.

Often the animated motifs on these cylinders—showing deities, grotesque creatures, animals, nobles, ceremonies, and human sacrifice—appear in imaginative tableaux which are obviously esoteric in nature. Michael D. Coe, who has studied this iconography at length, demonstrated that the subject matter depicted on these vessels pertains to death and the Maya Underworld—a realm known as *Xibalbá* or "place of fright." Other ceramics of this type, however, clearly show court scenes with sumptuously attired lords seated on thrones, women of high status, warriors, attendants, and a variety of activities associated with the ruling class. And a detailed analysis of Late Classic vases, plates, and bowls decorated with hieroglyphic inscriptions and mythological scenes rendered in a calligraphic style similar to the three surviving Maya codices was recently published by Francis Robicsek.

Based on his research, Robicsek believes that these "codex style" vessels were painted by artists who also produced Classic-period codices (now vanished), that they deal with myths pertaining to the Underworld, and that, when placed in their proper sequence, these ceramics comprise an actual codex—an episodic Maya "Book of the Dead." While there is much to support this intriguing hypothesis, it must be pointed out that all of the ceramics studied by Robicsek are looted pieces removed from their original archaeological context, and therefore some scholars feel that more research is needed to verify Robicsek's theory.

The narrative quality so evident in the scenes on Late Classic ceramics frequently carried over into murals that sometimes covered the interior walls of temples and palaces. Regrettably, few of these are known to have endured the ravages of decay; the most extensive are the celebrated frescoes at Bonampak in Chiapas (discussed in Chapter 9), but interesting paintings were also found at Uaxactún, Palenque, Chichén Itzá, Tancáh, Santa Rosa, and Tulúm. Judging from surviving examples, Classic-period murals—in contrast to the more rigidly stylized or symbolic frescoes dating from later centuries—were surprisingly dynamic, treating a wide range of subjects in vividly realistic terms. They exhibit innovative experiments in perspective and the use of foreshortening to create an illusion of depth, and some of them have provided archaeologists with a wealth of otherwise obscure details pertaining to rituals, costumes, musical instruments, sacrifices, warfare, and occasional vignettes of everyday life.

Among the minor arts at which the Maya excelled was the working of jade, a mineral greatly prized for its intrinsic beauty and ritualistic connotations. Offertory caches and tombs of important persons yield large quantities of jade in the form of jewelry, effigies, plaques, and mosaics. It was frequently used as inlays in stone and shell or as decorations set into human teeth (a mark of social prestige), and many jade artifacts are engraved with low-relief designs comparable on a small scale to the most accomplished stone sculpture. Maya craftsmen also carved bone, shell, and wood from which they fashioned a variety of ornaments and ceremonial items, and some areas manufactured exquisite vessels of alabaster and marble embellished with incising or reliefs. Skillfully made knives, spear points, and other implements were chipped out of flint and obsidian, though the most intriguing objects of this type are known as "eccentric flints"—oddly shaped blades resembling crescents, exotic plants, scorpionlike insects, or profiles of humans and animals, which were used in rituals.

We have almost no information about perishable arts such as weaving and featherwork, since nothing of this nature has survived except a few fragments of cloth. But considering the resplendent costumes and headdresses worn by elite figures depicted in sculpture and paintings, there is no doubt that these crafts were exceptionally advanced. Vivid pictorial details confirm that the Maya produced gorgeous feather capes, mantles, panaches, shields, banners, and excellent cotton textiles decorated with dyed and embroidered designs. Unfortunately, countless specimens of other fragile crafts, including basketry, leather goods, wood carvings, and lacquered gourds, were destroyed as a consequence of burial under moist conditions, leaving few traces of what must have once been remarkable creations.

Not until relatively late—sometime around A.D. 900—did metals assume any importance to the Maya. For the most part these were restricted to copper and gold imported from Panama, Costa Rica, Colombia, and Mexico (a few specimens of silver, zinc, and tin have come from the Guatemalan highlands); and metalworking techniques consisted primarily of filigree, lost wax or *cire perdue* casting, and repoussé. Objects of copper recovered from various sites include tiny bells, axes, celts, tweezers, figurines, tubes, disks, rings, earplugs, a small mask, and a single example each of an arrowhead and a fishhook. Gold was limited to ornaments and ritualistic items, and the largest number of gold artifacts discovered to date—primarily rings, beads, effigies, bells, cups, and embossed disks—were brought up from the famous Sacred Cenote at Chichén Itzá (see Chapter 12) into which they had been thrown as sacrificial offerings. An elite tomb uncovered in the ruins of Iximché, the former capital of the Cakchiquel tribe located fifty miles west of Guatemala City, yielded another spectacular cache of gold: forty beads, ten masks representing jaguars, and a headdress ornament resembling a crown.

Even a cursory view of Maya art reaffirms what we have observed in almost everything else about their culture: a staggering outpouring of time, energy, and resources inspired by religion and directed by a powerful ruling hierarchy. Conspicuously absent are images of the common man: the peasant farmers, the laborers who worked incessantly to erect and maintain the cities, or the anonymous artists whose talents so eloquently perpetuated the ideals of Maya civilization. Quite rightly, the late artist-scholar Miguel Covarrubias called it an "official" art, intended primarily for the glory of the gods and the aggrandizement of the elite classes. Only rarely does it abandon its obsession with deities, rituals, mythology, or exalted rulers to offer glimpses into the lives of ordinary people.

Somehow the aloof figures staring out from stone sculpture are as impersonal to us today as they must have seemed to an illiterate peasant centuries ago. We marvel at the sophisticated scenes painted on ceramics, the immense friezes adorning temples and palaces, or the rich treasures unearthed in tombs of long-forgotten lords. Yet for all that science can tell us about these magnificent works of art, the overall impression they create is one of absolute mystery. We are unfailingly awed by their technical brilliance, aesthetic ingenuity, and the unique world view they represent, but we cannot escape their overwhelming sense of remoteness.

Despite the large quantity of Maya art in museums throughout Europe and America, archaeologists are constantly haunted by the specter of creations long since lost to the effects of time: murals already hopelessly effaced, sculptured monuments eroded or smashed beyond recognition, or hieroglyphic codices rotting into oblivion in the damp vaults of undiscovered tombs. Moreover, countless objects of art are presently endangered by looters willing to commit acts of vandalism and theft in order to reap lucrative financial rewards offered by dealers seeking to exploit an inflated market in antiquities. Suddenly pre-Columbian art has become *de rigueur* among collectors; everything from ceramics and figurines to major monuments is being purchased on a no-questions-asked basis, often by persons to whom their "status'' or investment potential far outweighs aesthetic or historical considerations. Ironically, this situation, rather than environmental factors, now poses the most immediate threat to the preservation of Maya archaeological sites, and the problem is so serious that it has prompted legal action by various international law-enforcement, scientific, and cultural agencies in an attempt to end the ruthless decimation of this incomparable artistic heritage.

In 1952 a sensational discovery at Palenque dramatically illustrated the artistic and architectural heights achieved by the Maya during the Classic period. Along with Yaxchilán and Piedras Negras on the Usumacinta River, Palenque represents the climax of the Classic florescence in the western sector of the Maya area. Its sedate buildings and elegant sculptured monuments reflect aesthetic ideals of astonishing refinement, and many archaeologists consider it the most beautiful of all Maya ruins.

Today Palenque appears quite different from the way it did when Stephens and Catherwood explored the site in 1840. Its perimeter is still obscured by rain forest, and numerous structures lie buried under mounds of rubble, but the core of the city has been excavated and partially restored. Instead of the hazardous journey by muleback formerly required to visit Palenque, it can now be reached by automobile over a paved highway from Villahermosa, seventy miles to the northwest. A landing field has also been opened in the nearby village of Santo Domingo del Palenque, and from there taxis are available for the five-mile drive to the ruins along a narrow road that was once an Indian footpath.

What is presently known about Palenque's history has resulted from the efforts of numerous investigators. Among the early explorers who conducted surveys at the site were Alfred P. Maudslay, William H. Holmes, and Teobert Maler; and in 1923 the Mexican government assigned the American archaeologist Frans Blom to excavate the Great

Palace, which he attempted to restore to its original splendor. Other noted Mayanists, including Alfred Tozzer, Herbert Spinden, Sylvanus Morley, and J. Eric Thompson, have subjected Palenque to intensive studies, and large-scale excavations were carried out by the Instituto Nacional de Antropología e Historia under the supervision of Miguel Fernández. Four years after Fernández's untimely death in 1945, the continuation of the project fell into the capable hands of the late Alberto Ruz Lhuillier, a Cuban-born scholar affiliated with the Center for Maya Studies at the Universidad Nacional Autónoma de México. It was extremely fortunate that Ruz should have applied his talents to Palenque; his tireless enthusiasm and intense determination were perfectly suited to the challenge awaiting him.

Ruz was particularly intrigued by the Temple of the Inscriptions, the imposing structure standing atop a terraced pyramid in which Stephens and Catherwood had discovered five superbly carved hieroglyphic tablets. Ruz's curiosity was first aroused by the flagstone floor of the temple's interior chamber. Near the center of the room was an unusually large stone with two rows of circular holes drilled around its edges, all of them filled with plugs to conceal their presence. Archaeologists had long debated the possible significance of these holes, but no one could offer a satisfactory explanation for their use.

Ruz's examination of the chamber soon revealed a curious circumstance overlooked by earlier explorers: its walls appeared to continue on beneath the floor, as though another room lay below the upper level. Ruz decided to raise the drilled stone from the floor on a hunch that it might provide a key to some undisclosed architectural feature within the pyramid itself.

No sooner had his workmen lifted the heavy slab than the outlines of a narrow opening completely filled with rubble were visible underneath. At first it was impossible to tell whether it was actually a passageway connected to a lower room or simply a small subsurface crypt. But as the debris was removed, a series of stone steps plastered with stucco began to appear, leading down through a vaulted tunnel into the core of the pyramid. Ruz immediately resolved to follow the elaborate subterranean stairway to its end, despite the exhaustive labor involved in such an undertaking.

The task of clearing the stairs proceeded with maddening slowness. Heavy rocks blocking the passage had to be loosened and hauled up with ropes and pulleys. The heat and humidity in the vault were stifling, and fumes given off by the excavators' gasoline lamp mixed with choking dust made it impossible to dig for long periods at a time. By the conclusion of the first season's work in the summer of 1949, only twenty-three steps had been exposed, and there was no doubt that the passageway was much deeper than Ruz had anticipated.

As yet there was no way of knowing toward what the staircase was leading, though something had come to light that rekindled Ruz's expectations. Along one wall of the tunnel was a curious feature: a square hollow shaft or duct made of small stones set into lime mortar. What purpose it might have served was not known, but there undoubtedly had to be some motive for its construction concealed still lower in the pyramid's depths.

As the passage deepened, the obstructing rocks became heavier and were tightly cemented by encrustations of lime. Ruz surmised that the tortuous difficulty in reaching the bottom of the stairway resulted from deliberate intent on the part of its builders. When the passageway ceased to be used, it had been carefully sealed against intrusion by piling masses of rubble along its entire length. The flagstone was then set in place over the entrance in the temple floor, and the drilled holes by which it was lowered into position were filled with stone plugs. After Palenque was abandoned, the knowledge of the subterranean vault disappeared with its inhabitants. That much of the enigma now seemed certain.

By the end of the third season the stairway was opened to a depth of seventy-three feet. Still, there was not the slightest clue as to its original function. No inscriptions were found along the walls, and not a single fragment of sculpture had turned up in the tons of debris cleared from the vault. Up to that point the only thing unearthed was a small masonry box containing two jade earplugs lying on a red-painted stone, a discovery that, if anything, further complicated the questions in Ruz's mind.

During the summer of 1952 the excavators broke through into a

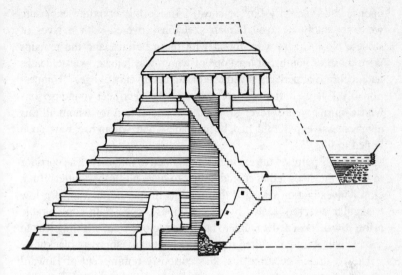

Cross section of the Temple of the Inscriptions, showing the passageway and location of the burial chamber. (After Ruz.)

corridor blocked at one end by a thick wall of tightly packed rubble. Beyond this they encountered another wall of cemented stones, and on the floor in front of it lay an offertory cache consisting of seven beads and two earplugs made of jade, three ceramic dishes, two shells filled with cinnabar, and an exquisite tear-shaped pearl a half-inch in diameter. Obviously these objects were intended as a ceremonial offering, but toward what mysterious end had they been placed in the otherwise empty corridor? Now it was imperative to penetrate the massive second wall obstructing the passageway if the dilemma was ever to make sense.

According to Ruz's own account, "the wall turned out to be more than twelve feet thick; breaking through it took a full week of the hardest labor of the entire expedition. The mortar held so firmly that the stones often broke before they separated, and the wet lime burned and cracked the workmen's hands. Finally we got through and came upon a rude masonry box or chest.'' Inside this cryptlike enclosure were six badly decayed human skeletons covered with a layer of stones. No artifacts were found with these burials, and the remains were those of youths, at least one of whom was female, whose deaths had occurred at perhaps seventeen or eighteen years of age. ''Unquestionably,'' Ruz continued, ''this was a human sacrifice, young persons whose spirits were forever to guard and attend him for whom all this entire massive pyramid had been made—and whom we now soon hoped to find.''

From this point on the excitement mounted in intensity. The corridor to which the steps led appeared at first to have no further outlet. But a closer investigation revealed the presence in the north wall of a low triangular doorway sealed by an enormous stone. With considerable effort it was loosened enough to be moved to one side, enabling Ruz to see beyond it into a vaulted room completely enveloped in blackness.

Now a drama occurred that was curiously reminiscent of Howard Carter's entrance into the treasure-laden burial chamber of Tutankhamen in 1922. Huddled together in the dimly lit passage, Ruz and his workmen grew tense with an expectation that only this kind of archaeological high adventure can evoke—the sudden discovery of splendors left by past civilizations, unseen for hundreds or thousands of years. Holding a floodlight, Ruz entered the darkened vault, and an instant later he knew his four seasons of patient labor had been lavishly rewarded.

It was some time before Ruz could aptly describe the sight confronting him: ''Out of the dim shadows emerged a vision from a fairytale, a fantastic, ethereal sight from another world. It seemed a huge magic grotto carved out of ice, the walls sparkling and glistening like snow crystals. Delicate festoons of stalactites hung like tassels of a curtain, and the stalagmites on the floor looked like drippings from a great candle. The impression, in fact, was that of an abandoned chapel. Across the walls marched stucco figures in low relief. Then my eyes sought the floor. This was almost entirely filled with a great carved stone slab, in perfect condition. As I gazed in awe and astonishment, I described the marvelous sight to my colleagues . . . but they wouldn't believe me until they had pushed me aside and had seen with their own eyes the fascinating spectacle. Ours were the first eyes that had gazed on it in more than a thousand years!"

The sculptured stone on the floor of the chamber measured slightly more than twelve feet long by seven feet wide, and its entire surface was carved with a complex bas-relief design. In its center was the sensitive figure of a man heavily laden with jewelry and wearing an elaborate headdress, reclining on the grotesque head of an earth monster. Above him arose a large ornate cross, its horizontal arms representing a two-headed serpent; at the top of the cross sat a mythological bird, and enclosing this tableau were rows of hieroglyphs containing a series of thirteen dates.

Its cruciform design is quite similar to relief carvings found elsewhere at Palenque, in the Temple of the Cross and the Temple of the Foliated Cross. As Ruz pointed out, these crosslike devices were probably symbolic of growing maize. Referring to the example in the Temple of the Inscriptions, he wrote: "We may presume that the scene synthesizes fundamental concepts of the Maya religion: the veneration of maize, a plant that needs human aid for its life, and, in turn, assures man's life; the mortal destiny of man, from whose sacrifices springs life in the aspect of the cruciform motif . . . [and] the cosmic frame that surrounds human existence, in which the stars govern the unalterable course of time." Ruz believed this theme might also symbolize "the yearning of man for an afterlife. One can't be sure whether the figure depicts mortal man in general or a specific individual for whom the monument was built. He is doomed by fate to be swallowed by the earth, on which he reclines. But in the hope of eternal life he gazes fervently at the cross, the symbol of corn and therefore of life itself."

The chamber in which this gigantic carving rested was roughly twenty-nine feet long by thirteen feet wide. Its steeply vaulted ceiling reached a height of twenty-three feet and was reinforced by five ponderous stones placed as buttresses against the crushing weight of the roof. Adorning the walls were nine human figures modeled in stucco relief, probably representing the gods of the Underworld. For almost thirteen centuries these images had peered out from beneath a curtain of white stalactites formed by lime deposits to preside over the silent chamber. Had they been placed there to witness rituals enacted by solemn priests, rites too sacred to perform before the multitudes? Or were they guardians of some undisclosed secret within the vault?

Examination revealed that the sculptured slab, which at first appeared to lie on the floor of the room, actually rested on an immense block supported by six rectangular pieces of stone. A suspicion awakened in Ruz's mind that the gigantic monolith under the slab held the key to the original purpose of the hidden chamber. To test this theory it was first necessary to ascertain whether or not the block was solid. By drilling a hole into one corner Ruz quickly determined that it not only had a hollow core, but its interior contained traces of red paint. Obviously the carved slab would have to be raised.

Utilizing the only suitable equipment at his disposal, Ruz had jacks placed under each corner of the five-ton stone, reinforced by logs to provide added leverage. "As the slab was lifted, inch by inch," he recalled, "we were surprised to find that a smaller inside cover lay below it. Also of stone and smoothly finished, this inner cover was about seven feet long and thirty inches wide. It was of a peculiar curved outline, with one end flared like a fishtail. And at either end was a pair of round holes, fitted with stone plugs exactly like those we had found in the temple floor far above us. By now we knew that these were lifting holes.

"We worked on, breathless with excitement. Every time we jacked the great carved top up an inch we slipped a section of board under it so that, if a jack slipped, the massive sculpture would not fall. When we had raised it about fifteen inches, my curiosity got the best of me. . . ."

Ruz squeezed his way under the slab and removed the plugs from the inner cover. Through the tiny openings he could barely distinguish what lay inside. "My first impression," he wrote, "was that of a mosaic of green, red, and white. Then it resolved itself into details— green jade ornaments, red painted teeth and bones, and fragments of a mask. I was gazing at the death face of him for whom all this stupendous work—the crypt, the sculpture, the stairway, the great pyramid with its crowning temple—had been built. . . . This, then, was a sarcophagus, the first ever found in a Mayan pyramid."

Although the bones were badly decayed, Ruz estimated that they were those of a male, about forty years old, and approximately five feet eight inches in height—unusually tall, considering that Maya men averaged around five feet two inches. His teeth had been painted red, but they were not filed or inlaid with jade, obsidian, or pyrite in accordance with a widespread practice among the elite classes, and Ruz could not determine if his skull was artificially deformed as was customary.

By far the most spectacular aspect of the burial was the rich treasure of jade ornaments placed on the dead man at the time of interment. Among these were a diadem fashioned of tiny disks, headdress decorations, and earplugs shaped like flowers with dangling appendages made from two pieces of mother-of-pearl fitted together and polished to give the illusion of enormous pearls. Around the neck was a collar

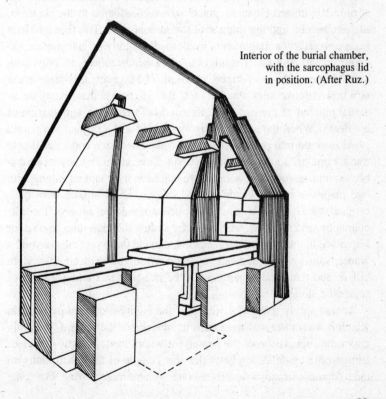

Interior of the burial chamber, with the sarcophagus lid in position. (After Ruz.)

of beads in the form of spheres, flowers, pumpkins, and a snake's head, and below this a breastplate or pectoral consisting of 189 finely polished jade tubes. Every finger of both hands was adorned by jade rings still in place over the bones; on the wrists there were cufflike bracelets, each composed of two hundred small round beads; and near the feet lay two large beads perhaps once attached to sandals. Originally the corpse had held a jade sphere about three inches in diameter in its left hand and a cube of jade in the right (possibly symbols of rank), and scattered among the remains were two beautifully carved human effigies and a plaque representing a bat. In keeping with Maya burial rites, a single jade bead had been placed in the mouth to ensure that the man's spirit could purchase food in the afterlife.

Before interment the body had been wrapped in a cotton shroud and sprinkled with red cinnabar, traces of which adhered to the skeleton, the ornaments, and the interior of the sarcophagus. The face had then been covered by a magnificent mask made entirely of jade mosaic except for shell and obsidian inlays used to simulate the eyes. Now considered one of the most superb creations of Maya art, this mask had a strikingly lifelike aura about it, and Ruz suggested that it may be an actual portrait of the deceased prepared beforehand in anticipation of his death. When the sarcophagus was sealed and the great sculptured stone lowered into position, a polished slate necklace and a small jade mask were left on the floor of the crypt. Several pottery bowls, probably containing food and water, were placed in the chamber, along with two exquisite human heads molded in stucco and broken from their original bases. Rubble was then piled around the edge of the sarcophagus, and the room was sealed by sliding the triangular stone door into place in the narrow entrance. Just outside the crypt, the six youths whose spirits were intended to guard or serve the dead man were killed, and their bodies jammed in the masonry box under a layer of cemented stones.

Almost surely the burial vault and the eighty-foot-high pyramid in which it was concealed were built in advance of the funeral, probably under the supervision of the person for whom the tomb was intended. But glyphic evidence suggests that the Temple of the Inscriptions on the pyramid's summit was erected later as a mortuary shrine. For some reason the memory of the deceased was not allowed to fade with the passing of time. In order to maintain a direct link with the burial chamber, the curious duct encountered by Ruz along the wall of the stairway was constructed of stone and mortar. Beginning at the side of the sarcophagus in the form of a serpent's head, it extended into the adjacent corridor and continued up the entire length of the passage to the floor of the temple. It is assumed that through this hollow tube passed the incantations of priests to the spirit of the man below, and perhaps they received in turn some darkly mysterious confirmation of their acceptance. Ruz termed the device a "psychic duct"—a direct line between the living and the unknown realm of death.

We cannot be sure exactly when the stairway leading to the crypt was filled with debris and permanently sealed. At first it was thought to have been a preordained act to secure the tomb against any immediate threat of desecration. However, later excavations showed that Palenque was subjected to a strong wave of outside influence from Mexico's eastern coast during the century just prior to its final abandonment. Hence there is reason to suspect that the tomb—certainly the city's most important religious shrine—might have been closed only as a precaution against the threat of foreign intruders.

Even though details such as this may never be fully clarified, Ruz's discovery provided an enormous amount of information about various aspects of Maya civilization. The structural complexity of the Temple of the Inscriptions, with its interior stairway, hidden crypt, and "psychic duct," offers a remarkable example of Maya architectural skills. New dimensions were added to our knowledge of Maya art, for the huge carved slab covering the sarcophagus, together with the two stucco heads placed near it as offerings, are among the finest examples of Classic sculpture ever uncovered, not to mention the magnificent array of jade ornaments taken from the grave. Also inherent in Ruz's findings were further indications of the position enjoyed by the hierarchy, a circumstance dramatically illustrated by the Herculean effort inspired by the veneration of a single high-ranking individual—engineers, artists, stonemasons, and laborers working devotedly to construct his final resting place.

Using techniques of hieroglyphic decipherment originally worked out by Tatiana Proskouriakoff (see Chapter 7), the epigraphers David H. Kelley and Floyd Lounsbury announced in 1974 that the nobleman whose tomb Ruz had discovered could be identified by a name glyph which they translated as Pacal (meaning "Shield"). According to their studies, Pacal became the ruling lord of Palenque on July 29, A.D. 615 (9.9.2.4.8), when he was twelve years old, and remained in power until his death on August 30, 683 (9.12.11.5.18), at the age of eighty. But Ruz vigorously disputed the phonetic translation of Pacal's name glyph, and suggested instead that he be called "8 Ahau" after the day of the 260-day sacred year or *tzolkin* on which he was born. In addition, Ruz challenged the eighty-year lifespan ascribed to Pacal or 8 Ahau, arguing that the presumed dates of his birth and death were incorrectly interpreted—a position he felt was further supported by his conclusion that the skeletal remains in the tomb were those of a man about forty. Nevertheless, the majority of scholars, citing the difficulty of determining the age of adult skeletons, have accepted the dates advocated by Kelley and Lounsbury, along with the reading of his name glyph as Pacal. It has also been established that the human figure depicted on the sarcophagus lid represents an actual portrait of Pacal reclining on a grotesque mask of the god Itzamná, a scene symbolizing the dead ruler's journey into the Underworld.

On the basis of current research by a group of epigraphers led by Lounsbury, Linda Schele, and Peter Mathews, we know that Pacal was succeeded by his forty-eight-year-old son, Chan Bahlum (Serpent Jaguar), and upon his death in 702 (9.13.10.1.5) a younger brother named Kan Xul ascended to power. Hieroglyphic texts indicate that it was Chan Bahlum who dedicated the Temple of the Inscriptions as a memorial to his father, Pacal, and that he was also responsible for building three of the most beautiful buildings at Palenque—the Temples of the Sun, the Cross, and the Foliated Cross. In fact, it is now possible to reconstruct a substantial amount of information concerning Late Classic dynasties at Palenque (as well as those of other major cities), and scholars have compiled a list of important rulers and their ancestors, including several women of extremely high status. Out of the maze of historic texts carved on Palenque's monuments have come such names as Chac Zutz, Kuk, Chaacal, Lady Zac Kuk (the mother of Pacal),

Ahpo Hel, and Kan Ik; but we still know relatively little about these intriguing nobles other than the dates of their births, deaths, and accession to power, their relationships to one another, the identities of certain patron deities associated with them, and a few of their accomplishments.

Interestingly enough, the "royal" tomb in the Temple of the Inscriptions is not the only elaborate burial of this kind unearthed in the Maya area, although it is certainly the most spectacular. Excavators have found a number of elaborate Classic-period graves throughout the lowlands, usually concealed in stone-lined vaults underneath plazas, platforms, and temples. For example, while digging at Tikal in the 1960s, archaeologists from the University of Pennsylvania discovered a series of richly appointed tombs. Among the grandest was a vaulted chamber under the base of Temple I (also known as the Temple of the Giant Jaguar), a terraced pyramidal structure in the Great Plaza which soars to a height of 155 feet above the center of the city. Inside the well-hidden sepulcher lay the skeleton of Ah Cacau (originally called Ruler A), a powerful lord who reigned over Tikal from 682 (9.12.9.17.16) until sometime between 723 and 734. Ah Cacau's body had been placed on a masonry bench covered by a woven mat, and he was surrounded by mortuary offerings of exceptional beauty: polychrome vessels, pearls, ornaments of oyster shell and jade, and a bundle of finely carved and incised bones. Around his neck were strands of massive jade beads and tubes (a total of sixteen pounds of jade was found in the tomb), and lying near the skeleton was one of the supreme masterpieces of Maya art—a jade mosaic cylindrical vase covered by a lid embellished with incised glyphs and a small human head that may represent a portrait of Ah Cacau.

More recently, a team of scientists from the Royal Ontario Museum headed by David Pendergast opened an elite tomb in a pyramid designated as Structure B-4 at Altun Ha in Belize. Judging by its contents, it was obviously the grave of an important ruler or priest who was interred amid a rich assemblage of ceramics, ornaments, ceremonial flints, and objects of jade, including exquisite necklaces, pendants, and the largest piece of jade ever found in the Maya area: a nearly life-size head of the sun god, Kinich Ahau, which weighs 9.7 pounds and was skillfully carved in bold relief. And in the spring of 1984 a sensational discovery was announced by the archaeologist Richard E. W. Adams and the National Geographic Society. While exploring the site of Río Azul in northeastern Guatemala, Adams and his associates broke through into a subterranean tomb that had narrowly escaped being ransacked by looters. On its walls were beautifully preserved hieroglyphic inscriptions painted on stucco, and the floor was littered with finely made pottery placed alongside a badly decayed skeleton. The vessels were typical of funerary offerings usually found in elite tombs—except for one, which was unlike anything ever encountered: a rounded jar equipped with a stirrup-handled lid that fit over the neck of the vessel and was locked into place by twisting it into ridges or grooves. Adorning this "screw-top" jar was a band of glyphs painted in bright blue over a coating of stucco, an inscription that when deciphered may shed additional light on the tomb's occupant.

Elite tombs have revealed a wealth of information about various aspects of Maya culture, especially since scholars can now read many of the inscriptions associated with ruling dynasties. Undoubtedly hundreds of such tombs still lie concealed under overgrown temples and palaces, and we can only speculate as to the treasures they contain. Usually their discovery is a matter of luck, as was the case with Alberto Ruz's decision to probe beneath the Temple of the Inscriptions. Yet it is certain that other tombs—perhaps more lavish than anything found to date—will be located, and we can be equally sure that with each such discovery our awareness of the splendors of Maya civilization will continue to heighten.

7 · GODS, PRIESTS, AND RULERS

Who were the gods whose veneration inspired the Maya to such marvelous accomplishments? Unfortunately, the information on this subject, extracted from ethnohistoric documents, hieroglyphic codices, and excavations, is both complex and ambiguous, largely because the Maya worshipped a bewildering array of deities. Even their exact number and order of importance is not clear. Inconclusive evidence suggests that a god named Hunab Ku may have stood at the pinnacle of the Maya pantheon, yet everything about Hunab Ku's role is strangely amorphous. Various authors refer to him abstractly as a supreme being, the creator of the universe, and a deity so sacred he was incorporeal and played no part in everyday human affairs. Some students believe Hunab Ku was actually a post-Conquest phenomenon, invented by the Maya under the influence of the Christian concept of a single, all-powerful Creator.

Other sources tell us the supreme god was called Itzamná. Quite possibly Itzamná and Hunab Ku were manifestations of the same deity, and Itzamná has sometimes been identified as Hunab Ku's son. Whatever their relationship, if any, Itzamná was looked upon as the creator of human life, the inventor of books and writing, and the patron of science and learning. He was considered the lord of the day and night, the ruler of the heavens, and the embodiment of both earth and sky. He also appears to have been the chief patron of the Maya ruling elite, who are often shown holding symbols of office emblazoned with two-headed serpents representing Itzamná. In the codices he appears as an aged man with a pronounced Roman nose, toothless jaws, and hollow cheeks. Elsewhere he assumes unmistakable reptilian traits; the name Itzamná literally means "iguana house," and he is commonly depicted in sculpture as an anthropomorphized lizard, snake, crocodile, or dragonlike monster.

Immediately below Itzamná in prominence were Ah Kinchil or Kinich Ahau, the powerful sun god (who may have been another manifestation of Itzamná); Ah Puch, the "Lord of Death," whose fleshless nose and lower jaw, exposed spine, and spotted body symbolized the fearful specter of death; Ek Chuah, the guardian of merchants and travelers; Xaman Ek, ruler of the North Star; Yam Kax or Ah Mun, the youthful corn god who is always portrayed wearing a headdress representing the life-giving maize plant; and Ix Chel, the patroness of medicine, childbirth, and floods to whom an important shrine was erected on Cozumel Island.

Rainmaking, thunder, lightning, and storms were under the control of Chac, a long-nosed creature with volutes or fangs in the corners of his mouth, whom we see in the codices producing rain by urinating on the earth or pouring water on it with gourds or pottery vessels. Each of the thirteen heavens of the Upper World had its patron deity, as did the nine lower realms of the Underworld. Another class of gods known as *Bacabs* are often shown in Maya iconography as old men with upraised arms, since it was believed they held up the sky. Special deities presided over hunting, fishing, war, poetry, music, weaving, and suicide, in addition to which there were gods associated with various planets, the moon, human sacrifice, the numbers from 0 to 13, and the nineteen months, twenty days, and *katun* cycles of the calendar.

Because these supernatural beings exhibit a curious mixture of human physical features with those of animals, reptiles, and birds, they appear in Maya iconography like fantastic monsters conjured out of the depths of some unearthly realm. Inherent in their nature were dualistic traits that expressed themselves in conflicting attitudes toward mankind, resulting in acts of kindness or wrathful vengeance according to unpredictable whims. Some gods readily altered their physical characteristics and roles, or assumed manifestations during the day that changed radically at night. To further complicate matters, most gods were envisioned both individually and with multiple identities. For example, Itzamná was thought of either as a discrete entity or as four separate deities involving night-day and earth-sky aspects. Native sources speak of the rain god Chac singularly or as having four distinct manifestations, and this idea is again illustrated by the four *Bacabs,* one of whom is stationed at each corner of the sky.

In Maya cosmology the earth was conceived as a flat, four-sided surface lying between thirteen heavens and nine underworlds, which were arranged in layers. At the geographical center of the earth grew a huge ceiba tree, with smaller trees located at its four outlying corners. Each direction corresponded to a particular color: white to the north, yellow to the south, red to the east, and black to the west. Specific deities were associated with these directions and colors, and a bird of the appropriate color supposedly nested in the tree at each corner of the earth. Apparently the Maya envisioned the world as resting on the back of a gigantic crocodile floating in a lily pond (a view shared with the Aztecs), and they believed that the earth had been created several times in the past, only to be destroyed again by calamities.

The Maya perceived themselves as inhabiting the center of a three-level vertical axis consisting of the Underworld, earth, and sky—a concept clearly depicted in Classic-period iconography through the use of motifs involving Underworld, earthly, and celestial imagery. It was believed that mankind existed at the center of both this threefold vertical axis and a four-sided horizontal plane defined by the cardinal directions. Inherent in this world view was a perception of reality wherein time, space, the physical world, and supernatural realms were continuous, interconnected parts of a universe in which human beings and gods interacted on all levels.

Ordinary mortals could scarcely hope to correctly interpret the will of the gods or devise the proper means of placating them. Instead this was the function of a sacrosanct priesthood whose training, mystical powers, and understanding of magic, ritual, science, and prophecy enabled them to intercede with the divinities on mankind's behalf. We have no direct evidence bearing on specific responsibilities of priests during the Classic period, and it has been suggested by some archaeologists that the ruling elite may have fulfilled this role by virtue of special training in religious matters. Nevertheless, in view of the abundance of religiously oriented art and the obvious importance of ritualism in every aspect of life as far back as the Preclassic era, it seems likely that priests—or some type of specialized religious practitioners—emerged as an integral part of Maya society at an early date. We know that powerful priesthoods existed at the time of the Conquest, and it is reasonable to assume that these were the outgrowth of an ancient tradition.

According to Landa's *Relación,* the highest-ranking priests in Yucatán were called *Ahau Can Mai* or *Ah Kin Mai.* Some post-Conquest documents refer to them simply as *Ah Kin* (''He of the Sun''), and they unquestionably enjoyed a powerful position in Maya society. Landa's description of the high priests' functions includes divination, prophecy, medicine, and the execution of ceremonies. Other important aspects of their responsibilities involved instructing candidates for the priesthood in astronomy, mathematics, hieroglyphic writing, calendrics, and rituals, as well as assigning new priests to fill vacant offices. Entrance into the clergy was usually a matter of heredity, and since priests did not practice celibacy, their offices were inherited by their eldest sons or other close male relatives. It was also possible for the second sons of nobles to become priests if they showed an inclination toward this profession.

Aiding the high priests with their tasks were *chilans* (sometimes spelled *chilams),* or prophets whose duty was to study divinatory almanacs, interpret mystical omens, and predict future events. Another class of priests—the *nacoms*—was charged with the grisly job of cutting out the hearts of sacrificial victims, and they were assisted in this by elderly subordinates known as *chacs* (named after the rain god), who held the victims' arms and legs at the moment of sacrifice. Shamans called *h-men* or *ahmen* specialized in prayers, sorcery, and curing illness; and several early sources mention that various duties within the temples such as sweeping floors and tending sacred fires were performed by the equivalent of ''vestal virgins''—young unmarried girls of noble birth.

It is questionable whether the populace in general had much comprehension of the deeper philosophic aspects of their religion, or of the intellectual pursuits of the priesthood. Almost surely they did not have access to important temples and shrines, though they frequently participated in special rites as determined by a strictly observed ceremonial calendar of events. Each of the eighteen months and the five-day *Uayeb* that comprised the vague year had specified rituals, as did certain periods of the *tzolkin*, the endings of *katuns*, the new year, seasons for planting and harvesting, and numerous other occasions. At such times the cities were crowded with peasants whose homage to the appropriate gods expressed itself through prayers, dances, chanting, offerings to idols, and the burning of copal incense. Nearly every ritual was preceded by fasting (meat, chili peppers, and salt were particularly taboo), sexual abstinence, and purification rites. Once under way, however, many ceremonies involved feasting, drinking an intoxicating beverage called *balché*, bloodletting (usually done by piercing the ears, nose, lips, tongue, or sexual organs with stingray spines, thorns, or obsidian blades), and possibly the use of hallucinogenic mushrooms or peyote.

Sacrifices played a vital part in Maya ritualism. Animals such as iguanas, crocodiles, turtles, dogs, peccaries, jaguars, and turkeys were occasionally sacrificed, and Landa observed that these offerings involved either whole animals—alive, freshly killed, or cooked—or in some cases only their hearts. But the supreme sacrifice was human life itself, and all too frequently humans were consigned to be slaughtered in the course of elaborate rituals. Such scenes are clearly depicted in sculpture, ceramics, and murals, and this gruesome practice grew out of the conviction (adhered to throughout Mesoamerica, especially among the Aztecs) that human blood was essential to sustain the gods. Victims for these rites were provided by slaves, captured enemy soldiers, bastards, criminals, or orphans, and included adults and children of both sexes. Actually, children were often preferred because of what Landa termed their lack of ''carnal sin''; if necessary they were sometimes abducted or even purchased from neighboring cities, the usual price being from five to ten stone beads per child.

Landa gives a vivid description of a common method of human sacrifice wherein the victim, his body painted blue (the sacrificial color), was led to the summit of a pyramid and stretched over a stone altar, with his arms and legs firmly held by four *chacs*. Next the *nacom*, using a flint or obsidian knife, cut open his chest, tore out the heart, and handed it to a high priest whose task was to anoint the faces of idols with its blood. Finally the corpse was thrown down the temple steps to a waiting priest who flayed it and danced in the skin, after which the onlookers ate the rest of the body, reserving the hands and feet for the officiating priests.

During another ritual known as the "arrow sacrifice," the victim—stripped and painted blue—was tied to a stake amid a group of dancers armed with bows and arrows. Upon a signal from a priest, each dancer passed in front of him, shooting at his heart until, according to Landa, "they made his whole chest . . . like a hedgehog full of arrows." Other sacrificial techniques included hanging, drowning, beating, mutilation, and decapitation, and one particularly grisly scene painted on a Late Classic vase shows a victim being disemboweled.

Although formidable barriers of heredity, education, and wealth separated the ruling hierarchies from the majority of the populace, Maya society appears to have been considerably more integrated than was suggested by earlier studies. Archaeological and documentary evidence alike indicate the existence of social strata divided between an hereditary elite (nobles and priests) and lower classes consisting of peasants and slaves, with another category made up of artists, tradesmen, and civil administrators occupying a somewhat middle position in the social scale. Yet this may prove to be an oversimplified view of Maya society. Many scholars now argue that further class distinctions existed within these three categories, and that commoners enjoyed a higher degree of social and economic mobility than was previously suspected (see Chapter 8).

One device for gaining increased status might have been a *cargo* system of the type extant today among the Tzotzil Indians in the highlands of Chiapas. Under this arrangement adult males rise to positions of authority by holding a series of *cargos* or public offices (civil and religious) on a rotating basis, although if a comparable system operated among the ancient Maya—as some students believe—it would have applied only to minor administrative or ceremonial posts and not to the upper echelons of elite power. Another avenue whereby commoners probably acquired higher status involved the production of arts and crafts, since it is difficult to imagine that persons engaged in the creation of such items as carved jade, polychrome pottery, sculpture, hieroglyphic books, murals, or the lavish clothing worn by the upper classes were anything but specialists. Very likely these occupations were hereditary, though it may have been possible for talented outsiders to enter these professions by serving as apprentices. Successful merchants and highly esteemed warriors also appear to have attained an elevated station in Maya society, while unskilled laborers and the mass of peasant farmers constituted the lowest rungs of the social ladder—discounting slaves and prisoners, who had no rank whatsoever.

Given the obvious need for tradesmen, artists, and administrators, the idea that these groups enjoyed an elevated social status seems entirely reasonable. In his recent book, *Ancient Maya Civilization,* Norman Hammond constructed an interesting model of these middle-class strata and the system under which they operated:

The ruler of the realm . . . would clearly be able to exert control only through an administrative class, and the existence of such a class may therefore be postulated from the mere existence and florescence of Classic Maya culture. The function of its members would have been to translate the ruler's directives into appropriate administrative action: decisions as to which resources of men and materials were to be allocated to a particular task, and the dissemination of necessary information about its performance.

The higher bureaucracy would have been within constant reach of the ruler, and below it we may propose a lower, executive bureaucracy responsible for the actual execution of directives . . . beyond the immediate control of the central administration. Such officials would be responsible for the assembly of the labor force, specialist craftsmen, and raw materials for a building project, or for the conscription, arming, and supply of a raiding or defensive force. This would necessarily operate at a local level, and some of the minor ceremonial centers probably would have acted as their bases of operation. Whether their position was purely administrative or whether, as seems more likely, it was associated with a high local social status (similar to that of the lord of the manor in medieval England or the district commissioner in the nineteenth-century British Empire), we cannot know for certain. Similarly we cannot know the extent to which a population was obliged to its local overlords as well as to the ruler, although Richard Adams has recently suggested that a feudal system of obligation is likely to have existed among the Classic Maya.

Many of the directives, whether from the central or local government, were doubtless concerned with the construction, decoration, and maintenance of public buildings—temples, ball courts, and all other non-residential structures clustered in the ceremonial precinct—and these activities in themselves would, as elsewhere in the preindustrial world, have been carried out by specialist artisans, working under a system of public patronage but also doubtless capable of undertaking private commissions. The kind of life described by Benvenuto Cellini in his *Autobiography* may not have been so very different from that of a topflight Maya craftsman.

Information on the structure of Maya society during the Classic period is extremely limited, but various post-Conquest sources give us a rough idea of its organization as it existed early in the sixteenth century. In Yucatán the most influential member of the ruling elite was the *halach uinic* or "true man." Anyone holding this position did so for life, and upon his passing the office was inherited by his eldest son or brother. In the event he had no suitable heir, a successor was elected by a council of lords from candidates chosen among noble families. Each major city was governed by a *halach uinic* in whom supreme political authority rested, including ultimate responsibility for civil affairs, relations with neighboring cities, and the administration of justice. So esteemed was his position that a cloth was always held up before his face to prevent anyone from speaking to him directly. As there were ceremonial aspects to many of his duties, the *halach uinic* was also a priest (or at least well versed in ritual procedures), and he may have been considered a god-king endowed with semidivine powers.

To assist in governing outlying villages the *halach uinic* selected magistrates known as *batabs* (axe bearers). Essentially they functioned as provincial mayors, keeping a close rein on local government and judicial matters, and overseeing the collection of tributes paid by the peasants to the hierarchy. Occasionally the *batabs* commanded detachments of soldiers which served as a kind of palace guard, but ordinarily in time of war the military forces were led by specially elected officers.

Immediately under the *batabs'* jurisdiction were administrative assistants called *ah kulelob*. Each town also had several *ah cuch cabob* or councilors who acted as representatives of local precincts. Other officials included the *tupiles* or constables charged with law enforcement, and the *ah holpopob*, whose position involved mediation at public meetings, leading dance rehearsals, chanting during festivals, and taking care of musical instruments.

All of these posts were held by members of the nobility (known collectively as the *almehenob*) and were attained either through inheritance or by selection on the basis of family and social status. Aside from their political and religious authority, some nobles were undoubtedly merchants, military leaders, slaveholders, and private landowners; others may have been renowned artists or architects under whose supervision important public works were executed. Abundant confirmation of their privileged status is seen in the aloof manner in which they are portrayed in sculpture and paintings, and the extreme disparity between the splendid costumes, jewelry, elaborate tombs, and other symbols of personal wealth displayed by the ruling hierarchy as compared with the meager possessions of the peasants. Furthermore, all knowledge of astronomy, mathematics, hieroglyphic writing, and the esoteric aspects of ritualism apparently remained entirely in the hands of the upper classes, leaving the vast majority of peasants illiterate.

Interesting insight into the archaeological background of this hereditary aristocracy grew out of an important breakthrough in glyphic decipherment announced in 1960 by Tatiana Proskouriakoff, an eminent specialist in Maya art and architecture who was affiliated with the Carnegie Institution. While studying a collection of sculptured stelae from Piedras Negras on the Usumacinta River in northwestern Guatemala, she noticed that on the basis of similarities in iconography they could be divided into seven groups, each of which had been erected at consecutive intervals in conjunction with a specific temple or palace. Unfailingly, the earliest stela in a given series depicted a young man seated in a niche enclosed by astronomical signs and the figure of a two-headed, serpentlike monster or celestial dragon, probably representing Itzamná. Just below the niche was a design resembling a ladder draped with a cloth or mat, and footprints leading up the ladder indicated that the man had recently climbed to his seat. Accompanying this "ascension motif," as Proskouriakoff called it, was an inscription showing an "inaugural date" along with glyphs relating to events such as the individual's birthday, his accession to power, and in some cases the names of his wife and children. The longest period of time covered by the dates on any group of stelae fell within an average human's life span, and each set of monuments related to a single individual and his family. In effect, then, these stelae recorded a succession of seven rulers who had reigned at Piedras Negras between A.D. 613 and 795 (9.9.0.0.0. to 9.18.5.0.0.)—a discovery of far-reaching implications, since it provided the first definite proof that certain inscriptions pertained to historical occurrences rather than to information that dealt exclusively with ritualism, astronomy, and calendrics, as had previously been assumed.

Subsequently, Proskouriakoff was able to demonstrate the existence of similar material on lintels and stelae from the neighboring city of Yaxchilán. Inscribed on these monuments were narrative scenes and hieroglyphs involving members of a powerful "Jaguar" dynasty, especially a prominent ruler named Bird Jaguar, whose military exploits over an adversary known as Jeweled Skull were clearly portrayed.

Several years later, David H. Kelley, applying the principles worked out by Proskouriakoff, reported inscriptions on monuments from Quiriguá tracing a sequence of three, and possibly five, separate dynasties. Further research at Quiriguá by Robert Sharer and Christopher Jones has given us a considerable body of information on an important ruler designated as Cauac Sky, who came to power in A.D. 724 and extended Quiriguá's influence over a wide area that included Copán. Indeed, Cauac Sky appears to have defeated Copán as the result of a military campaign in 737. He was also responsible for securing control of a vital trade route along the Motagua Valley, inaugurating a massive building program at Quiriguá, and erecting many of the city's justly famous monuments.

59 Ceramic figurines from the island of Jaina, off the coast of Campeche. These elegant, small-scale sculptures, which vary from 4 to 8 inches in height, were excavated from tombs at Jaina, a site that served as a necropolis for members of the elite class. Noted for their realistic detail, these figurines were made both by hand and in molds. They were originally painted in a variety of colors, and many were designed to be whistles. Late Classic.

60 Seated dignitary wearing large ear spools and a pectoral, Jaina. Note the decorative facial scarification, a widespread practice among the Maya. Late Classic. Height, 7 inches.

61 An old man embracing a young woman, Jaina. A number of figurines from this island repeat the theme of an elderly man caressing a young woman. Their meaning is not known, but it has been suggested that the aged figure is a god and the theme is related to a mythical or cosmological event. Late Classic. Height, 10¹/₈ inches.

62 *Above left:* Jade plaque depicting a lord on a throne, Toniná, Chiapas. Late Classic. Height, 4½ inches.

63 *Above right:* Jade plaque showing a lord seated in a framed niche, found in the vicinity of Nebaj, Guatemala. Late Classic. Height, 5⁹/₁₆ inches.

64 *Below:* Jade plaque from Nebaj. This plaque, one of the masterpieces of Late Classic jade carving, depicts a dignitary conversing with a dwarf. Width, 5¾ inches.

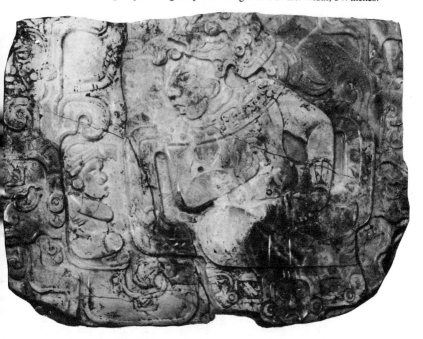

65 Onyx marble bowl, probably from Campeche. Scarcely an eighth of an inch wide at the rim, this exquisite vessel is incised with three figures holding religious symbols and encircled by a band of hieroglyphs. The incised lines have been accentuated with a dark pigment. Late Classic. Height, 4⁹/₁₆ inches.

66 Figure of a ballplayer, Jaina. He wears the typical protective devices used by Mesoamerican ballplayers—a padded arm guard, a knee guard, and a U-shaped stone yoke, with a serpent's head, around his waist. The deer's head in his hand may have been part of a helmet. Late Classic. Height, 5⁷/₈ inches.

67 Limestone disk from Chinkultik, Chiapas. A kneeling ballplayer, encircled by a band of hieroglyphs, is shown returning an oversize rubber ball, which bounces off his heavily padded hip. This disk was carved in A.D. 590 and may have been used as a ballcourt marker. Diameter, 21⅝ inches.

68 Stela 7, Machaquilá, Guatemala. A remarkably well preserved portrait of a ruler is seen in ceremonial regalia and holding a manikin-scepter. Late Classic.

69 A stucco head representing a stylized jaguar, Toniná, Chiapas. Late Classic. Height, 13½ inches.

70 Detail of a limestone relief panel showing a priest with an offering of birds, Jonuta, Tabasco. Late Classic.

71 Two views of a polychrome cylindrical vase from Altar de Sacrificios, Guatemala. The narrative paintings on this vase, which is acknowledged to be one of the finest ceramic vessels ever created by the Maya, may record the funeral ceremony of a noblewoman in whose tomb it was placed as an offering. *Left:* A lord—possibly Bird-Jaguar, a ruler from the nearby city of Yaxchilán—dances in a jaguar-skin costume.

Right: A fat, bald man in trousers decorated with a snakeskin pattern is shown dancing while a large boa constrictor arches over his head. The interpretation of these scenes has been the subject of considerable speculation, and some archaeologists believe that they represent a mythical event enacted in the Underworld. A hieroglyphic text indicates that the vase was painted in A.D. 754. Height, 6⅝ inches.

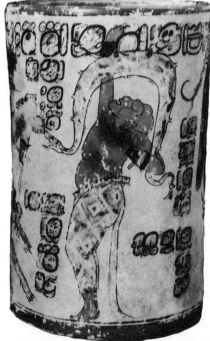

72 Carved shell pendant believed to be
from Jaina. The torso of a young noble
rises from the body of a fantastic fish decorated with incised glyphs. Late Classic.
Height, 3¹/₈ inches.

73 Jade plaque from Altun Ha, Belize.
Eight inches in height, this is the largest
jade plaque found thus far in the Maya
area. A ruling lord, wearing a birdlike
headdress, is seated in profile on a throne
that represents the sun god, Kinich Ahau.
The large head below the throne is the
Cauac Monster—a symbol of the Underworld into which the sun god disappears at
night. Late Classic.

74 Figure of a kneeling dignitary, probably from Tabasco. One of the few surviving examples of Maya woodcarving, this piece dates from the sixth or seventh century A.D. Height, 14¾ inches.

75 Polychrome plate, probably from Campeche, embellished with the figure of a bird. Late Classic. Diameter, 12½ inches.

76 Stela 3, Seibal, Guatemala. Carved sometime near the end of the ninth century A.D., this monument exhibits pronounced non-Classic traits that can be attributed to influences from Yucatán or the Mexican Gulf Coast which penetrated the southern lowlands during this time and may have contributed to the collapse of its cities. Note, for example, the absence of the elaborate costumes worn by elite figures in Classic sculpture, the non-Classic profile of the central figure, and the uncharacteristic division of the stela into three sharply defined panels.

77 Structure 1, Xpuhil, Campeche. This building is typical of the Río Bec architectural style in its use of massive ornamental masks over doorways and false towers in the form of pyramid-temples.

78 Alabaster vase with carved scrolls and animal-effigy handles, Ulúa Valley, Honduras. Postclassic. Height, 5¾ inches.

79 Désiré Charnay and an Indian companion climbing a Maya ruin. Charnay was among the first explorers to observe similarities in the art and architecture found at the Toltec capital of Tula, in central Mexico, and at Chichén Itzá, suggesting that Toltec culture had penetrated Yucatán.

80 Chichén Itzá, Yucatán, as it appeared about A.D. 1100. In the center of the main plaza stands the Temple of Kukulcán, from which a causeway leads to the Well of Sacrifice; to the left is the Temple of the Warriors, and to the right are the Temple of the Jaguars and the Ball Court.

81 Temple of the Warriors, Chichén Itzá, as drawn by Frederick Catherwood. The sculptured head of a feathered serpent in the foreground, originally attached to the balustrade of a stairway, represents the important Mexican god Quetzalcóatl, whom the Maya called Kukulcán.

82 Temple of Kukulcán—also known as El Castillo—Chichén Itzá, after partial restoration. Note the feathered serpents at the base of the stairway.

83 Limestone head of a feathered serpent, the emblem of the Mexican god Quetzalcóatl, or Kukulcán, Chichén Itzá. Postclassic. Height, 26³/₈ inches.

84 Temple of the Warriors, Chichén Itzá. The columns in front of the building are carved with figures of Mexicanized warriors, images of the Toltec-Itzá who invaded Yucatán during the Postclassic period.

85 *Left:* Relief carving of a Toltec-Itzá warrior, Temple of the Warriors.

86 *Below:* Limestone panel depicting a jaguar eating a human heart, a Mexican-inspired theme found on the walls of several structures at Chichén Itzá. Postclassic. Height, 41½ inches.

87 The Observatory, or El Caracol, Chichén Itzá, as it looked when drawn by Frederick Catherwood in 1842. The structure is believed to have been an astronomical observatory, and its dome-shaped tower contains a circular stairway leading to observation points from which the sun, moon, and certain stars could be studied along fixed lines of sight.

88 The Observatory after excavation and restoration. In the distance are the Temple of Kukulcán *(left)* and the Temple of the Warriors *(right)*.

89 Limestone sculpture of a *chacmool,* Chichén Itzá. Although *chacmools* were widely produced throughout Mesoamerica, the function of these curious figures is uncertain. The image is invariably that of a male, reclining on his elbows, with his legs drawn up at a sharp angle; the head is usually turned outward, and a round bowl is held on the stomach. The figures may have been used in sacrificial rites or as ritual guardians at the entrances to temples. *Chacmools* almost identical to this one were excavated at the Toltec city of Tula, in central Mexico. Early Postclassic. Length, 63 inches.

90 La Iglesia, Chichén Itzá. This ornate structure, misnamed "the Church," exhibits the characteristic features of the Puuc architectural style, which was widespread in parts of the Yucatán Peninsula during the Late Classic period. The lower sections of Puuc buildings were plain and faced with finely cut stones that were often coated with plaster. The façades, in contrast, were mazes of geometric designs, animal and human forms, and gigantic long-nosed masks of the rain god, Chac.

91 The Red House, Chichén Itzá. This beautiful example of a Puuc-style building was originally covered with red plaster. The roof is embellished with Chac masks separated by geometric frets.

92 Limestone standard-bearer, Chichén Itzá. Statues such as this were designed to hold wooden poles in their hands to which banners or flags were attached, and they were usually placed at the entrances to temples or palaces. Early Postclassic. Height, 37²/₅ inches.

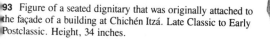

93 Figure of a seated dignitary that was originally attached to the façade of a building at Chichén Itzá. Late Classic to Early Postclassic. Height, 34 inches.

94 Edward Herbert Thompson.

95 Doorway of the Nunnery, or Las Monjas, Chichén Itzá.

91 The Red House, Chichén Itzá. This beautiful example of a Puuc-style building was originally covered with red plaster. The roof is embellished with Chac masks separated by geometric frets.

92 Limestone standard-bearer, Chichén Itzá. Statues such as this were designed to hold wooden poles in their hands to which banners or flags were attached, and they were usually placed at the entrances to temples or palaces. Early Postclassic. Height, 37²/₅ inches.

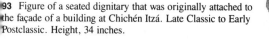

93 Figure of a seated dignitary that was originally attached to the façade of a building at Chichén Itzá. Late Classic to Early Postclassic. Height, 34 inches.

94 Edward Herbert Thompson.

95 Doorway of the Nunnery, or Las Monjas, Chichén Itzá.

96 *Above:* Well of Sacrifice, or Sacred Cenote, Chichén Itzá. Sacrificial victims were thrown into the water from the small temple in the foreground. *Below left:* Embossed gold eyes and a mouthpiece from a mask found in the Sacred Cenote. Postclassic. *Below right:* Gold pendant in the shape of a frog from the Sacred Cenote. Postclassic.

97 View of Uxmal, Yucatán, showing the Nunnery Quadrangle *(center)* and a massive pyramid-temple known as the House of the Magician *(right)*.

98 Palace of the Governors, Uxmal. The façade of this building, a superb example of Puuc-style architecture, is decorated with approximately 20,000 pieces of cut stone. When John Lloyd Stephens visited the palace in 1840, he was prompted to write: "If it stood this day on its grand artificial terrace in Hyde Park or the Garden of the Tuileries, it would form a new order...not unworthy to stand side by side with the remains of Egyptian, Grecian, and Roman art."

99 Detail of the Palace of the Governors.

100 Palace of the Governors, seen through an entrance to the Nunnery Quadrangle. In the foreground is a typical corbeled arch with capstones at the top. The slanting sides are supported by the weight of the rubble core inside the walls.

101 A section of the Nunnery Quadrangle, Uxmal.

102 The Great Palace, Sayil, Yucatán. Although only partially restored, this structure clearly illustrates the use of multiple stories, columns, and false columns, which are characteristic of some buildings in the Puuc region of Yucatán.

103 The Palace, Labná, Yucatán. The remains of a causeway are visible at the lower left; it originally connected the Palace with another complex of buildings on the opposite side of the plaza.

104 *Above:* The Arch, Labná, gateway to a complex of palace-type structures. Note the use above the two small doorways of models representing thatched-roof domestic houses. *Below:* The Arch as it appeared when visited by Stephens and Catherwood in 1842.

105 El Mirador, Labná. Still visible on the temple's façade are tenons that originally supported carved stone decorations.

106 Temple of the Seven Dolls, Dzibilchaltún, Yucatán. Inside this Late Classic building archaeologists found an altar containing seven small ceramic figures, each depicting a human with a physical deformity. A complex frieze with masks and serpentine forms once adorned the façade.

107 Effigy censer, Mayapán, Yucatán. Possibly a representation of the god Itzamná, this ceramic censer was originally painted in a variety of colors. Late Postclassic. Height, 23 inches.

108 Fragments of effigy censers from Mayapán. *Above right:* A polychrome mask identified by the long nose and different-colored eye patches as the merchant god, Ek Chuah. Height, 6¾ inches. *Right:* Head of the deity Itzamná. Height, 8 inches. Late Postclassic.

109 Effigy vessel depicting a man on the back of a turtle with a human head emerging from its mouth, Mayapán. Late Postclassic. Height, 7⅛ inches.

110 A temple at Tulúm, on the coast of Quintana Roo, an important Postclassic trading center.

111 Temple of the Frescoes, Tulúm. On the interior walls a series of Mexican-influenced murals was discovered.

112 *Above:* Mosaic mask made of turquoise, jade, conch shell, and tortoiseshell; reportedly found in Yucatán. Late Postclassic. Height, 5¾ inches.

113 *Right:* An incense burner adorned with the face of the Mexican rain god, Tlaloc, Cave of Balankanché, Yucatán. Postclassic. Height, 12 inches.

114 Yucatecan Indians worshiping in the Cave of Balankanché.

115 Lacandón women from a village near the ruins of Bonampak, Chiapas.

116 An Indian woman weaving with a backstrap loom, San Antonio Aguas Calientes, Guatemala.

117 Tzotzil Indians at Zinacantan, Chiapas.

Guided by Proskouriakoff's revolutionary breakthroughs in glyphic decipherment, scholars are rapidly establishing dynastic sequences for many Classic-period cities. As discussed in Chapter 6, Palenque's ruling lineages have begun to emerge from centuries of obscurity, together with those at Piedras Negras, Yaxchilán, Bonampak, Calakmul, Quiriguá, and Copán. But nowhere do we find a more detailed record of a Maya hierarchy than at Tikal, whose royal tombs and monuments have allowed archaeologists to reconstruct the city's ruling dynasties over a period of almost four hundred years. Beginning with the reign of Jaguar Paw early in the fourth century A.D., Tikal was dominated by a succession of haughty nobles known to us as Curl Snout, Stormy Sky, Kan Boar, Jaguar Paw Skull, Woman of Tikal, Double Bird, Shield Skull, Ah Cacau, and Yax Kin—names derived mostly from pictorial elements in their identifying glyphs, which have yet to be accurately deciphered. As a group, these rulers built Tikal into the greatest of all Classic-period centers in the southern lowlands, one whose influence was felt throughout the Petén and in many outlying regions. Tikal's elite were unexcelled for their wealth and status, as evidenced by the grandeur of the temples, palaces, monuments, and treasure-filled tombs built to glorify their memory and enshrine their accomplishments.

At Tikal, as elsewhere in the lowlands, the power of the upper classes reached awesome proportions during Late Classic times. In their role as divinely sanctioned sovereigns, they presided over important religious functions; supreme political authority rested in their hands; all major buildings and monuments were erected at their direction; they held a priority on the production and distribution of luxury items; the finest examples of Maya art were created for their pleasure and aggrandizement; they controlled long-distance trade; they regulated the procurement and distribution of natural resources; and they alone comprehended and utilized the full potential of astronomy, hieroglyphic writing, mathematics, and calendrics.

Joyce Marcus has eloquently summarized the position enjoyed by the elite stratum of Classic society. "The Maya nobility," she wrote, "had a monopoly on history; their genealogies were kept for centuries, their ancestors were revered as semidivine, their life crises were recorded in stone, and they were portrayed as named giants who frequently used the tiny bodies of unnamed commoners or captives as pedestals on which to stand. . . . More than half the known inscriptions dealt with the political history of the cities (such as the Hieroglyphic Stairway at Copán), the personal histories of their individual rulers . . . or their territorial organization . . . all set within a calendric framework.''

While little is known about sociopolitical systems during the Classic period, archaeologists have traditionally assumed that every major center, together with its supporting peasant settlements, comprised a politically autonomous city-state governed by local rulers. It was believed that the houses and cultivated fields of the commoners were randomly scattered on the outskirts of the ''ceremonial center,'' and there were sharply drawn boundaries between city-states. But recent studies of population density, settlement patterns, and hieroglyphic inscriptions have shown that this concept presents an overly simplistic picture of the situation, especially as it existed in the lowlands after about A.D. 500.

Unfortunately, it is exceedingly difficult to estimate the size of Maya cities, to define their exact geographical limits, and to calculate their populations. Such obstacles arise from the dense vegetation that hampers the task of surveying and mapping archaeological sites, plus the fact that not all structures (particularly residences) left visible remains. Nor is it always possible to know whether ancient dwellings contained single family units or extended families, or to determine whether every house in a specific area was occupied simultaneously or at different periods. Equally perplexing are a number of unanswered questions regarding the nature of Maya settlement patterns, the interrelationship between large centers and the many ''hamlets'' that dotted the region, and the order in which the cities can be ranked on the basis of population, ceremonial function, economic importance, and spheres of political influence.

Although current research has revealed a wide disparity in settlement patterns, it is possible to delineate certain fundamental elements that characterize Maya cities in general. As outlined by Robert J. Sharer in his 1983 revision of Sylvanus Morley's book, *The Ancient*

Maya, the basic settlement unit was the domestic house—identified as an oblong, rectangular, or round thatched-roof dwelling, usually raised on a low earthern platform, with walls made of wattle-and-daub or stone. It consisted of one or more rooms divided by partitions, and was designed to house a couple and their unmarried children.

Several of these houses were frequently grouped together, sometimes around open courtyards, to form a *residential complex* that probably included an extended family—that is, grandparents, parents, married children, siblings, or cousins living in separate quarters but in close proximity to each other. Occasionally these complexes contained houses that were larger and more elaborate than the average dwelling—perhaps the residences of family heads who carried out local civic or religious duties—and nondomestic structures such as elevated platforms are sometimes found in these compounds, probably the remains of family shrines.

Larger units, classified as *clusters,* were made up of approximately five to twelve residential complexes, and it is assumed that clusters were occupied by expanded lineage groups (such as clans, if they existed). Apparently the principal residences within a cluster belonged to the head of the lineage and his extended family, while the smaller houses were used by other families in the same lineage. Shrines and courtyards are common features of clusters, and several scholars have suggested that important members of these lineages may have utilized the services of retainers, servants, and craft specialists who lived in the outlying residential complexes.

Finally, the clusters were grouped around the aggregates of public buildings, ceremonial precincts, and elite residences that comprised a *center,* or city. In summarizing the nature of these most impressive of all Maya settlement units, Sharer concluded that despite their size (the likes of Tikal, Piedras Negras, Uaxactún, and Copán notwithstanding), the centers "merely represented larger and more complex versions of residential clusters. In fact some scholars have viewed the basic core of even the largest Maya sites as the residences (palaces) for the most wealthy and powerful ruling lineages, the large temple pyramids representing their ancestral shrines. Regardless of the varying emphases given to different functional aspects of Maya sites, the centers and their surrounding residential clusters define the remains of an ancient social and political system, or *community*."

A variation on this concept of ranked settlement units emerged from an extensive survey of sites in the northeastern Petén by William R. Bullard, Jr. Based on his research, he classified the smallest territorial subdivisions into *clusters* of five to twelve households that covered an area of perhaps 250 to 350 square yards. Next in size were *zones* comprising a number of contiguous clusters plus a minor ceremonial center containing small pyramid temples, platforms, and courtyards. Several adjoining zones were then grouped together to form a *district,* an expanse of approximately forty square miles dominated by a major city. Similar types of stratified settlement patterns have been observed in the valley of the Belize River, in Campeche, Quintana Roo, and Honduras, though there appears to have been a considerable amount of regional variation in the order in which settlement units were organized.

Nevertheless, in contrast to older, simplified models of Maya "city-states"—autonomous, entirely self-governed, and sharply divided between elite-dominated ceremonial precincts and outlying clusters of randomly arranged peasant habitations—archaeologists now recognize that some system of formalized territorial organization, along with a high degree of sociopolitical, religious, and economic interaction between its units, was universal throughout the lowlands, despite considerable disagreement as to exactly how these polities were structured.

Furthermore, as the larger centers became increasingly urbanized, they encompassed a sizable population of merchants, administrators, artisans, and craftsmen. Indications of this are particularly strong at Tikal, where hundreds of structures believed to have been residences or workshops of persons engaged in special trades were mapped within the city's central zone. Along with urbanization, the economic and religious influence of certain cities expanded, as did the wealth and power of their ruling elite—thus causing some of the major centers to exercise political control over neighboring cities.

In 1958 a German epigrapher, Heinrich Berlin, discovered the existence of what he termed "emblem glyphs"—hieroglyphic symbols presumably denoting either the names of individual cities or their ruling dynasties. While studying inscriptions from sites in the southern lowlands, Berlin noticed that a glyphic prefix known as the *ben-ich* sign, which is translated as "lord" or "lord of the mat" (a mat being the symbol of supreme political authority), repeatedly appeared with a variety of main signs or central elements (see Chapter 3). He also observed that each of these main signs occurred within a restricted geographical area and was associated with a specific city. On the basis of this information, Berlin correctly deduced that such glyphs represented names or emblems by which particular sites could be identified. In effect, they function like an official seal or coat of arms, and among the emblem glyphs already identified are those for Copán, Quiriguá, Palenque, Tikal, Yaxchilán, Piedras Negras, Calakmul, Naranjo, and Seibal.

Not long after the announcement of Berlin's discovery, epigraphers began to note that the emblem glyphs of several major cities appeared on monuments at sites located outside their normal spheres of influence, often in inscriptions associated with portraits of rulers or court scenes. The implications of this fact were startling. For the first time archaeologists had concrete evidence that some Maya cities became powerful enough to exact allegiance from smaller centers, thereby forming a kind of confederation of allied cities. If necessary this control may have been maintained by military force, a possibility supported by the many depictions of military exploits and captives in Classic-period art. Intermarriage was another means by which cities were linked, since we have absolute proof that ruling hierarchies in different areas were frequently related by blood. Quite conceivably, certain centers voluntarily united to form a viable political entity for reasons of economic advantage or mutual defense, with one city in the group perhaps serving as the capital or seat of government.

Because the emblem glyphs of larger cities often appear on monuments from smaller (and presumably "subordinate" sites), scholars have attempted to rank the importance of lowland cities according to the predominance and geographical distribution of their emblem glyphs. Using this approach, Joyce Marcus has proposed the existence in the Late Classic period of *regional, secondary, tertiary,* and *quaternary* centers. According to her findings, four regional centers—Tikal,

Copán, Palenque, and Calakmul—had emerged by A.D. 731, all of which, Marcus believes, controlled extensive territories administered under their jurisdiction by second-, third-, and fourth-order centers allied with them. In addition, this hierarchy of sites was constantly changing, and lower-ranking cities altered their status through population growth, military conquest, or the acquisition and spread of their own emblem glyphs—a factor closely tied to the prestige of their ruling families. With the emergence of this type of territorial control and administrative structure in Late Classic times, the Maya were approaching a level of political complexity usually associated with true states. It is highly doubtful, however, that the lowland cities were ever welded into a single political entity or "nation" governed by a supreme ruler, and nothing suggesting anything more than regional dominance has yet come to light.

Despite the emphasis on territorial control and intercity rivalry inherent in Late Classic society, there is no evidence of sustained, large-scale warfare during this period; at least we find no signs of conflicts widespread enough to devastate the countryside, destroy cities, or disrupt trade routes. Many cities were situated in terrain vulnerable to attack from all directions, yet the remains of fortifications are rare. A notable exception to this occurs at Becán in southeastern Campeche, where the site was encircled by a wide moat roughly forty feet deep and spanned by seven narrow causeways. Excavations at Tikal and Seibal revealed elaborate earthworks obstructing certain approaches to these cities, and defensive walls were recently found at several Classic-period sites in northern Yucatán—namely Uxmal, Chacchob, Aké, Chunchucmil, Muna, and Cuca—although these had apparently been constructed at a relatively late date. It has been suggested that wooden palisades, thorny entanglements, and deadfalls were used as defenses in some localities, but generally the presence of specialized defensive structures is not a prominent feature of Classic sites.

While warfare may have been limited in scope, militarism obviously played an important role in Classic-period society. Raids and skirmishes constantly took place, touched off perhaps by territorial disputes, feuds between rulers of neighboring cities, or the need for sacrificial victims and slaves. Such a conflict is vividly portrayed in murals at Bonampak, and scenes on pottery and sculptured monuments repeatedly depict combat and figures of prisoners or slaves kneeling before their captors. Some students believe that by the Late Classic period, warfare had become "institutionalized," with a military elite, semiprofessional warriors, and greatly expanded objectives aimed at outright conquest of neighboring cities, control of natural resources, and domination of trade routes.

Whatever its motivation, war was considered a ritualistic activity. It was invariably accompanied by ceremonies intended to enlist the support of appropriate gods (whose images were carried into battle by priests), and it occurred in an atmosphere of elaborate pageantry. Warriors shown in the Bonampak frescoes are clad in gorgeous headdresses, jade ornaments, and jaguar-skin capes, and are attended by individuals blowing wooden trumpets and holding feathered banners or parasols above their heads. Sixteenth-century Spanish chronicles tell of encounters with Maya soldiers—their bodies painted red and black—arrayed in plumed helmets and lavish costumes, carrying brightly colored standards, and attacking amid the eerie din of drums, conch-shell horns, whistles, and yells.

In addition to mercenaries known as *holcans,* warriors were conscripted from among the peasants, a task assigned to the *ah holpopob,* who acted as recruiters. Special scouts called *zabin* ("road weasels") were sent out to secure information regarding enemy defenses, and prior to every campaign women prepared large quantities of food which the troops carried on their backs. Judging from representations in sculpture and paintings, Classic-period weapons were limited to short spears tipped with flint or obsidian points, wooden clubs, flint knives, and shields. But in the Postclassic era, when warfare assumed an increasingly important role, a number of innovations entered the Maya arsenal: *atlatls* or spear-throwers, slings, two-handed wooden swords edged with obsidian blades, curirasses made of quilted cotton or tapir hide, and bows and arrows—all introduced from Mexico. Military tactics centered on ambushes, frontal assaults, or maneuvers designed to outflank the enemy, but once a conflict was under way it involved mostly hand-to-hand combat. Wars were generally of short duration, and fighting never took place at night—a truce being declared each evening until the following day. Anyone killing or capturing an officer of the opposing side was greatly honored; if a commander was killed or severely wounded, his troops usually retreated.

In the field, armies were supervised by officers known as *nacoms* or "war captains" (not to be confused with the priests responsible for carrying out human sacrifices). *Nacoms* were elected for a period of three years, and throughout their tenure in office they could not indulge in sexual relations, eat meat, or drink intoxicants. Enormous prestige was accorded a *nacom*, especially one renowned for his success in battle. Once a year a festival was held in his honor, during which, Landa reported, "they bore him in great pomp, perfuming him as if he were an idol, to the temple where they seated him and burned incense to him. . . ."

Landa further relates how victorious warriors cut off the lower jaws of dead enemy soldiers, skinned them, and wore the bones on their arms as tokens of military prowess; and elite figures depicted in Classic-period sculpture are sometimes shown wearing trophy heads. Yet the primary goal was to capture rather than kill as many of the enemy as possible, particularly high-ranking officers and nobles. Usually prisoners of elite status were reserved for sacrifice, while commoners were sentenced to slavery. Aside from captives taken in battle, orphans, debtors, and individuals convicted of theft or murder were cast into bondage, and the children of slaves were automatically condemned to their parents' fate. Occasionally a person enslaved for indebtedness was allowed to purchase freedom by paying the debt, and slaves were sometimes ransomed by their families, but slavery generally meant a lifetime spent as a laborer, a household servant, or a farmer in the service of the elite class.

Warfare was an undeniable fact of life during the Classic period, and it may have periodically erupted into intense campaigns that exceeded the limits of raids or skirmishes. But it is clear that normal activities were never seriously jeopardized. On the contrary, there is overwhelming evidence that this era—especially the centuries from A.D. 550 until the onset of the collapse in the southern lowlands shortly after 800—witnessed expanding populations, uninterrupted building, the free exchange of ideas, and vigorous trade.

Ever since Preclassic times, commerce had played a key role in the development of Maya civilization and contributed enormously to its political stability. Landa observed that "the occupation to which they had the greatest inclination was trade," and sixteenth-century explorers marveled at the vast network of commercial routes linking the entire region. Such commodities as flint, beeswax, honey, cotton textiles, rubber, copal incense, vegetable dyes, tobacco, vanilla, polychrome pottery, tortoise shells, feathers, and jaguar and ocelot skins were regularly exported from the lowlands to cities in the uplands of Chiapas, Guatemala, and El Salvador. In return, merchants from those areas brought jade, albite, obsidian, hematite, quetzal feathers, pottery, and cinnabar to sell in lowland centers. Groups living in coastal regions supplied salt, dried fish, shells, stingray spines, and pearls to inland districts. And sometime after about A.D. 900, objects of turquoise, copper, and gold began to be imported from Mexico, along with a variety of gold and copper items manufactured in Panama, Costa Rica, and Colombia.

Virtually all long-distance trade seems to have been organized by members of the elite classes, whose contacts with distant cities and management of natural resources enabled them to control this lucrative commerce. Local trade was largely in the hands of wealthy non-elite merchants, and successful artisans probably engaged in trade on a part-time basis, selling their own wares in the town market or in nearby cities. Goods were transported on the backs of slaves or porters along well-established land routes, or by sea and rivers in large canoes measuring up to fifty feet in length. Cacao beans constituted the principal currency and had a fixed market value; occasionally payment was made in stone or shell beads, red beans, feathers, or small, hatchet-shaped copper celts, and transactions based on credit were apparently common.

Some Postclassic cities contained specially designed marketplaces —most notably the Mercado at Chichén Itzá, a spacious building supported by round columns, where items for sale were displayed in individual stalls. No markets have been positively identified in any Classic sites (though a group of structures in the East Plaza at Tikal appears to have been designed for this purpose), but they may have consisted of thatched-roof shelters or stalls set up in open courtyards, in which case their remains would have long since disappeared. We do know, however, that certain cities on the periphery of the Maya area—Xicalango, Soconusco, Cimatán, and several more—grew into important commercial centers. Xicalango, on the shores of Laguna de Términos in Campeche, was especially famous as a distribution point for goods passing back and forth from Mexico to Yucatán, Guatemala, and Honduras. Recent studies have also established that Cozumel Island, off the east coast of Quintana Roo, served as a major "free port" for maritime traders during the Postclassic period.

Ancient Maya markets must have differed little from those of the present day: crowded, noisy, filled with visual delights and exotic smells, their stalls overflowing with a dazzling array of products ranging from food, clothing, and household wares to luxury items. Undoubtedly they served a secondary purpose as meeting places and public forums for the exchange of ideas. In native markets today, whether in Mérida, Antigua, San Cristóbal de las Casas, or anywhere else in the area, one hears discussions covering every imaginable subject of interest to local Indians. So it surely was in past centuries, for commerce served a vitally important function in Maya culture by encouraging contact with outside peoples, stimulating craftsmanship and specialization, and providing a broader economic base for large populations.

8 · FARMERS AND BUILDERS: GLIMPSES OF EVERYDAY LIFE

In sharp contrast to our knowledge of the upper classes of Maya society, archaeology has revealed few details concerning the ordinary people. Rarely do inscriptions, sculpture, and paintings focus on their activities, and excavations of former peasant dwellings have underlined the comparative simplicity of their lifestyle. Among the remains found in these "house mounds" are large quantities of utilitarian pottery used for cooking and storage, plus a variety of household implements—such things as axes, celts, knives, scrapers, spindle whorls, and grinding stones. Occasionally decorated ceramics, figurines, and ornaments are also unearthed, but the quality of these artifacts hardly compares with the extravagant treasures associated with the ruling elite.

Overshadowed as they were by the spectacular architecture, works of art, and intellectual feats surrounding them, it was nevertheless the peasants, the *yalba uinicob* (lower men) as they were known in Yucatec, who actually formed the backbone of Maya civilization. Without the benefit of their labors, the priests and rulers could scarcely have afforded leisure time for excursions into astronomy, calendrics, mathematics, or literature. Yet so few are the traces of the peasants' existence that we must rely upon early ethnohistoric works—primarily Landa's *Relación*—for almost everything we know about their lives.

No event held greater significance for the average Maya than the birth of a child. Not only were children considered a measure of personal wealth and good fortune, they also implied the direct sanction of the gods, especially Ix Chel, the patroness of childbirth, whose image was placed under expectant mothers' beds during labor. One's birthday was counted from the day of the *tzolkin* or sacred year on which he was born, a factor that also determined what deities were most inclined to favor or malign an individual throughout life. Infants were given a childhood name by a priest, who then cast a horoscope to aid in their upbringing. Later they assumed a *coco kaba* or nickname used by family and close friends, and took a formal name derived from their parents' surnames. Masculine names always began with the prefix *Ah* and feminine names with *Ix,* but after a man married he adopted the prefix *Na.*

According to Maya ideals of beauty, it was highly desirable to be cross-eyed; thus a nodule of resin or a small bead was attached to a child's hair which hung between the eyes and conditioned the pupils to focus inward. Shortly after birth an infant's head was tightly bound to wooden boards in order to flatten the forehead, as this too was considered a mark of attractiveness, especially among the upper classes. Older children had their earlobes, septums, lips, and one nostril pierced so they could wear a variety of ornaments.

When a boy reached the age of five, a white bead was braided into his hair; a girl of the same age received a string with a red shell dangling from it to wear around her waist. As symbols of virginity, these could not be removed until an elaborate rite marking the beginning of adolescence, which was performed when the boys were fourteen years old and the girls twelve. Drawing upon Landa's description, Sylvanus Morley recounted the details of this ritual in his book, *The Ancient Maya:*

> The day of the puberty ceremony was carefully selected; pains were taken to ascertain that it would not be an unlucky day. A principal man of the town was chosen as sponsor for the children participating; his duty was to help the priest during the ceremony and to furnish the feast. Four honorable old men were selected as *chacs*, to assist the priest. . . . On the appointed day, all assembled in the court of the sponsor's house, which had been newly swept and strewn with fresh leaves. An old man was assigned to act as godfather for the boys, and an old woman as godmother for the

girls. When this was done the priest purified the dwelling and conducted a ceremony to expel the evil spirit.

When the spirit had been expelled, the court was swept out again, fresh leaves were strewn about, and mats were spread on the floor. The priest changed his vestments to a handsome jacket and a miter-like headdress of colored feathers, taking in his hand an aspergillum for sprinkling holy water. This latter consisted of a finely worked short stick with rattlesnake tails hanging from it. The *chacs* approached the children and placed on their heads pieces of white cloth, which their mothers had brought for this purpose. The older children were asked if they had committed any sin or obscene act. If they had, they were separated from the others. . . . This concluded, the priest ordered everyone to be seated and to preserve absolute silence, and after pronouncing a benediction on the children, he sat down. The sponsor of the ceremony, with a bone given him by the priest, tapped each child nine times on the forehead, moistening the forehead, the face, and the spaces between the fingers and toes with water.

After this anointing, the priest removed the white cloths from the children's heads. The children then gave the *chacs* some feathers and cacao beans which they had brought as gifts. The priest next cut the white beads from the boys' heads. The attendants carried pipes which they smoked from time to time, giving each child a puff of smoke. Gifts of food, brought by the mothers, were distributed to the children, and a wine [*balché*] offering was made to the gods; this wine had to be drunk at one draught by a specially appointed official.

The young girls were then dismissed, each mother removing from her daughter the red shell which had been worn as a symbol of purity. With this, the girl was considered to have reached a marriageable age. The boys were dismissed next. When the children had withdrawn from the court, their parents distributed among the spectators and officials pieces of cotton cloth which they had brought as gifts. The ceremony closed with feasting and heavy drinking. . . .

Until they were married, girls continued to live with their parents, learning from their mothers how to cook, spin cotton yarn, weave, and perform other household duties. Unmarried men painted themselves black to denote their station in life and lived in communal houses where they were instructed in various crafts, studied the arts of warfare, played games, and openly consorted with prostitutes. Referring to these "bad public women," Landa reported that "the poor girls who happened to ply this trade . . . although they received pay for it, were besieged by such great numbers of young men, that they were harassed to death."

Marriage was permitted anytime after the puberty ceremony, but normally it did not take place until the men were about eighteen years of age and the girls reached fourteen or fifteen. Arrangements were made through the parents (sometimes years in advance), with the father of the prospective bridegroom initiating the search for his son's wife. To facilitate this, a professional matchmaker was employed to represent the husband in the matters of a worthwhile dowry and details of the ceremony. Great emphasis was placed on finding a girl properly trained in the domestic skills and manners befitting a suitable wife. When passing a man she was required to lower her eyes, turn her back, and step aside. A wife never ate or drank with her husband; she did not laugh at him or engage in long conversations, and only rarely, during certain festivals, did she dance with him. Girls were expected to be chaste before marriage, and those who violated this rule were whipped, rubbed with pepper, and held up to public ridicule.

Strict taboos prohibited unions between persons with identical paternal surnames, and a man could not marry his maternal aunt, his brother's widow, his stepmother, or, if he was a widower, his dead wife's sister. Very likely the restriction against marrying anyone with the same patronymic indicates the former existence of exogamous clans. Vestiges of such clans survive today among several Maya-speaking tribes in Guatemala and Chiapas, and a statement by Landa would seem to confirm their presence in Yucatán in the sixteenth century: ". . . the Indians say that those bearing the same name are all of one family, and they are treated as such, and on this account when one comes to a place which is not known to him and he is in need, he at once makes use of his name, and if there are any of the same name there, they receive him at once and treat him with the greatest kindness. And so no woman or man was ever married to another of the same name, for that was in their opinion a great infamy."

Once a marriage had been arranged, the wedding ceremony involved reciting the terms of the agreement as worked out by the participants' families, the blessings of a priest, and a banquet given by the bride's father. Afterward the husband was required to live with his wife's parents (or at least in a nearby house) for a period usually ranging from three to six years, assisting his father-in-law and thereby proving his abilities. Since marriage could be dissolved at any time merely by a declaration on the part of either the husband or wife, divorce was quite common. Only first marriages were celebrated by a formal ceremony; thereafter persons who had been divorced or widowed were free to simply take up residence with a new mate, an event customarily marked by a banquet given for their relatives and friends.

If a man was wealthy enough to afford multiple wives—almost always a member of the nobility—he sometimes did so, and slaves were frequently kept by the elite as concubines. Monogamy was the generally accepted custom among the peasant class, and Maya women were reported to be exceedingly jealous. "Some carried it so far," wrote Landa, ". . . that they lay hands on the women of whom they are jealous. And so angry and irritated are they . . . that some tear their husband's hair no matter how few times [he] may have been unfaithful."

Adultery on the part of women was considered a serious offense, punishable under certain circumstances by allowing the outraged husband to kill his wife's lover, if he so desired, by dropping a rock on his head "from a great height." One Yucatecan chronicler, Gaspar Antonio Chi, related how adulterers were "killed with arrows," and "he who corrupted any maiden or violated any woman received the death penalty." Even so, adultery and sexual promiscuity were fairly widespread, and Landa complained bitterly about the Indians' susceptibility to "weakness of the flesh."

Throughout Maya history the design of the typical domestic house remained essentially unchanged. Basically it consisted of a single-room unit—oval, round, or rectangular in shape—with walls made of poles, plastered earth (wattle-and-daub), or occasionally undressed stones; the roof was sharply pitched and constructed of thatched palm leaves supported by a framework of beams and saplings tied with lianas. High partitions divided the interior into two sections, allowing the rear half to be used as sleeping quarters and leaving the front for everyday activities. Adjacent to the main house there were often auxiliary buildings or shelters that served as kitchens or storage areas, and to ensure proper drainage, all of these structures stood on low platforms built of earth and stones.

The furniture the Maya used in their dwellings was apparently restricted to wooden stools and benches, and low beds made of tightly lashed poles covered with fiber matting. Food was cooked on stone hearths or in ceramic vessels, and meals were eaten while sitting on stools or mats spread on the floor. Every household also contained an assortment of utilitarian pottery, gourd receptacles, baskets, wooden chests, woven storage bags, stone implements, and *metates* and *manos* for grinding maize.

Landa's description of the way Maya cities were laid out indicates that the location of one's house was determined by social prestige: "In the middle of the town were their temples with beautiful plazas, and all around the temples stood the houses of the lords and priests, and those of the most important people. [Next] came the houses of the richest and those who were held in the highest estimation nearest to these, and at the outskirts of the town were the homes of the lower class. And the wells, if there were but few of them, were near the houses of the lords. . . ."

Unlike the splendid attire of the nobles and priests, the peasants' clothing reflected their humble status. Ordinarily the men wore nothing but a cotton loincloth (called an *ex* in Yucatec), though for cool weather or special occasions they put on a square-cut *pati* or mantle of cotton fabric. Women's clothing consisted of short skirts, *mantas* or shawls, and square-cut dresses worn with a petticoat—a garment identical to the *huipiles* so popular in Yucatán today. Both sexes wore rawhide sandals tied about the ankles with thongs or fiber cords. Men kept their hair long and wore it either straight or pulled back, with a bare spot burned on the top of the head; the women's hair was braided in a variety of ways and sometimes decorated with ornaments. Generally the only jewelry peasants could afford were necklaces, earplugs, pendants, and nose buttons made of jade, albite, shell, and amber. But

the use of perfumes, body paint, tattoos, and decorative scars was widespread among both elite and peasant classes, as was the practice of filing the teeth to points, which, Landa said, "they considered elegant." Often the nobility carried this obsession with adornment a step further by inlaying their front teeth with iron pyrite, obsidian, jade, or shell.

Of necessity the majority of Maya peasants were farmers, and a considerable amount of collective effort was devoted to the cultivation and preparation of food. As their ancestors had done in Preclassic times, they periodically cleared the forest from small plots of land to create *milpas* (an Aztec word meaning "cornfields"). Stone tools were used to cut down underbrush, saplings, and vines, but since it was virtually impossible to fell large trees with flint axes, they may have been ringed with fire several years in advance and left to die. When the bush was sufficiently dry it was burned off, and just before the onset of the summer rains, seeds were planted in shallow holes made with sharpened digging sticks. Using this method, a farmer could grow enough food in about four or five months to supply his family and pay tributes for the rest of the year. But after several seasons the land's productivity was depleted, making it necessary to prepare new fields; only by allowing worn-out plots to lie dormant for long periods and repeating the process of clearing and burning could they be recultivated. Known as *milpa,* swidden, or slash-and-burn agriculture, this technique remained unchanged for thousands of years, and except for the appearance of steel axes, machetes, and iron-tipped digging sticks, the same system is widely practiced in the region today.

Until recently, scholars envisioned *milpa* agriculture as the basis of Maya economy, an assumption that led to perplexing questions as to how a civilization so complex could have been supported by a primitive subsistence technology that was severely limited in productivity. But in the last few years new information has radically altered longstanding ideas about the nature of Maya agriculture. We now know that although *milpas* were important in supplying certain staple crops, a variety of other farming techniques were employed, especially during the Classic period when it became necessary to sustain ever-expanding populations. For instance, the large swamps or *bajos* found in many parts of the lowlands were often converted into arable lands by the use of raised fields. These were clusters of square or rectangular mounds elevated above the original surface by digging canals across the swamp in a gridlike pattern, then piling the earth between them to create fertile plots suitable for planting. In other areas, hillsides and ridges—normally difficult to cultivate because of erosion—were terraced with stone walls placed laterally along slopes to retain the silt and thus provide additional fields. Such innovations probably led to the utilization of mulches, fertilizers, and irrigation to make the soil capable of intense, long-term production, and there is reason to suspect that the Maya learned to increase their agricultural output by crop rotation, raising several types of plants in the same field simultaneously (intercropping), and obtaining more than one annual harvest of certain plants (multicropping). Undoubtedly they maintained orchards and small gardens adjacent to their houses (a tradition still carried on by present-day Maya groups); and in some parts of the Petén, thick stands of *ramón* trees near archaeological sites—particularly at Tikal—indicate a high degree of dependence on the plentiful breadnuts produced by this species, a food that required no specialized cultivation and may eventually have provided the primary source of vegetable protein in this area. In short, it is obvious that a variety of subsistence methods were exploited in response to differing ecological factors, and current research has shown Maya agriculture to have been far more sophisticated than was previously supposed.

Among the most important crops raised by Maya farmers were maize, beans, squash, sweet potatoes, manioc, tomatoes, chili peppers, avocados, chayote, jícama, sapote, amaranth, papaya, and cacao. In addition, tobacco, cotton, gourds, henequen, rubber (natural latex extracted from the *Castilla* tree), vanilla, copal resin, and a variety of wild fruits were harvested for both domestic consumption and export. Aside from game animals, birds, and fish, which supplied plentiful sources of meat, the Maya domesticated turkeys, ducks, stingless bees (kept in hives inside hollow logs), and several species of dogs, including a barkless variety bred for sacrificial use.

Traditionally the main meal of the day was eaten in the late afternoon, and the typical menu consisted of roasted meat, spicy stews, tamales, chili, red or black beans, vegetables, fruit, and chocolate. In the sixteenth century (and probably in prehistoric times as well), the cultivation of maize was the basis of Maya subsistence, and in one form or another it constituted a high percentage of the daily diet. Moreover, it was venerated as the very essence of life itself, and a passage from the *Popol Vuh*, the sacred book of the Quiché, tells how the gods fashioned mankind out of yellow and white corn. In preparing the kernels for use, Maya women first soaked them in limewater to remove the hulls. Next they were ground with *metates* and *manos* into a thick dough called *zacan,* which served as the base for various dishes, especially tortillas that were eaten in large quantities during the evening meal and for breakfast. *Zacan* mixed with water made a greatly relished drink called *pozole,* and a thicker version of this—a corn gruel or *atole*—was served hot and sometimes sweetened with honey.

Every family paid its share of tributes in goods and services intended to maintain the "establishment." Landa recounts how the houses of the lords (which were considerably more elaborate than ordinary dwellings) were built by the peasants "at their own expense." Apart from this, they planted, tilled, and harvested fields belonging to the nobility and shared with them the bounty from hunting and fishing. A portion of every season's crops—especially maize—was contributed to the hierarchy, along with regular tributes of commodities such as salt, cloth, honey, copal incense, fruit, and domestic animals. And since only a few months of the year were devoted to food production, the average man had a good deal of free time for construction projects, keeping the jungle cleared from the cities, and repairing buildings and roads.

Regardless of the burden of tributes and manual labor, it does not appear that the peasants were oppressed. As previously pointed out, all commoners did not necessarily share the same economic level. Quite possibly some achieved a higher degree of prosperity and social mobility through specialized skills or minor bureaucratic posts. In an article on this subject, Richard E. W. Adams listed a number of "middle class" occupational categories almost surely filled by peasants: scribes, accountants, musicians, entertainers, potters, sculptors, painters, costume makers, armorers, and stonemasons. Others might conceivably have become petty merchants, and J. Eric Thompson believed there was nothing to prevent a peasant who was particularly successful in a specialty from exchanging his goods for luxury items, acquiring a measure of personal wealth in the process.

Nor was all of the peasant's time consumed with work. Each month brought its religious ceremonies, festivals, and banquets, some of which, if the descriptions given by Spanish informants are correct, involved excessive drunkenness and sexual debauchery. Many rituals included dances with large numbers of participants arrayed in lavish costumes and carrying brightly colored banners and streamers. In most cases men and women danced separately, but Landa noted at least one exception to this—a dance called the *naual,* which he denounced as "not very decent." Another historical document, the *Relación* of Campocolche, states that the Maya had more than a thousand different dances. Other popular entertainments featured satirical plays and comedies presented on platformlike stages or in courtyards by masked actors and clowns, and there were storytellers who recited fables and legends to the accompaniment of drums, orchestral music, and songs. Apparently it was common for certain of these festivities to attract thousands of spectators.

Everyone took a passionate interest in the game known as *pok-a-tok* (its Aztec name was *tlachtli),* a sport played throughout Mesoamerica in courts similar to those described in Chapter 5. Basically it consisted of knocking a solid rubber ball from four to twelve inches in diameter through a stone ring placed midway along the wall of the court just above the players' heads. (In Classic-period sites, stone markers were used instead of rings, suggesting that the rules must have differed somewhat at that time.) Under no circumstances could the ball be thrown by hand or kicked; it had to bounce off the hips, shoulders, or forearms, which were heavily padded for protection. Two teams competed in these matches, and players demonstrating unusual skill were held in great esteem. Incredibly high stakes were wagered on the outcome of every game—including jade, gold, houses, and slaves—and the winning team was entitled to the jewelry and clothing of the spectators, who naturally fled the scene as quickly as possible once the match was decided. Various sources state that the losers were some-times sacrificed, and this would seem to be confirmed by a series of bas-reliefs in a ball court at Chichén Itzá showing players being de-capitated.

All misfortune and illness was viewed by the Maya as resulting from evil spirits or disfavor of the gods. Even today, witchcraft and dan-gerous omens are greatly feared, and many villages have medicine men whose duties include guarding against such forces. Among the Yucatecans, gourds filled with food are regularly put out for the invisi-ble dwarfs who are believed to cause sickness. Extreme caution is taken to avoid the *pishan* or souls of the dead, and the *x-tabai*—the spirits of beautiful young women with the power to lure men deep into the forest and steal their souls. Sylvanus Morley noted that if a Yucatecan dreams of red tomatoes, it means the death of a baby. Dreams involving a broken water jar signify death in one's family, and dreaming of pain, having a tooth pulled, or floating on air means a close relative will die. If a hunter sells the head, liver, or stomach of a slain deer, he will endanger his chances of killing other game; selling an animal he has killed to someone who throws its bones into a *cenote* will bring him ill fortune. Superstitions regarding lucky and unlucky days survive in the belief that anything undertaken on Tuesdays and Fridays is doomed to failure, or that the best time to plant *milpas*, gamble, or get married is a Monday or Saturday. Nine and thirteen are considered lucky numbers, a belief possibly stemming from their asso-ciation with the nine underworlds and thirteen heavens of ancient Maya cosmology.

When illness occurred, a sorcerer or priest was called upon to exam-ine the victim. He might prescribe a variety of treatments involving fetishes, divination, rituals, or potions, often with beneficial results. Extensive use was made of medicinal herbs, plants, mineral sub-stances, and potions with such unsavory ingredients as bat wings, red worms, animal excrement, urine, blood, crocodile testicles, and bird fat. In his book, *The Ethno-Botany of the Maya,* Ralph L. Roys gives a number of typical remedies translated from post-Conquest native sources, several examples of which are quoted as follows:

Toothache. Crumble the soot that clings to cooking stones and wrap it with cotton-wool; if it is a broken tooth, then let it be applied. The throbbing will cease. Or else grate with a fishskin the tooth of a crocodile and let it be wrapped with cotton-wool . . . and applied to the tooth that throbs. It will cease by this means. . . .

Pulling a Tooth. There is an iguana that is yellow beneath the throat. Pierce its mouth, tie it up and burn it alive on a flat plate until it is reduced to ashes. These ashes of the iguana you are to anoint. You shall set your forceps and then you shall draw the tooth without pain. Try it first on a dog's tooth, before you draw the man's tooth with the ashes of the iguana which is yellow beneath its throat.

Excessive Sneezing. Anyone who sneezes excessively so that it will affect the joints and veins, will, one day or night, die of it. You take a handful of orange leaves, boil them, apply (the liquid) to the foot and then you rub the body with the liquid also.

Insanity. Take the testicles of a black cock, mash and dissolve them in cold water and give it to him to drink at dawn before he takes his breakfast. Every day at dawn he is to drink it.

If the appropriate treatment failed and death seemed imminent, a final confession was made to the attending priest, who then prophesied how long the patient could be expected to live and what his prospects were regarding the afterlife. Death was greatly feared by the Maya, despite their belief that worthy individuals—those obedient to religious mandates and therefore favored by the gods—would eventually reside in an eternal paradise located among the thirteen heavens. Suicide, especially by hanging oneself, was looked upon as the greatest measure of personal sacrifice, an act ensuring the unqualified pleasures of immortality. Women who died in childbirth, priests, warriors killed in battle, and sacrificial victims could look forward to equally propitious rewards. Evildoers, however, were condemnd to *Xibalbá* (or *Metnal* as it was known in Yucatán), the Maya equivalent of hell—a demon-infested realm in the Underworld where the damned suffered never-ending cold, hunger, and torment.

In marked contrast to the elite class, peasants were usually placed in simple graves under the floors of their houses, which were frequently abandoned after their owners' deaths. Occasionally burials were made in stone-lined cists, *chultuns,* or caves, and children were sometimes interred in large pottery jars. In northern Yucatán, cremation was widely practiced among the aristocracy, perhaps because the limestone surface made the preparation of elaborate underground tombs too difficult. Almost always the bodies were wrapped in cotton shrouds, sprinkled with cinnabar, and buried either fully extended or in a flexed position, with the knees drawn up against the chest; in some cases the head was oriented toward the north, south, or east. Ornaments, pottery vessels (probably containing offerings of food), and objects formerly used by the deceased were put in the grave with the corpse, and cornmeal and a jade bead were placed in the mouth, a gesture intended to provide sustenance and money for the journey to the afterlife. "It was indeed a thing to see the sorrow and the cries which they made for their dead," wrote Landa, "and the great grief it caused them. During the day they wept for them in silence; and at night with loud and very sad cries, so that it was pitiful to hear them. And they passed many days in deep sorrow. . . ."

Overwhelming mysteries surrounded and awed the Maya peasant: the movements of the planets, the seasons, storms, birth, life, and death, all the manifest powers of the gods thrown up around him like an infinite mirror in which was reflected the frailty of his existence. Life was spent placating the ancient fear of the unknown which had followed mankind since the dawn of history. Entrapped in uncertainty and superstition, the Maya constantly sought religious sanction through rituals, the construction of lofty temples, and the guidance of rulers and priests whose esoteric knowledge gave them insight into mystical realms. To achieve this assurance, no sacrifice of time and effort was too costly.

Archaeologists have long been frustrated by the scarcity of information pertaining to certain aspects of Classic Maya culture. Almost nothing in the way of clothing, headdresses, furniture, or other perishable items has survived, and many facts concerning rituals, dances, warfare, and everyday activities could only be inferred from fragmentary data—mainly pictorial representations in sculpture and ceramic painting. Unexpectedly, however, the discovery of an inconspicuous temple in the rain forest of eastern Chiapas afforded a much more graphic insight into such details than anything previously unearthed.

For centuries this building lay concealed in a remote area inhabited by a Maya tribe known as the Lacandón. Immediately after the Conquest, these Indians had retreated into the wilderness in an effort to escape the Spaniards, and when a final attempt to subdue and Christianize them in 1790 ended in failure, they were, for all practical purposes, forgotten by the outside world. But by the mid-1900s this sector of Chiapas began to be exploited by chicle gatherers, mahogany cutters, and oil prospectors. As a result of this sudden influx, a variety of illnesses beset the Lacandón with disastrous consequences, and severe epidemics—added to a gradual exodus of younger Indians who migrated to nearby towns in search of improved living conditions—sharply reduced their population. Now largely confined to the region between the Jatate and Usumacinta rivers, the number of Lacandón once dwindled to about two hundred survivors, but with increased access to medical care in recent years, their population has slowly expanded.

Despite the constant pressure of disruptive influences, the Lacandón steadfastly cling to certain traditions practiced by their ancestors. One can still find groups living in thatched-roof dwellings, cultivating crops in *milpas*, making crude pottery, and weaving cloth on backstrap looms, though they also utilize many commercially produced items. Native religious practices continue to play an important role in their lives, and they sometimes carry out rituals or place offerings of maize, *balché*, and copal incense in long-deserted temples—to worship ancient gods and pay homage to their venerable legacy.

In the winter of 1945–46 an explorer named Giles G. Healey entered the jungles of Chiapas to photograph the Lacandón for a documentary film entitled *The Maya Through the Ages*, which had been commissioned by the United Fruit Company. While living in their villages, Healey observed that groups of Lacandón men occasionally made pilgrimages to secret shrines in nearby ruins. Intrigued by the prospect of filming rites conducted in temples still revered by descendants of their builders, Healey induced the Lacandón to reveal the location of twenty-one previously unknown sites by giving them shotguns, ammunition, and money. On one such occasion a guide led him deep into the rain forest along a path hacked out of the bush with machetes. In places no sunlight penetrated the canopy of trees, and the vegetation was so dense that it was not possible to see more than a few yards in any direction. Finally they reached an area littered with overgrown ruins—temples, altars, and monuments—rising like chalk-white phantoms out of a sea of jungle green.

In a courtyard at the foot of a terraced acropolis lay a massive sculptured stela broken into several pieces. Its central figure, etched in bold relief, depicted a dignitary laden with jade ornaments, holding a ceremonial staff, and surrounded by columns of hieroglyphic inscriptions. Flanking the stairway ascending the acropolis were two more elaborately carved stelae, and fragments of other monuments could be seen scattered about the ruins. On a platform near the northeastern corner of the acropolis stood an unpretentious flat-roofed building that, despite a thick mantle of trees and vines, had remained in a remarkably good

139

state of preservation. Its three doorways opened into small interior chambers, and above each entrance was a niche containing fragments of seated stucco figures. Visible on the upper façade between two of the doors were remnants of a weathered relief showing a standing human, and the outlines of an ornate mask still adhered to a section of the wall. Healey might never have seen this building had he not accidentally discovered it while hunting a deer that disappeared into a nearby thicket. Stopping long enough to inspect the structure's interior, he entered one of the doorways and found himself in a narrow vaulted room. When his eyes adjusted to the chamber's dim illumination, he suddenly became aware of faces peering at him from the walls. Gradually they assumed sharper delineation and muted colors, and he could see figures of richly costumed priests, nobles, musicians, and strangely masked impersonators surrounding him on all sides. In the next room he came upon a tableau of opposing armies locked in a furious battle, while on an adjoining panel prisoners of war were being judged by haughty chieftains. Magnificent paintings of dancers in exotic costumes, an orchestra, and scenes of human sacrifice adorned the third room, along with a group of nobles attended by retainers. What Healey had stumbled upon was a dazzling array of murals completely covering the walls of the building's three chambers.

Unknown to Healey, the existence of this site had been reported only four months earlier by two travelers, John G. Bourne and Carl Frey. Actually, Bourne had prepared scale drawings of its structures, but the jungle was so thick he had completely overlooked the building containing the frescoes. Hence, by sheer chance, Healey was responsible for revealing the most extensive murals yet discovered anywhere in Mesoamerica—a veritable "gallery" of pre-Columbian paintings which instantly provoked excited interest on the part of archaeologists and art historians alike.

In the winter of 1947 an expedition jointly sponsored by the United Fruit Company, the Carnegie Institution, and the Instituto Nacional de Antropología e Historia began an intensive study of the frescoes. Included among its staff were Healey, an engineer named Gustav Strömsvik, the archaeologists Karl Ruppert and J. Eric Thompson, and two artists experienced in mural restoration, Antonio Tejeda and Augustín Villagra Caleti, who set about making accurate copies of the paintings—a task requiring another expedition the following year to complete. At Sylvanus Morley's suggestion, the site was given the name Bonampak, a Maya term meaning "painted walls."

Because of its relatively small size—encompassing eleven major buildings situated on an acropolis, a single courtyard, and various unidentified mounds—Bonampak had obviously been a city of secondary importance. It was one of numerous settlements that once flourished in the Usumacinta Valley, and it had received cultural impetus from the nearby site of Yaxchilán, whose emblem glyph appears in Bonampak's murals. Tatiana Proskouriakoff wrote that Bonampak "could not have been more than a small center in a region crowded with other towns. It was without doubt merely a dependency of the much larger city of Yaxchilán. The stamp of the Yaxchilán style in its works of art is unmistakable, and the artists who for generations gave Bonampak its singular distinction were probably trained in the schools of the larger city."

Why Bonampak should have been graced with such outstanding artistic achievements we shall perhaps never know. Without considering for a moment the skill of its muralists, much of the sculpture at Bonampak is of exceptional quality. Proskouriakoff described the immense stela found in the city's main courtyard as "one of the largest and finest monuments ever set up by the Maya." Several of its other sculptured stelae and lintels are scarcely less sensitive in design and workmanship, and when the murals were finally executed, an already profound mastery of creative expression was brought to a dramatic climax.

What most distinguishes Bonampak's murals from frescoes elsewhere in Mesoamerica is their graphic realism. With a few notable exceptions—especially some of the wall paintings at Chichén Itzá—ancient murals in Mexico and Central America involve abstruse iconography. Usually they deal with mythology, gods, ritualism, cosmology, and other esoteric themes rather than scenes of actual life. For this reason the Bonampak frescoes have added a new dimension to our knowledge of pre-Columbian art; they represent a literal approach to their subject matter and are undoubtedly based on factual historical events. Varied aspects of Maya culture are vividly portrayed in a style largely unhampered by abstract symbolism or florid decorative embellishments. Instead, Bonampak's painters recorded a wealth of information concerning such details as costumes, musical instruments, warfare, human sacrifice, and rituals; and Sylvanus Morley was prompted to declare that "some of the figures . . . exhibit a degree of naturalism which western Europe did not achieve until several centuries later."

In copying the frescoes, the artists Tejeda and Caleti ran into formidable difficulties. Some areas were completely obliterated by decay, and the entire surface of the paintings was obscured by a layer of calcium deposited by moisture seeping through the building's walls. Any attempt to clean the murals would obviously have damaged them, so it became necessary to find a way to render these deposits transparent and bring out the full brilliance of the underlying colors. After lengthy experimentation it was discovered that the liberal application of kerosene produced the desired result, although the long-term effects of this procedure have proven disastrous.

While the paintings were being studied, an attempt was made to retrace the steps originally involved in their execution. Apparently the figures were first drawn with a light red line on the freshly plastered walls. Intervening areas had then been filled in with color, and the forms retraced and accentuated with heavier black outlines. Both Tejeda and Caleti believed the original cartoons were sketched on wet plaster, thereby achieving a true fresco technique. Brushes made of animal hair or feathers were probably used to apply broad areas of color, and rabbit fur may have served for painting more exacting details. A fairly extensive palette of colors had been derived from natural substances: reds and pinks were compounded of iron oxide, yellow was extracted from limonite or ocher, black from carbon, and brown from bitumen or asphalt. Until recently the source of the vivid blue used extensively by the Maya was unknown, but scientists now believe it was probably a mixture of indigo dye and a type of clay called attapulgite. Greens were presumably obtained by combining blue and yellow in varying amounts.

Of necessity the interpretation of the murals rests partly on conjecture, especially since the significance of many details can only be surmised and certain sections are permanently destroyed. A reexamination of the frescoes, begun in 1975 by Richard E. W. Adams, Robert C. Aldrich, and Deborah Klopfenstein, led to the tentative decipherment of some of the hieroglyphic texts accompanying the paintings which denote personal names and other information associated with specific figures, and future studies may yield historical data on the events shown in the murals. Date inscriptions indicate that they were executed around A.D. 750 to 800; therefore it seems reasonable to assume that they reflect a factual panorama of life at the very height of Classic-period splendor.

We see depicted on the walls of the east room a grand array of elite dignitaries dressed in full ceremonial attire, including what may be a *halach uinic* or supreme ruler surrounded by his wife and children. Nearby are dancers and their attendants in the act of putting on costumes adorned with exotic quetzal-feather decorations in preparation for a ritual. On a lower panel appears a group of earth-god impersonators wearing fantastic masks and flanked by musicians playing rattles, a drum, and trumpets, and beating on tortoise shells with deer antlers.

The scenes on the south, east, and west walls of the central room portray a raid on an enemy town. Hordes of elaborately attired warriors have hurled themselves against their opponents with relentless fury, seemingly for the purpose of taking captives, since no one is shown actually being killed. On the north wall the spoils of the preceding conflict are exhibited: the prisoners, stripped of all but their loincloths, sit before the victorious lords, awaiting the pronouncement of their fate—whether slavery or sacrifice.

In the west room the ceremony to which the events in the two previous chambers have led is finally enacted. The ecstasy of the participants has broken forth in frenzied dancing, the ebullient color of swirling costumes, and the blare of trumpets. Amid this scene is a dead captive whose hands and feet are held by attendants; a priest flails his limp body with a wandlike object. Watching from an opposite wall, a group of nobles adorned in floor-length white capes are apparently

143

discussing the ritual, and below them minor officials sit cross-legged, gesturing as if in conversation.

In appraising these frescoes, the French anthropologist Jacques Soustelle wrote: "Bonampak is a sort of pictorial encyclopaedia of a Maya city of the eighth century; the city comes to life there again, with its ceremonies and its processions; its stiff and solemn-looking dignitaries weighed down by their heavy plumed adornments, its warriors clothed in jaguar skins. Lively or violent scenes are . . . displayed side by side with gracious, familiar pictures of daily life. A complete cross-section of society—women, children, servants, musicians, warrior chiefs, dying prisoners, and masked dancers—that is what these painters . . . succeeded in depicting on those walls, lost today in the depths of one of the continent's most impenetrable jungles. . . . Only naïve illusion, born of egocentricity, could permit us to apply the word 'primitivism' to an art which, like any other, was, in its time and place, the supreme creation of a genuine culture."

A sense of urgency may have overcome Bonampak's artists as they labored to record the spectacle of their times. Proskouriakoff writes of a vague apprehension which pervaded their sensibilities: "As far as we know, this was the last brilliant chapter in the history of the region. We see at Bonampak its full pomp, its somewhat barbarous and elaborately designed ritual. . . . There is a bare hint, a mere suggestion in the dramatic scenes, and in the excitement of line foreign to the serenity of the Maya style, of an emotional tension which might have presaged a crisis; but there is, unfortunately, no sequel to the scenes. . . ."

Events throughout the Maya realm were rapidly assuming an ominous restlessness. Not long after A.D. 800 the crisis to which Proskouriakoff alludes began to erupt in the southern lowlands. Suddenly the Maya were on the brink of a shattering upheaval, and though their inhabitants could not foresee its consequences, the magnificent cities in this region had but a few years longer to exist.

Early in the ninth century, Maya civilization in the southern lowlands underwent a catastrophic decline. In one city after another, artistic, intellectual, and religious activity gradually came to a halt. New construction ended so abruptly in some sites that buildings and monuments were left unfinished. Even the practice of erecting dated stelae was terminated at successive locations, a circumstance that has provided an accurate chronology of this dissolution throughout much of the region. At the site of Toniná in Chiapas, the last known Long Count date was carved on a monument in A.D. 909.

Within roughly the century from A.D. 800 to 900, virtually all of the once-populous cities in the southern lowlands were deserted. Incredibly, the buildings were left untouched, almost as if their occupants had intended to return momentarily. Instead an immense stillness enveloped them, from which they never awakened. Underbrush slowly overtook the courtyards; vines and the roots of trees engulfed the pyramids, temples, and palaces, forcing their stones to split apart and crumble. Ultimately the jungle reclaimed the ill-destined Maya cities, totally forsaken at the very height of their glory.

In the absence of any clear-cut explanation to account for a disaster of such magnitude, archaeologists have advanced a number of theories. Had conquering armies from Mexico invaded the lowlands? Had they succeeded in overpowering the resplendent cities in their path of conquest, slaughtering many of their inhabitants and forcing the rest to flee? It was a distinct possibility in view of the Mexicans' inclination toward militarism, but one that was soon discarded for lack of evidence. Unexpected changes in climatic conditions, especially sharp increases in rainfall, were suggested as possible factors; and some students concluded that earthquakes had struck the lowlands with sufficient frequency to cause the abandonment of its cities. Epidemics were cited as another reason for the exodus, and several investigators believed an imbalance occurred in the sex ratio which caused the birth of progressively fewer females, eventually triggering a severe population decline. But none of these hypotheses was borne out by later research; there is no archaeological evidence of abnormal climatic changes, widespread earthquakes, or radical demographic changes.

Since this perplexing mystery had not been satisfactorily explained by external calamities, Sylvanus Morley felt that its solution lay within the framework of Maya civilization itself: social disintegration, civil strife, or economic failure. But what could have presaged an internal crisis of such far-reaching consequences? For Morley and some of his colleagues, the answer was to be found in the theory of ''agricultural exhaustion,'' the conviction that the *milpa* system, which Morley viewed as appallingly wasteful of land resources, simply could not produce enough food to sustain an expanding population. In *The Ancient Maya* (1946) he detailed this concept:

> The repeated clearing and burning of ever-increasing areas of forest to serve as corn lands gradually converted the original forest into man-made grasslands, artificial savannas. When this process was complete . . . when the primeval forest had been largely felled and replaced in time by these artificially produced grasslands, then agriculture as practiced by the ancient Maya came to an end, since they had no implements whatsoever for turning the soil—no hoes, picks, harrows, spades, shovels, or plows.
>
> The replacing of the original forest by man-made savannas . . . must have come about very gradually, reaching a really acute state at different cities and eventually causing their respective abandonments at different times, depending in each case upon variable factors such as the relative size of the population in question, respective periods of occupation, and general fertility of the surrounding areas.
>
> Other adverse factors following in the wake of the decreasing food sup-

ply, such as accompanying social unrest, governmental disorganization, and even religious disbelief, doubtless all played their respective parts in the collapse . . . but it appears highly probable that economic failure—the law of diminishing returns, another way of saying the high cost of living— was chiefly responsible for the final disintegration. . . .

But did the Maya actually exhaust their reserves of arable land? It became increasingly difficult to accept this premise in view of later findings to the contrary. Studies by the distinguished archaeologist Alfred V. Kidder demonstrated a salient fact in this regard: the soil along the Motagua River in western Honduras is revitalized annually by flooding. Whereas it was usually necessary to allow depleted *milpas* to lie fallow for several years, during which, according to Morley's theory, they reverted to grasslands, the Motagua Valley has been continuously farmed for centuries. Yet this region's two most important cities—Copán and Quiriguá—were among the first to be deserted early in the ninth century. Additional research by J. Eric Thompson showed that vacant lands tend to revert to forest rather than grass, and the large savannas found in some parts of the lowlands (once thought to be former *milpas*) are seldom in close proximity to ruined cities and therefore cannot be positively attributed to ancient cultivation. Further arguments against the principle of agricultural exhaustion have come from the recent discovery (discussed in Chapter 8) that the Maya were not solely dependent upon *milpas;* on the contrary, their utilization of hillside terraces, raised fields, orchards, and kitchen gardens—all of which could have been kept in constant production by the use of irrigation and fertilizers—greatly increased the potential for intensive agriculture over long periods. Moreover, there is considerable evidence that by Late Classic times several food sources were widely utilized that did not require specially prepared fields—principally breadnut, sweet potatoes, and manioc.

Along the Usumacinta River, the city of Piedras Negras in Guatemala lies almost completely hidden by jungle. Many of its monuments are among the finest ever created by Maya sculptors, and one especially outstanding piece is a beautifully carved dais originally used by elite dignitaries. At some time in the past it had been intentionally smashed, but the exact date of its destruction could not be ascertained. Another work of marvelous craftsmanship was unearthed at Piedras Negras, a sculptured wall panel depicting a high priest or ruler presiding over a hierarchic conclave. Again, its severely damaged condition had not resulted from natural causes: the head of each individual figure—fifteen in all—was knocked off, leaving sharp breaks in the stone. Excavations at Tikal by the University of Pennsylvania brought to light a number of stelae and altars showing deliberate mutilation similar to the monuments at Piedras Negras; a notable example was Stela 26 (called the "Red Stela" because it was painted bright red), which had been defaced, shattered, and buried under the floor of a temple amid its own fragments and a curious assortment of offertory objects.

Mayanists viewed the implications of these disclosures with heightening interest. Was it not reasonable to assume, they argued, that the willful destruction of objects intimately associated with long-established religious beliefs was indicative of defiance toward the hierarchy under whose supervision they were created? And since the cities functioned primarily as seats of religious and civil authority, did not the smashing of these monuments attest to uprisings by the peasants against their elite overlords, resulting in the eventual desertion of these centers?

A number of archaeologists advocated this hypothesis as the long-sought resolution to the enigma surrounding the collapse of Classic culture. J. Alden Mason, writing in the *Bulletin of the University of Pennsylvania Museum* in 1943, stated that the most likely explanation of the problem was "war and civil strife. Probably the people, weary of the yoke of the priesthood, with their interminable demands for building and ceremonies, revolted. At Piedras Negras, at any rate, the archaeological evidence definitely indicated that the ceremonial furnishings were intentionally damaged, the monuments mutilated, and its ceremonial center abandoned."

Other Mesoamerican cultures fell victim to internal disturbances at roughly the same time. Teotihuacán, once the most powerful city in Mexico, had been burned around A.D. 650, after which it was slowly deserted. In Oaxaca, the great Zapotec capital of Monte Albán declined about A.D. 700, and by A.D. 1100 the site of Tajín in Veracruz—formerly the center of a wide sphere of influence in eastern Mexico—had collapsed. In each case, scholars originally attributed the cause of these upheavals to internal weaknesses stemming in large part from popular rebellions against oppressive ruling hierarchies, a view now regarded as a drastic oversimplification.

In a revised edition of Morley's *The Ancient Maya,* published in 1956, George Brainerd expounded on this theory: ". . . the causal element for the Maya decline may be restricted and defined if we assume that the contemporaneous decline of other Classic New World civilizations was influenced by historically related causes. . . . Just as peoples in widely spaced areas of aboriginal America developed similar formal governments ruled by priests, they may have tired simultaneously of this way of life. The lower classes must have revolted, and the word must have traveled. Such a drastic change may well have been caused by the formation of an organized set of new ideas as the purpose of existence—a new philosophy."

In his book *The Rise and Fall of Maya Civilization,* J. Eric Thompson examined the question of why the power of the hierarchy might have been undermined. Among the ideas he suggested was the possibility that the mystique of their esoteric pursuits eventually wore thin in the eyes of the overburdened multitudes. What value to illiterate Maya peasants were abstract realms of mathematics, calendrics, and astronomy, particularly when such knowledge was kept sequestered exclusively among the priest-rulers? Too long had the masses remained in a state of servitude; too exacting was the endless labor required to construct temples and palaces, tend the fields of wealthy nobles, pay tributes, and supply luxury goods. And too blatant were the tricks with which the priests wove their cabalistic patterns of psychological control, the system of religious punishments and rewards intended to coerce the populace into strict obedience.

For centuries the masses had willingly submitted to the ruling elite, until perhaps the shadow of despotism and degeneracy brought about an outcry for rebellion. Once this disenchantment set in, it is possible that something as simple as a crop failure in one or two localities, a natural catastrophe, or an astronomical phenomenon such as an eclipse which the priest failed to predict prompted a serious loss of faith in the hierarchy. Events of this kind could easily have touched off revolts, with the result that the authority of the elite was overturned, and the cities—the supreme symbols of upper-class power—were sacked and abandoned.

Lately there has been a trend among Mayanists not to attribute the demise of Classic culture to any single cause, and a great deal of speculation has focused on a combination of underlying factors. In essence, this was the prevailing view at a seminar held in October 1970 at the School of American Research in Santa Fe, New Mexico, which brought together eleven scholars to discuss the subject in the light of current archaeological data.

Briefly, the participants in this conference emphasized a variety of social, political, and economic conditions thought to have rendered the Maya susceptible to a sudden upset and decline. For instance, recent excavations at numerous sites have underlined the extraordinary complexity of Late Classic society. By this time the aristocracy and priests alike had become enormously powerful, wealthy, and self-serving, a fact amply confirmed by the lavish splendor of their tombs, representations of dynastic succession on monuments, and the proliferation of palace-type structures and luxury items. No doubt they directly controlled a vast segment of the economy, including foreign trade and the local distribution of raw materials and food. Along with this sharp increase in elite power and prosperity, the number of retainers and minor administrators swelled tremendously, placing additional demands upon the peasants for food and commodities necessary to support the hierarchy. Very likely these conditions resulted in ever-widening gaps and antagonisms between the upper and lower classes, and much of the work required by the elite may finally have been carried out by enforced labor.

Everywhere there are indications that the Late Classic period witnessed greatly expanded population pressures, together with a marked acceleration in the number and size of cities. Ritualism and intellectual pursuits had reached a peak of activity, and there was apparently a considerable amount of competition between the major centers and their respective hierarchies, a tendency to challenge each other in sheer magnificence of architecture, monuments, and luxury goods such as jade, featherwork, and ceramics. Eventually this rivalry may even have erupted into widespread intercity warfare, leading to a further drain on manpower and food reserves.

All of these circumstances imposed a tremendous burden on land, natural resources, and available labor, particularly since Maya technology probably lacked the capacity to accommodate these demands. In turn, this could easily have caused land use to be mismanaged, thereby bringing about acute shortages of food and a heightened susceptibility to disease. Significantly, skeletons from some Late Classic burials reveal evidence that peasants were smaller and less healthy than the aristocracy, suggesting that the latter had requisitioned more than its share of dwindling food supplies. And an analysis of skeletal remains from graves at Altar de Sacrificios by Frank P. Saul, an anatomist with the Medical College of Ohio, showed traces of scurvy, anemia, and periodontal disease, all attributable to malnutrition.

Each of these problems—overpopulation, exaggerated demands by the elite for goods and services, intercity rivalry, widening gulfs between social classes, and decreasing food supply—contributed to what have been termed "stress factors," which left Maya civilization precariously balanced on the edge of catastrophe. Given such circumstances, any of several situations might have provoked a chain reaction ending in a general collapse. Severe famine or outbreaks of disease could have resulted in a massive economic failure, a Maya version of the Great Depression, causing the cities to be deserted as repercussions from these events spread throughout various levels of society. If the peasants had finally revolted against authoritarianism, it is possible that they not only destroyed the elite class, but also disrupted the whole superstructure of trade, political administration, religion, and intellectualism controlled by the nobility, leaving little or no skilled leadership in any of these realms. Moreover, all of the previously cited "stress factors'' may have been involved simultaneously, interacting with each other to produce a situation of insurmountable chaos.

Further clues bearing on the problem have recently emerged from research by Harvard University at Seibal, located on the Río Pasión in the south-central Petén—findings that have revived earlier speculations regarding outside invaders. Investigations revealed the sudden appearance of a complex of non-Classic traits at this city during the ninth century. Included among these are ceramic figurines of a strikingly alien type, and two varieties of pottery called Fine Orange and Fine Gray, known to have originated along the Gulf Coast of Mexico, presumably somewhere in Tabasco. Even more intriguing, a series of stelae were erected at Seibal between about A.D. 850 and 900 portraying elite figures whose faces differ radically from those characteristically depicted in Classic sculpture, resembling instead carvings from eastern Mexico or Yucatán. Foreign architectural features are also associated with these monuments, particularly a curious round structure and the use of columns, which are both typical of certain archaeological sites in Mexico.

Inescapably, such facts point to some degree of intrusion into the southern lowlands in the ninth century, either directly from Mexico or by way of Maya groups in Yucatán who had already been exposed to strong Mexican influences. Sizable quantities of Fine Orange and Fine Gray pottery have also turned up at Altar de Sacrificios, Yaxchilán, Piedras Negras, and Palenque, leading archaeologists to view these penetrations by outsiders as fairly extensive. Whether this influx of non-Classic elements took the form of a military invasion or a gradual infiltration of people and ideas is not clear. In any case, with the unstable conditions already existing in Maya society, such incursions could easily have spread havoc throughout the region and set in motion a conspiracy of malefic events: further overtaxation of food and other resources, disruption of normal trade relations, conscription of manpower for prolonged military service (effectively removing them from food production), displacement of the hierarchy, and even forced resettlement of conquered populations, perhaps in northern Yucatán. If this was actually the situation, then the Maya may have succumbed to a combination of outside pressures and demoralizing internal tensions, a circumstance so often responsible for the downfall of civilizations.

At present, no one can say with certainty why Classic Maya culture collapsed so suddenly. Existing evidence is far too fragmentary for absolute conclusions to be drawn. Only one thing is certain: whatever the reasons behind this catastrophe, they were irreconcilable with the destiny of the Maya. Never again would their civilization regain its former brilliance; its once-splendid Golden Age was forever gone.

11 · CHICHÉN ITZÁ:
THE HOME OF ALIEN GODS

What, then, became of the survivors of these disastrous events? Had they continued to live in the midst of their decaying cities, eventually reduced by circumstances to a primitive existence? Or had they deserted the region completely and moved elsewhere? For years, most Mayanists envisioned the southern lowlands as having quickly reverted to an uninhabited wilderness in the aftermath of migrations that carried the remnants of its population into Yucatán, but a considerably different picture of the situation has emerged from subsequent research.

Excavators working at Uaxactún discovered that people had lived in or near that city long after it ceased to function as a major center, even using some of its buildings as dwellings and burial places. Similar findings were unearthed at several sites in Belize and northern Petén, especially at Tikal, where deposits of refuse in temples, intrusive graves beneath the floors of Classic structures, older monuments reset upside down as if the inscriptions could no longer be understood, and the appearance of a new type of pottery—the Eznab Ceramic Complex—all point to a partial occupation of the site after its collapse early in the ninth century.

T. Patrick Culbert, a member of the University of Pennsylvania's Tikal Project in the 1960s, has poignantly summarized the final chapter in the history of this once-great city in his book, *The Lost Civilization: The Story of the Classic Maya,* in which he describes the life-style associated with the Eznab Ceramic Complex (A.D. 830–900):

Of the several hundred housemounds [residential remains] that have been tested by excavation in Tikal and its vicinity, *not one* shows any hint of Eznab occupation. All of the Eznab debris comes from in and around palace structures. But the Eznab people were not living like the kings of yore, for the lack of maintenance had begun to tell, and on occasion roofs collapsed on the unhappy inhabitants of the rooms below. When this occurred, the debris was not even removed; if some sheltered space remained, the larger stones were shoved out of the way and occupation continued amidst the rubble. Instead of being swept and refreshed daily, as must have been the case in better days, courtyards, stairways, and even the corners of occupied rooms accumulated unsightly piles of garbage—a gold mine for archaeologists, but hardly up to centuries-old Maya standards of cleanliness. Like barbarians living untidily among the ruins of vanquished cities, the Eznab population survived for a time. But they were neither conquerors nor outsiders; they were, instead, the impoverished descendants who probably still recounted tales of the days of Maya glory. And not many were left to enjoy these tales, for I would calculate, from the number of rooms occupied, that the population of Tikal . . . could have been no more than ten percent of the total reached . . . less than a century earlier. . . .

The Tikal of Eznab times was not a rejection of Maya patterns, but rather a Tikal gone poor; survivors carried on as they could, clinging to the same elite centers for living, and worshipping in the same sacred places. The best they could manage, however, was so impoverished that it became almost a parody of what had once been. Even these pitiful survivors . . . were unable to endure, and after a century and a half they, too, disappeared, leaving Tikal empty and alone except for the teeming lesser life of the regenerating forest.

What finally happened to the inhabitants of the southern lowlands we do not know. Some may have migrated into Yucatán and Belize, where numerous cities continued to flourish after A.D. 900; others could have found their way southward into the highlands or to distant parts of Mexico. In Culbert's opinion, most of them—perhaps a million people—simply died out. "Lest this interpretation conjure up garish pictures of streets and jungles piled high with rotting corpses," he wrote, "I should hasten to note that we are dealing with a period of four or five generations. It is an inescapable demographic fact that *all* of every population dies each generation, so the loss of a million Maya need not have been an overnight catastrophe. A far less spectacular but more likely mechanism of population loss can be generated by more subtle changes in birth and death rates. A decline in fertility and increases in death rates in crucial population segments such as young women or infants and children can work drastic changes in population totals over a period of several generations."

Whatever the reasons, the southern lowlands underwent a steady decline in population from about the middle of the ninth century onward, leaving behind small, isolated groups who survived for only a short time. Despite halfhearted attempts to make use of deserted temples and resurrect religious monuments (ostensibly to maintain contact with ancient gods), these peoples never produced art or architecture remotely comparable to the creations of their illustrious predecessors. Every aspect of their existence reflects a weak imitation of former glories, an almost desperate effort to preserve rapidly fading links with their past without the benefit of an educated elite or strong political authority. As for what became of the ruling class, whose power, wealth, and semidivine status had reached its peak on the eve of the collapse, we know nothing; all signs of their former greatness suddenly vanished from the archaeological record. Along with the cities they once ruled, and the dazzling artistic and intellectual achievements over which they had presided, their memory was slowly but inexorably engulfed by the ubiquitous rain forest.

Yet the presence of ruins of a different character throughout Yucatán affirms that Maya civilization endured there long after its demise in the southern lowlands. Originally this region was believed to have remained uninhabited during the Classic period, or at most had contained only widely scattered settlements that were nothing more than provincial outposts by comparison with the thriving centers to the south. After their collapse, large numbers of survivors were thought to have migrated into the upper half of the peninsula, imparting to this sector the intellectual, artistic, and technical genius of their lustrous heritage. Here, between approximately A.D. 900 and 1200, these immigrants supposedly founded magnificent new centers: Uxmal, Chichén Itzá, Kabáh, Sayil, Labná, and dozens more whose ruins comprise one of the most spectacular arrays of archaeological monuments anywhere in America. With these hypothetical events there emerged what scholars called the "New Empire" (in contrast to the "Old Empire," a term formerly used to designate Classic culture in the south)—a brilliant resurgence of Maya traditions infused with renewed vitality.

Succeeding years of research have demonstrated the inaccuracy of this concept. When more was learned about the date inscriptions from Yucatán, those which could be securely fixed in Maya chronology fell between A.D. 475 and 889, a clear indication that long before the southern lowlands were deserted, Yucatán was inhabited by people versed in hieroglyphic writing and calendrics. As excavations in the region broadened in scope, a number of sites were found to contain pottery closely related to the typical wares associated with Classic horizons to the south, including polychrome vessels imported directly from the Petén; and several ruins in Yucatán produced Preclassic ceramics, notably at Komchén and Dzibilchaltún, where levels of occupation dating back to around 800 B.C. are well defined.

Scholars had previously attached much importance to certain marked differences between Yucatán's sites and those farther south with regard to building techniques, decoration, and city planning, viewing these as proof that the northern cities were considerably later in date. Generally the arrangement of temples, palaces, and courtyards had been less formalized in Yucatán than was customary in the southern lowlands. Fewer terraced pyramids had been erected, and the elegant, comparatively simple embellishments used to decorate buildings in the south had been supplanted by highly ornate exteriors as exemplified by the Chenes, Río Bec, and Puuc styles (see Chapter 5). In Yucatán great emphasis had been placed on the construction of concrete walls faced with a veneer of cut stones; the erection of multistoried "apartment" type structures was fairly widespread, and there was an increased use of columns, especially to support doorways. But as the evolution of Maya architecture became better understood, these peculiarities were viewed as less indicative of a radical departure from older traditions than had originally been supposed. It was shown that most of the architectural conventions seen in Yucatán sprang directly from Classic prototypes and represented regional variations that had developed at an early date.

Such factors necessitated a broad revision of prior theories concerning the "New Empire." Contrary to the idea that Yucatán had remained either a wilderness or a sparsely inhabited province during the Classic period, archaeologists now know that many of its cities flourished at the same time as those in the south. No longer do they look upon such ruins as Uxmal, Chichén Itzá, Labná, and Sayil as crowning jewels in a "renaissance" wrought by survivors of the "Old Empire." Nearly every aspect of their art, architecture, inscriptions, and ceramics appears to have been firmly rooted in Classic traditions, and there is no doubt that the region had supported a heavy population even in Preclassic times.

Furthermore, some students felt that when the great centers in the southern lowlands were finally surrendered to the rain forest, most of Yucatán's sites were also abandoned at about the same time and for equally mysterious reasons. If emigrants from the south had in fact migrated northward after the collapse of their cities, their fortunes may have been no more promising once they reached Yucatán. Very possibly the same disaster that overtook Yaxchilán, Palenque, Tikal, Uaxactún, Copán, and the rest of the southern cities had spread into the northern end of the peninsula, again leaving its centers empty and their inhabitants scattered in small agrarian communities.

Before his untimely death in 1971, E. Wyllys Andrews IV, who conducted an intensive study of Yucatán's prehistory under the auspices of the Middle American Research Institute at Tulane University, seriously disputed this hypothesis. He contended that a number of northern cities—specifically those in the Chenes, Río Bec, and Puuc districts—should be viewed in a different chronological context than was previously supposed. Based on a variety of archaeological data, Andrews speculated that these sites had not risen to prominence until relatively late in the Classic period and were occupied for several centuries afterward. Actually, he saw them as representing an extension of Classic civilization that somehow survived its demise farther south, stimulated perhaps by an influx of refugees from the Petén and the

Usumacinta Valley who began migrating northward early in the ninth century. Given the ascendancy of the Chenes, Río Bec, and Puuc cities during what he termed the "Florescent" phase in Yucatán—dating from roughly A.D. 900 to 1100—Andrews argued that Maya culture never really "collapsed" in the north, undergoing instead a vigorous upsurge resulting in the rapid proliferation of new settlements for several hundred years after its eclipse in the south.

In the years since Andrews's death, scholars have expended a great deal of effort in attempting to clarify the chronology of Yucatán's archaeological sites. Essentially this research has verified Andrews's contention that the thread of Classic culture survived its dissolution in the south by several centuries. Our evidence for this comes from dates recently assigned to many of Yucatán's most important ruins on the basis of their art, architecture, and ceramics, which show an unbroken continuum with Classic traditions—magnificent sites like Río Bec, Xtampak, Becán, Xpuhil, Edzná, Oxkintok, and Cobá. We know, too, that the superb Puuc-style cities such as Uxmal, Kabáh, Labná, and Sayil represent yet other manifestations of Classic culture in Yucatán.

It is equally clear that these centers were definitely *not* abandoned during the ninth century as was once believed, and indeed most of them continued to thrive until around A.D. 1000 or somewhat later. Archaeologists are also certain that the "collapse" of Classic Maya civilization did not occur suddenly; instead it was a prolonged process that began in the southern lowlands during the ninth century and slowly spread northward over the next two hundred years. As a result, the traditional chronology (still widely used in the literature) that places the end of the Classic period at A.D. 900 is only accurate in relation to the southern lowlands. To compensate for this problem, many scholars now refer to the era from A.D. 800 to 1000 as the "Terminal Classic" period—a designation that approximates Andrews's "Florescent" phase and more appropriately reflects the disappearance of Classic culture in the northern lowlands.

All of this raises another perplexing issue. Why were so many major cities in Yucatán abandoned at all? Did they fall victim to the same conspiracy of events that undermined their southern neighbors, or did they face a different set of problems stemming from their particular environment, geographical location, and internal pressures? We cannot fully answer these questions, but their solutions appear to be largely related to outside influences that began to emerge in Yucatán sometime after A.D. 900. In the aftermath of the disaster that had overtaken the southern lowlands, the political, economic, and spiritual fortunes of the Maya were radically altered by foreign intrusion that swept over them from the direction of Mexico. Suddenly, Maya civilization found a temporary renewal of its former vigor redirected by alien ideals. It was a virile, cogent stimulus, but one whose origin was so deeply cloaked in mythology that it eluded scientists for years.

Chichén Itzá, the sprawling ruined city seventy miles east of Mérida, had long been an archaeological puzzle. Its existence was known since the time of the Conquest, but other than the desultory efforts of a few early explorers, it was not systematically studied until 1924, when the Carnegie Institution began a ten-year program of excavation under Sylvanus Morley's supervision. Even before then, however, a curious paradox had been observed among its ruins: in contrast to numerous older buildings of predominantly Puuc style, much of the architecture at Chichén Itzá reflected strangely non-Maya elements.

These spurious structures included the impressive Temple of Kukulcán (also called El Castillo), the Temple of the Jaguars and its adjoining Ball Court, the Temple of the Warriors, the Mercado or marketplace, and a circular building known as El Caracol, an astronomical observatory not unlike its modern counterparts in outward appearance, with a spiral stairway leading to fixed observation points inside a domelike tower. Ironically, these famous buildings have come to epitomize Maya civilization in the minds of the general public, yet they incorporate foreign concepts wholly out of character with traditional Maya architecture: the use of colonnades, interior courts or peristyles, rooms divided by columns, and a type of exterior wall treatment known as *talud-tablero*—rectangular inset panels placed on an outward-sloping base.

Another innovation at Chichén Itzá was the construction of square platforms, two of which probably served as stages for ceremonies or theatrical performances. Nearby stands a third platform, T-shaped in outline and decorated with rows of human skulls carved in low relief.

Nothing like it had ever been encountered in the Maya area (they have since been found at Uxmal and Dzibilchaltún), though similar platforms were excavated at several locations in central Mexico. In fact, Spanish chroniclers reported seeing a structure of this type in the Aztec capital of Tenochtitlán; it was known as a *tzompantli,* and it held racks on which the skulls of sacrificial victims were publicly displayed.

Aside from these architectural features, a number of new sculptural motifs were evident at Chichén Itzá. Adorning temple walls and columns were depictions of warriors whose dress and physical appearance differed sharply from the usual images portrayed by Maya artists: enigmatic figures wearing quilted cotton armor, with pectorals in the form of butterflies or birds, and carrying shields, *atlatls,* spears, and flint- or obsidian-tipped clubs. Massive columns and balustrades sculptured to represent feathered serpents flanked the doors and stairways of temples. Rows of eagles and crouched jaguars clutching human hearts were carved in bold relief on walls. Several buildings contained figures of seated men designed to hold standards or flags in their outstretched hands; and there were anthropomorphic statues with upraised arms known as "Atlantean" figures, used to support altars and door lintels, together with so-called *chacmools* or representations of reclining men with raised heads and knees, holding shallow basins on their abdomens.

Because all of these non-Maya architectural and sculptural traits were closely associated with Toltec culture, which had once dominated central Mexico, only one plausible explanation could seemingly account for their presence at Chichén Itzá: they were indelible imprints left by Toltec invaders who had conquered the city and implanted the seeds of a radically different culture. A mural in the Temple of the Jaguars depicts lines of battle drawn between Maya defenders and attacking warriors whose costumes and weapons match the Toltec figures shown so profusely in Chichén Itzá's sculpture. Ironically, the Maya are pictured falling in defeat before an enemy!

Suddenly a question arose that had long perplexed archaeologists. Several post-Conquest documents, including the *Books of Chilam Balam* and Landa's *Relación,* mentioned the important role played in Yucatán by a people called the Itzá. Supposedly they had settled at

Chichén Itzá (which bears their name) in the tenth century, and transformed it into a powerful center whose influence spread over a vast area of the surrounding territory. Judging from Maya chronicles, there can be no doubt that the Itzá were regarded as intruders, for they are described as "foreigners," "tricksters and rascals," and "those who speak our language brokenly." But these references concerning the Itzá are at best a confusing mixture of history and folklore, making them exceedingly difficult to verify. As a result, it has proven impossible to reconstruct an accurate chronology of events relating to the Itzás' arrival in Yucatán, or even to determine their exact identity—whether they were actually the Toltecs or some other Mexican group, perhaps from the coastal regions of Tabasco and Campeche. For that matter, it has only been in the last forty-five years that the Toltecs themselves have emerged from obscurity and their great capital, the legendary Tollán, was finally brought to light.

Myths concerning Tollán were common in Mexican folklore. Among the first European chroniclers to mention this site was a Franciscan friar, Bernardino de Sahagún, who referred to it in his monumental work entitled *A General History of the Things of New Spain*, also known as the Florentine Codex. For years after the conquest of Mexico, Sahagún had labored at transcribing the language, history, and customs of the Aztecs into a bilingual record, using their own Nahuatl tongue and Spanish. With much the same determination as Landa showed in pursuing his studies of the Yucatecans, Sahagún worked among the Aztecs, questioning them about every aspect of their culture. One point was consistently reaffirmed by his native informants: their art, architecture, calendar, and religion—in short, almost everything they accomplished—had been strongly influenced by peoples who inhabited central Mexico long before the Aztecs rose to power in the fourteenth century. Unfailingly, these precursors were identified as the Toltecs, whose capital, Tollán, was reportedly one of the most magnificent cities in Mexico. So highly skilled were the Toltecs, wrote Sahagún, that "nothing they did was difficult for them. . . . They cut green stone [jade], and they cast gold, and made other works of the craftsman and the feather-worker. . . . And these Toltecs enjoyed great wealth; they were rich; never were they poor. Nothing did they lack in their homes. . . .''

A sixteenth-century Aztec noble, Fernando de Alva Ixtlilxochitl, an interpreter for the Spanish viceroy in Mexico City, compiled a lengthy version of his people's history which also stated that the stimulus underlying the rise of Aztec culture was largely derived from the Toltecs. Ixtlilxochitl portrayed them as masters of art, architecture, calendrics, medicine, and engineering, with a fierce dedication to religion and a love of rich pageantry. Toltec laws were said to have been strict but justly enforced, and their most important priest-king was the famous Quetzalcóatl, the ''living divinity who dwelled among the builders of Tollán.''

In weighing the validity of these accounts, scholars were confronted with certain ambiguities. Native sources generally agreed that the Aztecs were profoundly influenced by Toltec culture as originally derived from Tollán. Moreover, scattered throughout the Valley of Mexico and its environs were archaeological remains far older than those of Aztec origin, the most spectacular being the ruins of Teotihuacán, thirty miles north of Mexico City. For lack of a more definitive term, this ancient substratum was initially designated as ''Toltec,'' and virtually every pre-Aztec site in central Mexico was directly attributed to Toltec inspiration.

But subsequent research has ruled out this concept. We now know that the Toltecs did not occupy this region exclusively, prior to the coming of the Aztecs. Other peoples were equally responsible for its rich archaeological heritage, and the Toltecs themselves were relative latecomers. Like the Aztecs, they inherited much of their culture from earlier groups, especially the inhabitants of Teotihuacán, who had controlled central Mexico for centuries.

Until recently it could not be said with certainty who the Toltecs were; nor was it known where their capital of Tollán was located, or whether the long-missing city ever existed at all. Some archaeologists dismissed the whole problem as a myth and even denounced the hypothetical use of the word ''Toltec,'' insisting that since no such culture had been positively defined, its application was unjustified. Others, however, were not so willing to disregard the value of legend in reconstructing historical events, and they proceeded to search for Tollán's ruins.

Roughly fifty miles north of Mexico City, in the state of Hidalgo, the town of Tula de Allende nestles in a sun-parched valley. On a promontory overlooking the dusty village, dozens of rubble-covered mounds marked what had once been a vast complex of temples, terraced pyramids, plazas, and ball courts. Sahagún and Ixtlilxochitl had both identified this site as Tollán, and in 1880 a French traveler and antiquarian, Désiré Charnay, noted with more than passing interest how closely many of the monuments and sculptural motifs he saw while visiting Tula were duplicated at Chichén Itzá. But it was not until 1940 that excavations were undertaken at Tula by the Mexican archaeologist J. R. Acosta, who was to continue his research for twenty years.

Hardly had Acosta started to dig before Charnay's astute observations were resoundingly confirmed. Out of these explorations at Tula gradually emerged the entire panorama of traits so clearly identified with Chichén Itzá. Here were the same images of warriors clad in quilted armor who had carried the bitter taste of conquest to Yucatán. Identical reliefs of eagles and jaguars feeding upon human hearts moved across the walls of Tula's pyramid-temples, and there were buildings with colonnades, peristyles, *talud-tablero* facings, Atlantean figures, standard-bearers, *chacmools,* and representations of the plumed serpent—emblems of the Toltecs' adored god-king Quetzalcóatl. (Recent excavations at Tula by Eduardo Matos also uncovered the base of a skull rack, or *tzompantli,* a grim reminder of the Toltec obsession with human sacrifice.) So striking were the parallels between Tula and Chichén Itzá that it seemed as though the same artists and architects had worked at both locations.

Acosta's findings left no doubt that Tula was the original site of Tollán, and archaeologists have since been able to clarify many aspects of Toltec history. Apparently the Toltecs' ancestry included two groups of immigrants who settled at Tula (already an established town) sometime after A.D. 600. One of these tribes, the Tolteca-Chichimeca, were Nahuatl- and Otomi-speaking peoples that migrated from northern Mexico; the origin of the second group, the Nonoalca, is unknown, though some early documentary sources identify them as learned priests, merchants, and craftsmen from southern Veracruz and Tabasco who allegedly spoke Nahuatl, Mixtec, Popoloca, Mazatec, and Maya. Richard A. Diehl, a leading authority on Toltec history, wrote that this linguistic diversity "suggests that [the Nonoalca] were not a single ethnic group but rather 'civilized' people who migrated to Tula from almost everywhere except the northern frontier. They probably included middle- and upper-class people from Teotihuacán, Monte Albán, Xochicalco, Tajín, and other centers, who were forced to search out new lives when their home communities declined in power and importance."

Under the leadership of sagacious kings, Tula grew into a sprawling city of perhaps thirty thousand inhabitants, and its influence spread through central Mexico until virtually every tribe in the region proudly claimed Toltec ancestry. Even so, the city finally fell victim to famine, civil strife, and chaos, the causes of which are not clear, and sometime around A.D. 1170 it was permanently abandoned, causing its survivors to migrate to other areas. If we can believe native accounts, a large number of people had departed from Tula almost two centuries earlier, led by the celebrated Quetzalcóatl after he was driven from his homeland by forces allied to the war god Tezcatlipoca. This exodus presumably took place in the year 987, and according to various sources Quetzalcóatl and his subjects made their way to Yucatán and established themselves at Chichén Itzá.

In addition to unresolved questions surrounding the Toltec-Itzá migrations into Yucatán, scholars have also been confronted with complex problems involving the origin of Quetzalcóatl, a culture hero whose remarkable accomplishments are described in numerous myths. His name is a combination of the Nahuatl words *quetzal* (the magnificently plumed bird native to the Guatemalan highlands) and *cóatl* (snake); hence he is symbolically depicted as a serpent adorned with feathers. Native accounts refer to him as both a deity of extreme importance and the first ruler of Tollán, and he was revered throughout Mexico and Central America for his wisdom, gentleness, and patronage of art, literature, agriculture, and science. Sahagún wrote that the

Aztecs believed Quetzalcóatl "created the world; and they bestowed upon him the appellation Lord of the Wind, because they said that Tonacatecotli [a powerful creator-god] . . . breathed and begat Quetzalcóatl. They erected round temples to him. . . . They said that it was he who formed the first man. . . . He alone had a human body like that of men; the other gods were of an incorporeal nature."

When Quetzalcóatl was finally defeated by the jealous warrior god Tezcatlipoca and driven from Mexico, some legends say that he vanished into the sea near Veracruz. Others proclaim that he ascended into the heavens and became the planet Venus. Still another version states: ". . . the man whom they called Quetzalcóatl . . . taught [his followers] by word and deed the way of virtue, saving them from vice and sin, giving them the laws and good doctrine; and to restrain them in their lusts and lewd ways, had instituted fasting amongst them. . . . But seeing how little fruit his doctrine brought forth, he had gone away by the same road he had come, which was to the East, vanishing on the coast of Coatzacoalcos, and as he departed . . . he had said to them that at a future time . . . he would return, and then his doctrine would be received and his sons would be lords and owners of the land. . . ."

Quetzalcóatl's fame extended far beyond the limits of Toltec influence. He was worshipped at Teotihuacán, where one of the city's principal structures—the Temple of Quetzalcóatl—was erected in his honor. To the Maya of Yucatán he was known as Kukulcán, the Quiché called him Gucumatz, and his veneration became as profound in these regions as it was in Mexico.

Writing of Quetzalcóatl's appearance in Yucatán, Landa reported: "It is believed among the Indians that with the Itzás who occupied Chichén Itzá there reigned a great lord named Kukulcán, and that the principal building, which is called Kukulcán, shows this to be true [a reference to the Temple of Kukulcán or El Castillo]. They say that he arrived from the west; but they differ among themselves as to whether he arrived before or after the Itzás or with them. They say that he was favorably disposed, and had no wife or children, and that . . . he was regarded in Mexico as one of their gods and called Quetzalcóatl: and they also considered him a god in Yucatán on account of his being a just statesman; and this is seen in the order which he imposed on

Yucatán after the death of the lords [the overthrow of Maya rulers by the Toltec-Itzá], in order to calm the dissensions which their deaths had caused in the country.''

Had such a man as Quetzlacóatl actually existed? Native documents are quite specific in telling us how a revered leader named Topiltzin-Quetzalcóatl once ruled Tollán. Some historians feel that because of his renown as a statesman he may have been deified by succeeding generations, or his office may have carried with it the connotation of a god-king. What seems more likely is that long before the Toltecs' rise to power, Quetzalcóatl was already an important deity in Mexico (which would account for his veneration at Teotihuacán), and an early Toltec chieftain—possibly an entire dynasty—adopted his name, perhaps as a means of investing himself with Quetzalcóatl's powers.

Unquestionably the worship of Quetzalcóatl-Kukulcán in Yucatán was ushered in by the influx of Mexican culture that swept over the area in the tenth century, although archaeologists do not agree on details of when and how the cult was introduced. As previously stated, early historical accounts pertaining to these events are contradictory and lack a sound chronological basis. This is due in part to problems arising from the use during the Postclassic period of the abbreviated Short Count calendar or *u kahlay katunob* (see Chapter 3), which recorded only twenty-year *katun* cycles. Yet the *Books of Chilam Balam* place Kukulcán's arrival at Chichén Itzá in *Katun* 4 *Ahau*, one of the few Short Count dates that we definitely know corresponds to A.D. 967–987, and on the basis of information recorded in certain native manuscripts, many authorities believe 987 was the year Quetzalcóatl's banishment from Tula supposedly took place.

All of which brings us once more to the fundamental questions of who the Itzá really were, the date of their arrival in Yucatán, and their relationship to the Toltecs. A number of Mayanists are of the opinion that the Itzá and Toltecs were separate groups, and that the veneration of Quetzalcóatl-Kukulcán was introduced by the Toltecs *after* the Itzá incursion at Chichén Itzá had already occurred. J. Eric Thompson, who studied this problem in depth, identified the Itzá as a group called the Putún or Chontal, a Maya-speaking people who inhabited the coast of Tabasco and Campeche. Famed as long-distance traders and seamen, the Putún had absorbed strong Mexican influences and probably spoke Nahuatl in addition to their own dialect. According to Thompson's hypothesis, the Putún expanded into Yucatán and settled at Chichén Itzá around A.D. 981, bringing with them many earmarks of Mexican culture. When Quetzalcóatl and his Toltec followers arrived at Chichén Itzá from Tula in 987 (assuming this event actually took place), they were cordially received by the Putún-Itzá, whose own Mexican affinities encouraged them to enter into an alliance with the Toltecs.

In contrast to this viewpoint, other students see the Itzá as latecomers to Yucatán. In his book *The Maya*, Michael D. Coe suggests that the Itzá (who he thinks were led by a later ruler also using the name Kukulcán) did not arrive from Mexico until A.D. 1224–44, long after the Toltecs infiltrated Chichén Itzá and were adopted into the mainstream of Yucatecan culture. Since Chichén Itzá was deserted by about this time, Coe believes the Itzá settled there only briefly before they moved eastward and founded the city of Mayapán, which figures prominently in the final phase of Maya history.

On the basis of recent research, however, Thompson's chronology of events—which places the Itzá in Yucatán by the tenth century—has gained wide acceptance. In addition, there is no longer much doubt that the Putún and the legendary Itzá were the same group, and investigators have now confirmed that Putún-Itzá influence was far more extensive than previously supposed. Even though they were of Maya ancestry, the Putún had been almost completely Mexicanized by virtue of the fact that their homeland lay in the coastal lowlands of Tabasco, and they maintained close commercial ties with the peoples of central Mexico—including the Toltecs. As warriors and merchants they were extremely aggressive, and throughout the Postclassic period they controlled trade routes that extended from the Gulf Coast of Mexico around the Yucatán Peninsula to Honduras. It is also probable that the Toltec influences so firmly imprinted on the ruins of Chichén Itzá may be attributable to the Putún. Quite possibly they either fostered incursions into Yucatán by the Toltecs (with whom the Putún regularly traded) or they were allied with Toltec warriors brought in by the Putún-Itzá to protect their far-flung trading networks.

Nor was Yucatán the only scene of Putún incursions into Maya territory. By the middle of the ninth century the Putún had penetrated the southern lowlands, pushing their way up the Usumacinta River and along the Río Pasión to Seibal and Altar de Sacrificios. With them came new types of ceramics—the widely distributed trade wares known as Fine Orange and Fine Gray. And the strange Mexicanized portraits of elite figures on monuments at Seibal dating from A.D. 850 to 900 almost certainly represent Putún lords who seized control of the city, probably hastening its collapse in the process (see Chapter 10).

Whatever its source, there is little doubt that the Toltec-Itzá colonization of Yucatán involved some degree of military conquest, as shown by scenes at Chichén Itzá depicting battles and the sacrifice of Maya captives at the hands of Mexican invaders. Along with profound aberrations in art, architecture, religion, and sociopolitical structure incurred by this alien intrusion, some of Yucatán's cities may have been abandoned as a result of these external pressures. Here indeed could be the answer to the question previously posed as to why so many of Yucatán's flourishing cities—Uxmal, Labná, Sayil, Edzná, Cobá, and the like—were abandoned around A.D. 1000. Very likely the Toltec-Itzá incursions engulfed them in a calamitous upheaval, disrupting long-established trade routes, toppling their ruling hierarchies, or subjecting them to military conquest. On the other hand, some cities obviously continued to flourish under the new regime, and aside from Chichén Itzá, whose size and advantageous location encouraged the Toltec-Itzá to make it their capital, such places as Izamal, Motul, Dzibilchaltún, Maní, and Cozumel Island became key centers of Toltec-Itzá authority.

Along with the new sculptural and architectural features already mentioned in relation to Chichén Itzá, other significant innovations entered Yucatán as a consequence of foreign intrusion. Gold, copper, and turquoise were brought in from Mexico, and two distinctive varieties of ceramics came into widespread use: highly polished vessels known as X-type Fine Orange and a unique ware called Plumbate, the only glazed pottery ever manufactured in Mesoamerica—both of which were widely traded by the Putún. Among the invading armies were well-organized military orders using the eagle and jaguar as their symbols. Newly introduced weapons included cotton armor, *atlatls,* slings, and obsidian-edged swords, and there was an increased emphasis on militarism in all phases of political and religious life. Human sacrifice began to be practiced on a scale never approached in the Classic period, with the ruthless Toltec-Itzá soldiers assuming a vital ritualistic function as providers of captives for sacrificial purposes.

New gods and ceremonies also appeared, involving not only the cult of Quetzalcóatl-Kukulcán but several other Mexican deities as well: Tonatiuh, the sun god; Chicomecóatl, the maize goddess; Tlaloc, the rainmaker; Xipe-Totec, god of sacrifice; and even Quetzalcóatl's archrival, the powerful Tezcatlipoca or "Smoking Mirror." In his 1956 revision of Morley's *The Ancient Maya,* George Brainerd wrote: ". . . respect for the piety of Kukulcán and the luxuriance of religious construction at Chichén Itzá suggest that the Maya may have lent their talents and labors willingly to the furtherance of a new religion. Perhaps the Toltec conquest of Yucatán was accomplished as much by religious evangelization as by military force."

In time, Mexican influences made their way into almost every aspect of Maya culture, and Chichén Itzá became the focal point from which they extended over a large section of the peninsula. Even so, native traditions did not disappear under this foreign domination; nor were they subjected to the kind of deliberate annihilation later inflicted by the Spaniards. Intermarriage and cultural exchange led to a gradual fusion of Maya and Mexican traits, and the conquerors had enormous respect for Maya technology and craftsmanship. Everywhere at Chichén Itzá we see Toltec-style buildings and monuments executed according to Maya techniques. Images of rigidly posed Mexican warriors and chieftains are shown opposite serene Maya lords, and there are buildings adorned with long-nosed Chac masks of typical Puuc design alongside the feathered-serpent emblems of Kukulcán. Like the Roman conquests in Europe and the Near East, the Toltec-Itzá invasion of Yucatán resulted in a synthesis of artistic styles, religious beliefs, and customs in which the thread of Maya civilization continued to survive.

But the great Classic tradition had ended. Inevitably the infusion of alien customs, the introduction of innovative approaches to art and architecture, and the acceptance of Mexican religious concepts brought about sweeping changes in the old order. Factors were now at work that would drastically restructure Maya culture in the three centuries prior to the Spanish Conquest, and it was not long before a new system of values far removed from those of the past began to emerge.

12 · THE WELL OF SACRIFICE

Because of its prominence as the seat of Toltec-Itzá power, Chichén Itzá was the center of artistic, religious, and economic activity in Yucatán for more than two hundred years. Several sixteenth-century Spanish authors claimed that it was equally renowned as a shrine, and in time of drought, pestilence, or similar misfortunes, pilgrims from distant areas visited the city in order to carry out human sacrifices in which victims laden with jade, gold, and precious stones were hurled into the now-celebrated Sacred Cenote, an ominous pool of water said to be the abode of gods, especially the rain deity Chac. For years, however, this intriguing tale had remained nothing but hearsay until a scholar-diplomat named Edward Herbert Thompson attempted to verify its grim details and in so doing made archaeological history.

When Thompson assumed the post of United States consul in Yucatán in 1885, he was barely twenty-five years of age. A native of Worcester, Massachusetts, he had been educated in business and engineering, but as a young man he developed an abiding interest in archaeology. In 1879 he published an article in *Popular Science Monthly* entitled "Atlantis Not a Myth," in which he advocated the well-worn idea that the American Indians were descended from survivors of the apocryphal lost continent. Although he later rejected this theory, the article brought him to the attention of influential officers of the American Antiquarian Society and the Peabody Museum at Harvard University, who engaged him to conduct a vaguely defined plan of archaeological research in Yucatán and arranged for his appointment to the consulate in Mérida.

Like John Lloyd Stephens, Thompson regarded the responsibilities of a diplomatic career as secondary in importance to his enthusiasm for antiquities. Scarcely had he arrived in Mérida before he launched a series of explorations at various ruins, particularly Uxmal and Labná, where he surveyed structures, carried out small-scale excavations, and made casts of monuments and the façades of buildings, which were displayed at the Chicago World's Fair in 1893. But eventually the focal point of his research became the acres of overgrown structures and mounds that marked the site of Chichén Itzá—the place, he wrote, "that was to be the scene of my life-work."

A few years after his arrival in Yucatán, Thompson negotiated for the purchase of the abandoned plantation on which Chichén Itzá was located. In his autobiography, *People of the Serpent,* he described his first impression of the ruined city that was to be his home for almost three decades:

The gradual ascent and winding of the trail between the boulders and the big trees seemed so like familiar forest rambles at home that it came over me almost with a shock to realize that the boulders I passed by so carelessly had cut surfaces and were once carved columns and sculptured pillars. Then, just as I began to understand that the level, forest-covered surface beneath my feet was a terrace made by ancient man, I peered upward to a great stone mass that pierced the sky, and all else was forgotten. A pyramid with terraced sides, paneled walls of cut limestone, and broad stairways leading upward, was crowned by a temple. Other buildings, high mounds and broken terraces, were buried in the forest and only the dark green knobs on the horizon told where they stood.

Pen cannot describe or brush portray the strange feelings produced by the beating of the tropic sun against the ash-colored walls of those venerable structures. Old . . . furrowed by time, and haggard, imposing, and impassive, they rear their rugged masses above the surrounding level and are beyond description.

The ruined group of Chichén Itzá covers a space of fully three square miles. Over all this territory are scattered carved and square stones in countless thousands and fallen columns by the hundreds; while the formless remains and outlined walls of huge structures fallen into decay are seen on every side. Seven massive structures of carved stone and adamantine mortar still tower erect and almost habitable. Their façades, though gray and haggard with age and seamed by time, sustain the claim that Chichén Itzá is one of the world's greatest monuments of antiquity.

During his exploration of the city, Thompson's attention was drawn to the ruins of a pyramid similar in design to the nearby Temple of Kukulcán, except that it was much smaller in scale. Now called the Tomb of the High Priest, each of its four terraced sides was ascended by a stairway flanked with stone balustrades representing open-jawed serpents. In characteristic fashion, its summit formerly supported a small temple, although nothing remained of this ceremonial superstructure other than four elaborately carved columns. While clearing rubble from the base of these pillars, Thompson stumbled upon two highly polished capstones embedded in what had once been the floor of the temple.

Beneath these stones he discovered a square shaft descending approximately twelve feet into the core of the pyramid. Faintly discernible on the floor of this vault were portions of a human skeleton surrounded by broken pottery bowls. The burial rested on a smooth flagstone similar to those which had sealed the crypt's entrance, and below this were four more graves superimposed upon one another. "In the third grave," wrote Thompson, "I found a handful of copper bells, small in size, and turned to verdigris. In the fourth grave I found a necklace of handsomely cut and finely polished rock-crystal beads. The floor of this last grave was on a level with the base of the pyramid, and I naturally concluded that, as the pyramid rested on the limestone ledge rock of the region, my work of excavation was automatically ended. Then I observed that the stone floor tiles still persisted, and lifting them, I discovered to my surprise a series of steps hewn out of the living rock down into a chamber. . . . The stairs were covered and the chamber filled with wood ashes. The only way I could enter . . . was by lying flat on my back and pushing my feet ahead of me through the ashes and into the chamber. . . ."

Slowly Thompson worked his way into the narrow crypt. Intermingled with the refuse he cleared from the vault were a number of jade beads, some of which looked as though they had been burned. Otherwise the room turned out to be empty except for a square stone resting against one wall. When Thompson attempted to move the slab it unexpectedly gave way, revealing a black hole in the floor underneath it. A flood of cold air rushed out of the cavernous opening, blowing out the candles and leaving Thompson and his Maya assistants in "utter darkness in the bowels of the earth."

"Don Eduardo," cried his workmen, "this is surely the mouth of Hell!"

"Not so," he replied. "Since when has the mouth of Hell given forth a breath as cold as this wind?"

By a curious irony this logic appealed to the terrified Indians. Years of Christian teaching had instilled in them the concept of Hell as a blazing inferno where the condemned suffered fiery ordeals. Had they still adhered to the beliefs of their ancestors that Xibalbá, or the Underworld, was a place of unbearable cold, they would surely have fled in terror as the cold air issued from the ominous black pit.

The opening was roughly circular in outline and three feet in diameter. By lowering a lantern attached to a tape line, Thompson estimated its depth to be fifty feet. "I had two of the natives grasp each of my feet at the ankle," he recalled, "and then, head downward, my body swinging like a pendulum with my tape and light below me, I managed to get a good idea of the place. . . .

"After getting back my breath, I told my workers that we would quit for the day and go home, but would return very early on the morrow prepared to go down into that hole. I also warned them not to tell anybody what we were doing lest they laugh at us and call us crazy. As a matter of fact, I was certain that we had made a very important find, and I did not want any more witnesses than I could help."

By dawn Thompson's crew had assembled at the pyramid for the day's adventure. A block and tackle was mounted above the opening in order to haul up the debris from the pit. Equipped with a knife between his teeth, his pockets bulging with trowels, brushes, and candles, Thompson was lowered by a rope through the opening into the pit.

No sooner had he switched on his lantern than he encountered an unexpected treasure: an alabaster vase filled with polished jade beads and an exquisite pendant. Moments later his assistants scrambled down the rope to join him, and during the hours that followed they were lost in the feverish excitement of discovery. One after another, magnificent relics were exhumed from the debris littering the floor of the crypt. Scattered about were shells inlaid with mother-of-pearl, pottery vessels, and a ceremonial flint blade that Thompson described as resembling "the votive stone sickles of the ancient Druids"; there were also numerous large oval pearls, many of which had lain undisturbed for so long that they fell to powder at the slightest touch. Later Thompson recorded an interesting postscript to these discoveries:

We ate and drank as the spirit moved us and then continued with the work until I could feel that a weariness was creeping over us. I gave the signal to stop work and get ready to go up into the outer world. When we reached the temple platform with our trophies, we saw a strange sight.

It was eleven o'clock in the evening. . . . A darkness as of midnight was all about us and on the plains beneath, the families of my workmen were crying and lamenting, with my wife and children trying in vain to calm them.

"No use!" they wailed. "The master and all of our people are dead and gone. The Great Serpent has taken them and we shall never see them again!"

Great was the rejoicing when we triumphantly appeared with our trophies and came down to them.

This was one of the red-letter days in my life as an archaeologist. I had discovered and investigated what was probably the sepulchre of a high priest of the Mayas. . . .

The five graves in the vertical shaft above . . . what of them? Whose bones, decayed and turning to dust, rested in the graves when I first uncovered them? Were they the acolytes or the servants of the high priest whose bodies were so placed as to guard in death as they served in life this high and sacred personage? Or were they priests of a lower order, whose friends sought for them by this last close contact a higher place in the future life? Who knows?

But a discovery of far greater magnitude awaited Thompson's restless curiosity. In the midst of his speculations he was seized by an obsession that was to endanger his life, subject him to ridicule, and ultimately result in disastrous legal difficulties. It was also to place him among the foremost contributors to Maya research.

Leading from the north side of the Temple of Kukulcán was the outline of an ancient road or *sacbe* known as the Sacred Way, which extended for three hundred yards through the city's main plaza to a huge natural well. Formations of this kind, called *cenotes* (from the Yucatec term *dzonot*), provide the major source of surface water in northern Yucatán; they are fed by underground drainage systems and form wherever the porous limestone crust has collapsed to expose the subterranean water table. It was probably this *cenote* that gave Chichén Itzá its present name. Literally the Yucatec word *chi* is translated as "mouth" and *chen* signifies a well, thus Chichén Itzá means "the mouth of the well of the Itzá." The oval-shaped *cenote* measured roughly two hundred feet in diameter and was encased by vertical limestone walls rising to a height of sixty-five feet above the surface of its murky green water. This was the well to which native folklore so often referred—the Sacred Cenote whose mysterious depths were rumored to contain a treasure.

Landa himself had stood at the brink of this evil-looking pool and recalled its secrets as told by his Indian informants: "Into this well they . . . had the custom of throwing men alive as a sacrifice to the gods, in times of drought, and they believed that they did not die though they never saw them again. They also threw into it a great many other things, like precious stones and things which they prized. And so if this country had possessed gold, it would be this well that would have the largest part of it, so great was the devotion which the Indians showed for it."

Most antiquarians had dismissed Landa's statement as nothing more than a legend unworthy of serious consideration. But Thompson did not share their skepticism. "The thought of that grim old water pit," he wrote, "and the wonderful objects that lay concealed within its depths became an obsession with me. . . ."

Then he came across another account, written in 1579 by Diego

Sarmeinto de Figueroa, who had visited Chichén Itzá during his tenure as *alcalde* of the nearby town of Valladolid:

> The lords and principal personages of the land had the custom, after sixty days of abstinence and fasting, of arriving by daybreak at the mouth of the Cenote and throwing into it Indian women belonging to each of these lords and personages, at the same time telling these women to ask for their masters a year favorable to his particular needs and desires.
>
> The women, being thrown in unbound, fell into the water with great force and noise. At high noon those that could cried out loudly and ropes were let down to them. After the women came up, half dead, fires were built around them and copal incense was burned before them. When they recovered their senses, they said that below there were many people of their nation, men and women, and that they received them. When they tried to raise their heads to look at them, heavy blows were given them on the head, and when their heads were inclined downward beneath the water they seemed to see many deeps and hollows, and they, the people, responded to their queries concerning the good or the bad year that was in store for their masters.

A daring plan was taking shape in Thompson's mind. If he was to test the validity of the myth that had so captivated his imagination, it would be necessary to probe beneath the *cenote*'s waters for relics of the gruesome homage supposedly paid by the Maya to their gods. But before proceeding with his formidable undertaking, Thompson journeyed to Boston, where he sought instruction in deep-sea diving and familiarized himself with various types of underwater equipment. Next he assembled a portable derrick and dredging apparatus suitable for his specialized needs, a device easily mounted at the well's edge and operated by a hand winch.

"Not until then," he wrote, "did I appear before the Honorable Stephen Salisbury of Worcester, Massachusetts, and Charles P. Bowditch of Boston, both officers of the American Antiquarian Society and of Harvard University of which the Peabody Museum is a part. To them I explained the project and asked the moral and financial aid of the two organizations they represented. . . . I found both of these gentlemen very reluctant to put the seal of their approval upon what they clearly believed to be a most audacious undertaking. They were willing to finance the scheme, but hesitated to take upon themselves the responsibility for my life.

"I finally argued them out of their fears, and all other obstacles having been overcome, the dredge and its equipment were duly installed on the platform to the right of the shrine and close to the edge of the great water pit, the Sacred Well."

Before beginning the dredging operation, Thompson determined the area of the pool most likely to contain human remains by throwing in logs the approximate size and weight of a man attached to a rope and measuring the depth to which they sank. With a group of Indians to manage the heavy machinery, the dredge was brought into position over the designated spot and slowly lowered into the water.

For days the dredging continued with endless repetition; the heavy steel bucket disappeared into the *cenote*'s somber depths only to reappear with nothing but mud, leaves, and decayed wood in its jaws. "At times," reported Thompson, "as if to tantalize me, the dredge recovered portions of earthen vessels undeniably ancient. I resolutely threw aside the thought that these might be the proofs I sought. Potsherds, I argued, were likely to be found anywhere on the site of this old city, washed from the surface deposits by rains."

Not long afterward something came to light that rekindled Thompson's fading expectations. "I rose in the morning from a sleepless night," he wrote. "The day was gray as my thoughts and the thick mist dropped from the leaves of the trees as quiet tears drop from half-closed eyes. I plodded through the dampness down to where the staccato clicks of the dredge brake called me and, crouching under the palm-leaf lean-to, watched the monotonous motion of the brown-skinned natives as they worked at the winches. The bucket slowly emerged from the heaving water that boiled around it and . . . I saw two yellow-white, globular masses lying on the surface of the chocolate-colored muck that filled the basin. As the mass swung over the brink and up to the platform, I took from it the two objects and closely examined them."

Undoubtedly they had been fashioned by human hands, but Thompson was uncertain what their purpose might have been. He broke one in half and tasted it; then it occurred to him to hold the substance over a smoldering fire. Instantly a pungent fragrance filled the air, and Thompson suddenly remembered a detail from a native legend he had once read. "Like a ray of bright sunlight breaking through a dense fog came to me the words of the old *H'men*, the Wise Man of Ebtun: 'In ancient times our fathers burned the sacred resin—*pom*—and by the fragrant smoke their prayers were wafted to their god whose home was in the Sun.'

"These yellow balls of resin were masses of the sacred incense *pom* [copal], and had been thrown in as part of the rich offerings mentioned in the traditions."

Thereafter each dredgeload of slimy mud contained new affirmation of his conviction. Out of the pit's murky water came a profuse array of objects bearing the unmistakable imprint of Maya craftsmanship: pottery vessels, incense burners, wooden spear-throwers, fragments of stone sculpture, jade figurines, beads, and pendants. True to Landa's prediction, there were dozens of artifacts made of copper and gold, including tiny bells, rings, a golden bowl and cups, effigies, sections of a mask, and skillfully embossed disks. "Objects of nearly pure gold," Thompson noted, "were encountered, both cast, beaten, and engraved in repoussé, but they were few in number and relatively unimportant. Most of the so-called gold objects were low-grade alloy, with more copper than gold in them. That which gave them their chief value were the symbolical and other figures cast or carved upon them." Aside from this spectacular array of relics, the dredge finally brought up the ultimate proof Thompson had hoped to recover; human bones and skulls appeared amid the other treasures so long immersed in the watery shrine—the remains of sacrificial victims cast into the well in the manner Landa and Figueroa had described.

After several months the dredging operations reached an impasse; the basin began to emerge with nothing but silt and sticks caught in its steel jaws, and Thompson knew it had eaten its way to the rocky floor of the pool. Having anticipated such an eventuality, he now planned to descend into the *cenote* and explore the hidden crevices that the dredge was too large to reach. The necessary diving equipment was already at his disposal, and he had previously engaged two Greek sponge fishermen to assist with his precarious explorations. To the horror of the Indians who crowded around the well's rim, the three men embarked upon their subterranean quest. "As I stepped on the first rung of the ladder," recalled Thompson, "each of the pumping gang, my faithful native boys, left his place in turn and with a very solemn face shook hands with me and then went back again to wait for the signal. It was not hard to read their thoughts. They were bidding me a last farewell, never expecting to see me again. Then, releasing my hold on the ladder, I sank like a bag of lead, leaving behind me a silvery chain of bubbles."

Gradually the water changed from amber to green and finally to an impenetrable black. Thompson's submarine flashlight was unable to pierce the veil of darkness in which he was shrouded. He groped blindly along the floor until he located a ledge or crevice, then sifted its contents by hand. Here and there were steep mud walls laden with rocks and tree trunks; these proved to be a distracting hazard, for, as Thompson explained, "every little while one of the stone blocks, loosened from its place in the wall by the infiltration of the water, would come plunging down upon us in the worse than Stygian darkness. . . ."

For several weeks the divers continued their examination of the well. The Indians, who watched the proceedings with abject fascination, waited anxiously for the terrible disaster they were certain was imminent—outraged gods lurking in some unseen cavern beneath the surface would surely drag the intruders to a watery grave. But fortunately no serious mishaps occurred, and their dangerous venture resulted in more startling discoveries. Each time a diver reappeared from the depths, his pouch brimmed with artifacts: pieces of carved jade, nodules of copal incense, pottery, objects of copper and gold, human bones, and fragments of cloth miraculously preserved in the mud. Among the most interesting treasures were three ceremonial knives of the type used to cut the hearts from sacrificial victims. Only one was unbroken and its beautifully chipped flint blade was mounted in a carved wooden handle overlaid with gold representing two entwined serpents. Of the identifiable skeletons retrieved from the *cenote,* twenty-one were children between the ages of eighteen months and twelve years, thirteen were adult men, and eight were women.

Since almost all of the relics were broken, Thompson was of the opinion that the Maya had adhered to the common practice among ancient peoples of "killing" objects intended as funerary offerings, smashing them so their "spirits" could accompany the deceased with whom they were entombed. But the custom of breaking funerary items was not widespread among the Maya, and much of the damage noted by Thompson might have been caused by the height from which they were thrown into the well.

Judging from the abundance of material recovered in the *cenote*, human sacrifices had taken place there with ominous frequency. And because of the obsessive emphasis on sacrificial rites in Mexican religion, scholars were at first inclined to view the use of the pool for this purpose as a Toltec-Itzá innovation, introduced after their occupation of Yucatán. But this may not have been the case. Some of the carved jades from the well are definitely of Classic-period workmanship; one piece in the sculptural style of Piedras Negras was inscribed with a date of A.D. 706, and another, which is almost certainly from Palenque, bore an inscription equal to A.D. 690. Archaeologists are not sure whether these jades were brought to the Sacred Cenote from distant cities during the seventh and eighth centuries, or whether they had been kept through the years as treasured heirlooms or looted from Classic tombs, then cast into the well at a later time.

Despite the immense scientific importance of Thompson's discoveries, his years of exploration at Chichén Itzá ended with a series of unfortunate occurrences. During a revolutionary uprising that swept Yucatán in 1921, the hacienda where Thompson lived was burned while he was away in Mérida. Lost beyond reclamation was his valuable library, as well as many priceless artifacts recovered from his excavations. A few years later the hacienda was rebuilt and leased to the Carnegie Institution as the headquarters for its extensive program of research at Chichén Itzá, and today the building is part of a hotel situated adjacent to the ruins.

Legal difficulties then developed with the Mexican government over the rumored value of the articles reclaimed from the Sacred Cenote.

Some estimates placed the worth of the much-publicized gold objects in excess of $500,000, though Thompson steadfastly denied these reports, arguing that the actual value of the material could be judged only in terms of its contribution to science. But the Mexican authorities were unswayed by his protests, and because Thompson had shipped the collection to the Peabody Museum for safekeeping, he was promptly charged with stealing national treasures. Accordingly, his property in Yucatán was confiscated and held against payment of 1,036,410 pesos, an act that forced him to relinquish his ownership of the hacienda and forsake plans for future excavations at Chichén Itzá.

In his defense Thompson wrote: ". . . I should have been false to my duty as an archaeologist had I, believing that the scientific treasures were at the bottom of the Sacred Well, failed to improve the opportunity to bring them to light, thus making them available for scientific study instead of remaining in the mud and useless to the world. I should have been equally false to my duty as a scientist if, after bringing them to light, I had neglected to take all possible measures for their immediate security and permanent safety."

Although the litigation was unsettled at the time of Thompson's death in 1935, the Mexican supreme court later ruled that no existing laws had been violated by his actions. Even so, ethical questions surrounding the ownership of the material from the *cenote* remained a controversial issue, and in 1960 the Peabody Museum voluntarily returned ninety-four pieces from the collection to the Instituto Nacional de Antropología e Historia in Mexico City.

Ever since Thompson's operations at the Sacred Cenote ended in 1911, numerous proposals have been made to resume explorations there in the hope of finding more objects concealed beneath its waters. Finally, in 1960, an expedition jointly sponsored by the National Geographic Society and an organization of underwater sportsmen known as CEDAM (Club de Exploraciones y Deportes Aquáticos de México) undertook such a venture. With them came professional archaeologists, scuba divers assigned to the project by the Mexican navy, and an array of up-to-date equipment—principally a motor-driven airlift with which the divers could vacuum the silt from the floor of the *cenote* and pass it through screens designed to catch even the smallest artifacts.

But four months later the work was abruptly terminated because of a controversy over damage to valuable specimens caused by the powerful airlift, though by then some four thousand additional relics had already been recovered, including more bones of sacrificial victims, ornaments of jade, amber, and crystal, gold-washed copper rings, and a ceremonial knife with a gold-foil handle.

Another effort to explore the *cenote* was launched in 1967 by CEDAM and Norman Scott, an American underwater expert whose company, Expeditions Unlimited, had previously been involved in quests for sunken treasure in the Caribbean. With substantial financial backing supplied by a number of commercial firms and a wealthy Texan named F. Kirk Johnson, a twofold plan was devised. An attempt would first be made to drain the well using centrifugal pumps capable of handling 200,000 gallons of water an hour, thereby allowing archaeologists to excavate the thick deposits of silt covering the bottom. If this failed or proved too expensive, the alternate approach involved the use of complicated filtering devices to clear the water so divers could work unhampered by the pool's impenetrable darkness.

After repeated efforts the pumping operation was only partially successful; the porous limestone surface surrounding the *cenote* permitted the runoff to drain back through underground channels almost as quickly as it was removed. Nevertheless, the water level was lowered enough to expose what was called "Thompson's bank," a huge mound consisting of the silt and debris brought up by Thompson's dredge and later dumped back into the well. Under careful excavation and screening it was found to contain hundreds of artifacts overlooked by Thompson and his native workmen.

Fortunately, the plan to clear the *cenote*'s water by means of chemicals produced remarkably good results. Utilizing chlorine to kill the algae and other organisms normally infesting the well, its water was then circulated through filtering tanks filled with diatomaceous earth to remove impurities. Eventually the pool was rendered sufficiently clear to enable archaeologists with scuba gear to systematically probe the floor while underwater photographers recorded many of their finds *in situ*.

Among the objects retrieved by these procedures were two stone standard-bearers in the form of crouched jaguars, gold effigies, disks, and rings, the soles from two sandals made of gold (presumably placed on the feet of sacrificial victims just before their deaths, since they showed no signs of wear), ceramic figurines, a carved antler representing a bird, and fragments of Late Classic polychrome pottery, their brightly painted scenes still clearly visible. Hundreds of human skeletal remains, a high percentage of them from children, were also found, along with the bones of deer, jaguars, turkeys, dogs, and other animals, indicating that these creatures were probably cast into the well as sacrificial offerings. Perhaps the most interesting items were the only known examples of ancient Maya furniture ever found: two low wooden stools, shaped somewhat like turtles and decorated with carvings of human faces emerging from serpents' mouths.

No doubt the Sacred Cenote has not revealed the last of its secrets, and future expeditions may challenge it again with even more sophisticated techniques. Nor was it the only well in Yucatán used for sacrificial purposes. In 1958, divers from the National Geographic Society explored another pool—the Xlacah Cenote—located amid the ruins of Dzibilchaltún. To everyone's amazement it yielded more than six thousand artifacts, including large quantities of pottery, several bone awls incised with hieroglyphs, a clay flute, jade ornaments, a small wooden mask, and the all-too-familiar human skeletons.

We can only guess whether or not other treasure-laden *cenotes* lie hidden elsewhere in Yucatán, but if the discoveries made by Thompson and his successors are any indication, the rapidly developing science of underwater archaeology may disclose countless surprises in the depths of these forbidding wells.

From about A.D. 1200 until the Spanish Conquest, the sequence of events in Yucatán is obscured in a mist of quasi-historical evidence gleaned from sources of questionable reliability. But one place reappears frequently in post-Conquest accounts relating to this era: the once-populous city known as Mayapán, a sprawling maze of debris-littered mounds thirty miles southeast of Mérida. For years it had remained a mystery. It was often mentioned in the *Books of Chilam Balam* and various Spanish chronicles, but archaeologists had not undertaken to explore its ruins.

Native sources spoke of Mayapán as having played an extremely important political role in the later phases of Maya history. Reportedly, it was here that the Itzá, under the supervision of the mighty Kukulcán, had founded a new capital after the abandonment of Chichén Itzá. Here, too, a ruling lord named Hunac Ceel was said to have established a dictatorship that subsequently brought a vast portion of Yucatán under his jurisdiction.

In his *Relación*, Landa gave the following account of the city's origin:

This Kukulcán established another city after arranging with the native lords of the country that he and they should live there and that all of their affairs and business should be brought there; and for this purpose they chose a very good situation, eight leagues further in the interior than Mérida is now, and fifteen or sixteen leagues from the sea. They surrounded it with a very broad stone wall, . . . leaving in it only two narrow gates. The wall was not very high and in the midst of this enclosure they built their temples, and the largest, which is like that of Chichén Itzá [El Castillo], they called Kukulcán, and they built another of a round form, with four doors, entirely different from all the others in that land. . . . In this enclosure they built houses for the lords only, dividing all the land among them, giving a town to each one, according to the antiquity of his lineage and his personal value. And Kukulcán gave a name to this city—not his own name as the Ah Itzás had done at Chichén Itzá, but he called it Mayapán, which means "the standard of the Maya." . . . Kukulcán lived with the lords in that city for several years; and leaving them in great peace and friendship, he returned by the same way to Mexico. . . .

In the *Books of Chilam Balam* we read how Yucatán was governed for almost two hundred years by a "triple alliance" consisting of the three most influential centers in the peninsula: Mayapán, Chichén Itzá, and Uxmal. The dates generally ascribed to this political union fall between A.D. 987 and 1185, although these vary somewhat according to discrepancies in conflicting versions of its history. Supposedly this "League of Mayapán," as it is called, brought about a high degree of political stability during its existence. Ostensibly the reins of government over the entire territory were held jointly by lords representing each of the League's three member cities. But frictions inevitably touched off intrigue and open revolt, resulting in a shattering upheaval that was to dissolve the League of Mayapán and provide the background for an obscure noble to seize control of Yucatán.

Archaeological research has failed to bear out the details of these events. For one thing, there is substantial evidence that Uxmal was abandoned by A.D. 1000 or shortly thereafter. Moreover, Mayapán had emerged as an important center only after Chichén Itzá lost its position of eminence as the peninsula's leading city sometime around A.D. 1200. Thus the three cities supposedly comprising the ruling triumvirate did not flourish simultaneously, at least not during the entire two hundred years of the League's hegemony. Still, it is not impossible that such a confederation once exercised a system of mutual control

over Yucatán, and that inaccurate recollections of its structure or con-
fusion as to the dates involved have obscured its history.

Whatever the truth may prove to be, the League of Mayapán's dissolution brings us to a fascinating if equally hazy juncture—the famous "plot of Hunac Ceel." If native accounts of this event can be
accepted literally, we encounter one of the most dramatic episodes in
the whole sweeping panorama of Maya affairs. Regrettably, however,
the references to Hunac Ceel in the *Books of Chilam Balam* are extremely vague, and there is disagreement among archaeologists over
the date of his rise to power.

From what we can gather, this curious drama began at Chichén Itzá
during the enactment of a sacrifice at the Sacred Cenote. For reasons
that are not clear, Hunac Ceel, a powerful lord of Mayapán, was
among the individuals cast into the well on this particular occasion;
perhaps he offered himself voluntarily or jumped into the water unexpectedly after the other victims drowned without delivering the divine prophecy so anxiously sought by the people waiting above. In any
case, Hunac Ceel reappeared from the depths of the pool, claiming that
he had personally spoken with the gods and received their prophecy.
Evidently this heroic act ignited the admiration of the onlooking
crowds, who brought Hunac Ceel up from the water and affirmed him
as their ruler. Immediately after his ascendancy, Hunac Ceel selected
Mayapán as the center of his authority, and using his family name he
established a dynasty there known as the Cocom. Next he sought to
eliminate the threat posed by the dissident lords of Chichén Itzá, especially its reigning chieftain—Chac Xib Chac.

Exactly how this was accomplished is again clouded by conflicting
accounts, but an interesting reference in the *Books of Chilam Balam*
would lead us to believe that Hunac Ceel exploited what amounted to a
sexual intrigue to further his lordly ambitions. He declared war against
Chichén Itzá when the untrustworthy Chac Xib Chac abducted the
bride of an ally, Ah Ulil, the ruling chief of Izamal. Other sources
differ as to the motives underlying the conflict, but whatever their ex-
cuse, Cocom legions overran Chichén Itzá and left the city so decimated that it was thereafter slowly abandoned. Next Hunac Ceel

reportedly attacked his erstwhile friend, Ah Ulil, in order to eliminate any potential challenge to his authority from Izamal.

From this point on, Mayapán became the most powerful city in Yucatán. Its armies were swelled by professional soldiers recruited from Tabasco—fierce Mexican mercenaries known as the Ah Canul, whose devotion to the Cocoms was purchased with guarantees of prestige and the spoils of military victories. To ensure the "loyalty" of Yucatán's other cities, their chiefs were forced to reside at Mayapán, where their policies and allegiances could be carefully watched. Surrounded by a walled city, defended by a private army, and with his potential enemies under close supervision, Hunac Ceel and his descendants maintained political control over much of the northern peninsula for roughly 250 years.

Despite a fairly effective centralized government at Mayapán, the Cocoms' rule was preemptive and often abusive, even to supposedly favored chieftains. Resentment and intrigue—the inevitable fissures in a decaying regime—gradually began to weaken the Cocoms' influence upon subordinate lords. Hostility toward the oppressive regime at Mayapán continued to grow until the partisans of one Ah Xupan, a member of the powerful Xiu family who ruled the territory around Uxmal, joined in a plot to overthrow the reigning Cocom lord. "This they did," wrote Landa, "killing at the same time all of his sons save one who was absent; they sacked his dwelling and possessed themselves of all his property . . . saying that thus they repaid themselves what had been stolen from them." Other accounts tell us in some detail how Mayapán was attacked and set afire by an army under the Xius' command about the year 1441.

Such was the brief outline of Mayapán's history as gleaned from the writings of Spanish and native chroniclers. It speaks of curious manifestations wholly foreign to older traditions: walled cities, professional warriors, and a centralized government. But how much could be accepted as actual fact? At best, the story's chronology was desultory and confusing, and its fragmentary details were drawn largely from folklore rather than historical records.

Obviously Mayapán's enormous size, its unique layout, and its prominent role in post-Conquest documents merited further study. With these facts in mind, a team of investigators from the Carnegie Institution set out in 1951 on a five-year project to excavate the city's principal buildings. Since the site proved to be even larger than previously estimated, it was a formidable undertaking; altogether Mayapán covered one and a half square miles, and the ruins of 4,140 structures were mapped within its boundaries. Out of the ensuing explorations there gradually emerged a remarkable set of circumstances not unlike those outlined in documentary sources.

Just as Landa had described it, the entire site was enclosed by a low stone wall breached by narrow, easily defended gates, although a total of twelve entrances were found, instead of only two as stated in the *Relación*. Within its central precincts stood the principal ceremonial structures, dominated by a pyramid patterned after the Temple of Kukulcán at Chichén Itzá, with terraced sides and four stairways flanked by feathered-serpent balustrades. Grouped around these temples were numerous rectangular buildings with colonnades and small interior rooms—perhaps the official residences of Cocom lords or the subordinate chiefs from neighboring cities who were required to live at Mayapán. Among the artifacts unearthed by excavators were finely worked flint arrowheads, which confirmed that the bow and arrow (previously unknown to the Maya) was used by Mayapán's armies, probably introduced from Mexico by Ah Canul mercenaries. In addition, the majority of Mayapán's structures had unquestionably served as dwellings, and the entire city was highly urbanized. Frequently the houses, many with front porticoes supported by columns, gave the impression of residential districts where nobles, craftsmen, and peasants lived in close proximity.

Especially interesting was the scarcity of major religious edifices at Mayapán. What few temples it contained are unimpressive in size and reflect extremely poor workmanship; thick layers of stucco were used to disguise crude masonry, columns were badly assembled, and flat beam-and-mortar roofs all but replaced corbeled vaults. In place of large-scale religious structures, there was an emphasis on small shrines or family oratories incorporated into individual residences, a fact interpreted by archaeologists as a sign that religion had lost much of its importance. Aside from this degeneration in architecture, Mayapán's sculpture was unimaginative and poorly executed (often consisting of weak imitations of Mexican-inspired works at Chichén Itzá), and its ceramics could scarcely have been more prosaic, except for ornate *incensarios* painted with garish colors.

Finally, there was positive proof of the city's destruction by fiery violence about the middle of the fifteenth century. The roof timbers of many structures showed evidence of burning; in some instances masonry walls were blackened by fire, and there were signs of extensive looting, attributable perhaps to the havoc wrought by the Xiu insurrection as related in native chronicles.

A summary of the findings at Mayapán reveals a city that bore little resemblance to the great centers of the past: it was a walled refuge garrisoned by paid troops, its supremacy maintained by force of arms, its inhabitants supported almost entirely by tributes, its art and architecture in severe decline, its rulers less in awe of their gods than of the intoxication of military power, its governing councils filled with displaced lords of subjugated provinces—puppets in function but political hostages in reality.

Elsewhere in Yucatán these influences had a profound effect, climaxed by a widespread disintegration in art and architecture and the rise of warrior-oriented societies. A trend toward urbanized cities protected against attack is obvious at several ruins in Quintana Roo, notably Xelhá, Ichpaatún, and the spectacular seacoast site of Tulúm, all of which are surrounded by walls. Other cities dating from this period are known to have been enclosed by what Spanish chroniclers described as wooden palisades and watchtowers.

Archaeologists have previously looked upon the upsurge of militarism during the Late Postclassic period (from A.D. 1250 to the Spanish Conquest), together with the decentralization of religious authority, the rise of political factionalism, and declining standards in art and architecture, as symptoms of a decadence that presaged the final collapse of Maya civilization—a counterpart of the moral and social disintegration associated with the final days of the Roman Empire. But a number of scholars, led by Jeremy A. Sabloff and William Rathje, now view this era in a very different light. "Instead of decline and cultural stagnation," wrote Sabloff and Rathje, "we see a cultural reorientation: a transfer of authority to new hands and a consequent pursuit of new objectives." In part, their conclusions are the result of excavations conducted in 1972–73 on Cozumel Island, a tremendously active Putún trading center that provided significant data on the importance of commerce in Late Postclassic society. While not disputing the increased role of militarism or the inferior art and architecture evidenced by cities like Mayapán, Tulúm, and Xelhá, Sabloff and Rathje argue convincingly that with the disappearance of the old elite class— which placed a high premium on architecture, monumental stone sculpture, hieroglyphic inscriptions, and luxury goods such as painted ceramics and jade ornaments—traditional values were reshaped by a pronounced emphasis on mercantilism aimed at mass markets.

Such changes stemmed from the impact of Putún traders, whose influence had by then penetrated into every facet of Maya culture. Under their guidance, long-distance sea trade—with Cozumel Island as its focal point—became a major economic factor leading to the establishment of a far-flung network of commercial centers throughout northern Yucatán. No longer interested in the aesthetic ideals, intellectual activities, and ritualism of earlier centuries, the Putún were more concerned with the promotion of commerce, the management of raw materials, and the manufacture of mass-produced pottery, cotton textiles, implements, and a variety of other items intended to supply the needs of an essentially non-elite population. Although the quality of these goods inevitably declined (at least by Classic-period criteria), the standard of living enjoyed by the peasants rose considerably as cheaper merchandise was made available over a wide area. In time, a new code of ethics involving commerce replaced elite-oriented values, causing archaeologists to think of the Late Classic as an era of cultural decay. From an elitist viewpoint this was undeniably true, but Sabloff and Rathje insist that a period of history marked by the appearance of an entirely new set of ethics (which they call "mercantile pragmatism"), the emergence of a complex economic system, and the rise of a powerful merchant class cannot be judged as "the decadent last gasp of a dying civilization."

Nevertheless, after the downfall of Mayapán in the mid-fifteenth century, Maya culture lapsed into a state of turmoil that set the stage for its demise at the hands of the Spaniards. Once again these events must be reconstructed from post-Conquest narratives, which provide us with only fragmentary information. We read how the one Cocom lord who survived the sacking of Mayapán (by virtue of being away on a trading expedition) led the remnants of his people to a new settlement known as Tibolón. Large numbers of Ah Canul, the Cocoms' mercenary guards, established themselves in the northwest corner of the peninsula. Some years before, a group of Itzá had journeyed southward into the Petén, where they founded the city of Tayasal at Lake Petén Itzá, and the remaining Xiu chieftains settled at Maní, a few miles south of Mayapán. Ironically, the word *Maní* signified "it is finished."

Within a short time thereafter Yucatán was divided into sixteen independent provinces, each ruled by a petty lord with a private army under his command. No centralized authority had the power to unite these political entities, and it was not long before territorial disputes turned the northern and eastern sectors of the peninsula into a series of opposing states. Open warfare erupted throughout the area. Villages were raided for sacrificial victims and youths suitable for forced military conscription. Occasionally the marauders, striking at night, would set fire to outlying fields in order to starve towns into submission, and it is probable that trade routes were disrupted, resulting in economic chaos. Ruling lords rose and fell in rapid succession, often displaced by conspiracies or outright assassination. In one celebrated incident that occurred as late as 1536, Nachi Cocom, the great-grandson of Mayapán's last ruler, succeeded in luring two Xiu chieftains and their retinue to a banquet, whereupon Nachi Cocom's warriors unexpectedly attacked them and slaughtered the entire party.

To the south, in the Guatemalan highlands, the story was essentially the same. Although the Maya in this region had maintained close ties with Mexico ever since the colonization of Kaminaljuyú by Teotihuacán in the fifth century A.D., they were subjected to renewed Mexican influences during the Postclassic period. As was the case in Yucatán, a variety of Toltec-derived traits appeared at this time in the highlands, including increased militarism, the Quetzalcóatl cult, large-scale human sacrifice, vigorous trade, and political factionalism that split the region into numerous tribes ruled by chiefs who traced their ancestry to the Toltecs. No doubt these Mexican affinities stemmed from Putún warrior-merchants who had penetrated the highlands perhaps as early as the ninth or tenth centuries via two separate routes—through the Usumacinta and Pasión valleys from the Gulf Coast of Mexico (the same way they reached Altar de Sacrificios and Seibal), and along the Motagua River from trading centers on the Caribbean coast of Guatemala and Honduras, especially the town of Nito at the mouth of Lake Izabal.

Furthermore, there appear to have been sustained contacts between the highland centers and Chichén Itzá in Postclassic times. It is known that large quantities of Plumbate pottery, a trade ware manufactured on the Pacific coast of Guatemala, were imported into Yucatán along commercial avenues controlled by the Putún. Native chronicles from Guatemala also contain references to Tula and Tollán, and a passage in the *Popol Vuh* tells how three Quiché lords visited Tollán to secure official acknowledgment of their right to rule:

> And starting on their journey, they said: "We are going to the East, there whence came our fathers." So they said when the three sons set out. One was called Qocaib, and he was the son of Balam-Quitzé, of the Cavec. The one called Qoacutec was son of Balam-Acab, of the Nihaib; and the other called Zoahau, was son of Mahucutah, of the Ahau-Quiché.
>
> . . . They crossed the sea when they went there to the East, when they went to receive the investiture of the kingdom. And this was the name of the Lord, King of the East, where they went. When they arrived before Lord Nacxit, which was the name of the great lord, the only supreme judge of all the kingdoms, he gave them the insignia of the kingdom and all its distinctive symbols. . . . And Nacxit ended by giving them the insignia of royalty, which are: the canopy, the throne, the flutes of bone, the *cham-cham*, yellow beads, puma claws, the heads and feet of the deer . . . snail shells, tobacco, little gourds, parrot feathers, standards of royal aigrette feathers, *tatam,* and *caxcon.*

According to some authorities, Nacxit was the name given by the Quiché to the legendary king of Tollán, Topiltzin-Quetzalcóatl and his lineage. But other sources identify Nacxit as both a ruling lord at Chichén Itzá and the god Kukulcán (Quetzalcóatl); and because the *Popol Vuh* recounts that the Quiché lords "crossed the sea," some students are persuaded that the Tollán referred to in the narrative was actually Chichén Itzá (which could easily have been reached by sailing from the Gulf of Honduras around Yucatán) and that Nacxit was a Toltec-Itzá lord whose jurisdiction extended all the way to the highlands.

Similarities in architecture and site planning are also evident in Guatemala and Yucatán. Late Postclassic highland centers often contained Mexicanized features, and one notable example—Zaculeu—has terraced platforms, buildings with *talud-tablero* walls (as seen at Chichén Itzá and Tula), terraced platforms, and a ball court, all strongly reminiscent of structures in Yucatán. Fortifications are a hallmark of these sites, and nearly every regional capital and smaller center in the highlands—cities such as Utatlán, Iximché, Chutixtiox, and Zaculeu—was situated on a defensible hill or promontory surrounded by deep canyons, ramparts, and walls. By this time warfare constantly raged throughout the area, and the two most powerful groups—the Quiché and Cakchiquel—were locked in a bloody struggle for supremacy.

Everywhere in the Maya region, art and architecture declined drastically as the Late Postclassic period progressed. With few exceptions, sculpture and ceramics were grossly unrefined; stone temples had largely been replaced by thatched huts, and hieroglyphic writing, astronomy, calendrics, and other intellectual pursuits were all but forgotten. No leaders arose to reverse the tragic destiny that had overtaken the Maya; no one challenged the egocentric schemes by which their rulers propelled them into constant warfare. Disunity, political intrigue, and moral decay had exacted their toll—and the prophets of disaster went unheard.

It was now the spring of 1517. The ships of Hernández de Córdova were nearing Cape Catoche off the northeastern coast of Yucatán. Soon the Maya caught their first glimpse of the mysterious Spanish vessels, which appeared to them like "mountains rising out of the sea on clouds,'' remembering perhaps that the prophecies of Chilam Balam had forewarned of this event:

> *On that day, a cloud arises,*
> *On that day, a mountain rises,*
> *On that day, a strong man seizes the land,*
> *On that day, things fall to ruin. . . .*

Hastily a meeting was held among the Maya chieftains at Cape Catoche. Later they sent a delegation to meet with the emissaries of Charles V, Emperor of Spain, *the most powerful man of his day!*

Suddenly, then, Maya civilization came to an end, overwhelmed by an outside threat even more ominous than its own internal difficulties—the Spanish Conquest. We can only speculate on what course it might have taken had these events not occurred. As for its past accomplishments, they were quickly engulfed in obscurity, leaving us to marvel at splendid relics of long-forgotten ages, a tradition of art, architecture, science, and literature unequaled in pre-Columbian America. Indeed, Sylvanus Morley once characterized the Maya as ''the Greeks of the New World,'' and numerous discoveries in recent years have justified his analogy.

Along with the material remains of their achievements, the Maya have left us a bewildering paradox that has plagued students from the outset of their investigations: everywhere we encounter undeniable miracles shrouded by countless unsolved mysteries. Despite the giant strides that brought Maya research out of the limbo of nineteenth-century romanticism, archaeologists face an enormous challenge. Future disclosures may someday enable them to piece together the whole fascinating panorama of Maya history, but if this is ever to be accomplished, vast areas must still be explored, dozens of key sites excavated, the hieroglyphic inscriptions deciphered, and a huge accumulation of data analyzed, all requiring a tremendous outlay of time and money.

In his excellent book, *The World of the Ancient Maya*, John S. Henderson summarized some of the fundamental problems still to be resolved:

Not one facet of Maya civilization is fully understood. Information on the Preclassic Maya world is naturally sketchy, but surprising gaps also mar reconstructions of later Maya societies. Along with archaeology, native traditional histories and early Spanish descriptions provide unusually full pictures of a few Maya societies at the period of the Conquest. Even in these instances, available information is not uniform. It reflects politics and economics in detail, other aristocratic concerns less well, and many aspects of culture not at all. In some parts of the Maya world, the archaeological record is entirely blank.

Even basic aspects of Maya civilization are puzzling. What were subsistence systems at the heart of Maya economics really like? *Milpa* farming, featuring maize, beans, and squash, was fundamental, but it was not standardized. What were the varied blends of accessory crops? How important were manioc and other root crops? What differences resulted from variations in soil, climates, scheduling, and the use of such techniques as terracing? *Milpa* farming was never the sole agricultural system. How important were ridged-field systems and other methods of intensive farming? To what extent did Maya farmers cultivate ramon, chicosapote, and other tree crops? What was the dietary importance of noncrop plants, fish, shellfish, and other wild foods?

Trade networks were vital to Maya societies. They distributed great quantities of raw materials and finished products. What perishable goods moved along these networks? How important was exchange of foods between communities and regions? By what social mechanisms did exchange operate? What balances of market and redistributive patterns characterized Maya economics? What role did political leaders play in administering subsistence activities and commerce?

Extreme differences in wealth and social status developed within Maya societies during the Preclassic period. How sharply defined were social groups? How extensive was occupational specialization? To what extent did it coincide with social ranking? What mechanisms of social mobility were available to common folk?

Maya civic centers boasted impressive concentrations of monumental art and architecture. They were seats of great political and economic power. To what extent were they urban? Tikal, Dzibilchaltún, and several other great centers housed populations that numbered in the tens of thousands. At

197

Mayapán and a few other late northern centers, dense concentrations of dwellings clustered inside community walls. Maya cities certainly embodied many of the economic and political functions of true cities, but none had the urban form of Teotihuacán, with a huge, dense population concentrated within a community laid out according to a rigid grid plan. Did the smaller and more dispersed populations of Maya centers enjoy different patterns of social relations? All of these questions, and many others, can be asked of every part of the Maya world in every period of its pre-Columbian history.

In the face of such numerous and far-reaching problems, the enigmas posed by Maya civilization seem overwhelming. Nevertheless, scholars are meeting the challenge more vigorously than ever before. With the accelerated pace of new projects, important breakthroughs are taking place with increasing frequency, and certain previously insoluble problems are gradually yielding to modern research. Improved field techniques and methods of laboratory study are being applied to specific questions, along with the talents of highly trained specialists representing many scientific institutions and a variety of disciplines. Excavations are currently under way at a number of important sites, and significant studies dealing with every aspect of Maya civilization are constantly appearing in print.

Hardly a year passes without new expeditions setting off in search of further revelations into what has become a singularly intriguing chapter in American archaeology. And whatever the difficulties to be overcome, other scholar-explorers in the tradition of Stephens, Maudslay, Thompson, and Ruz will continue to probe Maya ruins until their secrets are known, for the lure of such things is irresistible.

14 · BALANKANCHÉ: POSTSCRIPT TO AN ANCIENT CIVILIZATION

Regardless of the unresolved questions surrounding their history, we have seen that the Maya are not a "vanished race" as they are so often portrayed in nonscientific literature. More than two million Indians of Maya descent still occupy the region, and next to the Quechua peoples of Peru and Bolivia, they constitute the most populous surviving aboriginal culture anywhere in America.

Like their pre-Columbian ancestors, the contemporary Maya are divided into various peoples speaking related but often mutually unintelligible dialects, which presumably evolved from a single common language. Among the largest of these groups are the Yucatec, who number in excess of 350,000 and inhabit Yucatán, Campeche, and Quintana Roo. Immediately to the southwest in Tabasco and eastern Chiapas live the Chol, Chontal, and Lacandón, and scattered throughout the uplands of central and southeastern Chiapas are the villages of the Tzotzil, Tzeltal and Tojolabal. Guatemala's lofty highlands are populated mainly by the Quiché, Cakchiquel, Tzutuhil, Chuh, Aguacatec, Ixil, Mam, Uspantec, and Kanjobal; and two groups known as the Kekchi and Pokomchi occupy sections of central Guatemala, principally the Department of Alta Verapaz. Another Maya-speaking people—the Huastec—are found far to the north in the Mexican states of Veracruz and San Luis Potosí, where they apparently migrated centuries before the Conquest.

Over the years linguists have sought to classify Maya languages into separate dialects and larger subgroups or "families," but this has proved difficult since the distinctions between certain dialects are extremely subtle and the analytical criteria used by scholars is not always uniform. At present many linguists recognize twenty-eight Maya dialects (with two more recently extinct) divided into six subgroups—Yucatecan, Huastecan, Tzeltalan-Cholan, Kanjobalan, Mamean, and Quichean—though this classification probably does not represent all of the complex interrelationships that exist in Maya languages.

Modern Maya culture inevitably reflects the impact of prolonged contact with outside influences. Every major town has its Catholic church, public school, municipal buildings, stores, and an occasional movie theater, gas station, or tavern. The government of each settlement or *municipio* is generally patterned after Spanish colonial models and is subject to the jurisdiction of national and state laws. Near populous centers such as Mérida, Guatemala City, or San Cristóbal de las Casas it is not unusual to find Maya houses (many painted with garish soft-drink signs) equipped with radios, electric lights, steam irons, upholstered furniture, and similar accoutrements of contemporary life; and wherever roads have been opened through the countryside, trucks, automobiles, and buses are appearing in increasing numbers. Nowhere are the effects of acculturation more evident than in the marketplaces, which frequently display native goods—pottery, leatherwork, woven cloth, sandals, baskets, and sisal hammocks—alongside a vast assortment of commercially made items ranging from cooking utensils, hardware, and canned foods to clothing, shoes, cheap perfume, and costume jewelry.

Yet despite more than four centuries of economic exploitation, religious indoctrination, and social upheaval, the Maya have maintained a remarkable ethnic cohesion. Many groups still adhere to certain aboriginal traditions—to the extent that ethnological studies of their culture have provided valuable insights into a wide spectrum of pre-Conquest practices. In geographically remote villages, these links with the past pervade nearly every aspect of daily existence, and entering them, one is acutely aware of suddenly being thrust into a realm of "living" archaeology.

Almost everywhere the houses have remained virtually identical to the thatched-roof dwellings with lime-plastered earthen or stone walls that once surrounded ancient Maya cities. As in the past, there are often adjacent structures used for cooking or other domestic activities, and the houses are frequently grouped together to form compounds similar to those mapped in lowland archaeological sites. In many villages, pottery is still made using ancient techniques whereby the vessel is built up by coiling thin strips of clay and smoothed with a wooden instrument, after which it is coated with a watery clay slip and fired under piles of burning wood. In Guatemala and Chiapas, exquisite fabrics are woven on traditional backstrap looms, and throughout the area, animal hide and vegetable fiber are utilized to make sandals, baskets, matting, and a variety of other items of everyday use that have not changed in design or function for centuries. Women still grind maize into dough with stone *metates* and *manos* (though some villages now have machines for this purpose), and the men go to work in their fields carrying tortillas and gourds filled with *atole,* the age-old mixture of corn and water first mentioned by sixteenth-century Spanish chroniclers as one of the staples of the native diet. Among the larger and more cohesive groups—especially in Yucatán, Guatemala, and Chiapas—traditional dress prevails over non-Indian clothing; and there are numerous festivals and religious celebrations that involve pre-Columbian practices such as offerings, purification rites, fasting, and the burning of copal incense.

Even in physical appearance the average Maya are quite similar to their ancestors: small, rather stocky, with copper to medium brown skin, straight black hair, and broad faces accentuated by pronounced noses, high cheekbones, and dark eyes. One often encounters Indians with the "hooked" nose, downturned lower lip, and almond-shaped eyes characteristic of profiles depicted by ancient artists, and Sylvanus Morley observed that "many of the modern Maya of Yucatán so closely resemble the figures on monuments and in paintings that they could have served as models for them."

Notwithstanding the efforts of missionaries, Maya religious beliefs incorporate a curious mixture of native and Christian elements, including a strong emphasis on magic, witchcraft, curing illness, and divination. Native priests continue to play an important role, and almost every activity—including marriage, childbirth, planting crops, and hunting—is accompanied by ceremonies involving pagan deities. In the Guatemalan highlands the ancient 260-day sacred almanac is still used to determine planting seasons, and in a Chamula village in Chiapas an anthropologist named Gary Gossen found a wooden board with charcoal marks that recorded the sequence of days and months— the "folk equivalent," as Norman Hammond remarked, "of the sculptured inscriptions of the Classic Maya in its notation of the passage of time."

Agricultural methods have remained essentially unchanged for thousands of years; maize, beans, squash, chili peppers, and other staples are still planted in *milpas* with the same type of pointed digging stick used by the peasants for perhaps four thousand years. As they sow their fields, modern Maya farmers utter prayers, sing chants, and leave offerings to propitiate the same earth gods that nurtured their ancestors. In his *Rise and Fall of Maya Civilization*, J. Eric Thompson recalled a planting ritual he once observed in a Mopan village in Belize, which is typical of similar rites throughout the region:

The night before sowing, the helpers gather at the hut of the owner of the field. At one end of the hut the sacks of seed are laid on a table before a cross, and lighted candles are placed in front and to each side of a gourd containing cacao and ground maize. The seed is then censed with copal, and afterwards the hut, inside and out, is completely censed. The men, who have brought their own hammocks, lounge in them, passing the night in conversation and music and the enjoyment of a meal served at midnight. Sometimes the group prays in the church for a good crop. The purpose of this vigil is to insure that the crop will not be endangered by the incontinence of any member of the group (the Mam, the Chorti, the Kekchi, and other Maya groups observe periods of continence of up to thirteen days at sowing time).

Looking back thirty years, I can see the group, most of them deep in shadow, for the guttering candles throw only a small circle of light. One or two are sitting in their hammocks; a third is lying back in his hammock with one foot dangling over the edge. Everyone is wrapped in a thin blanket, for the April night is cold and the chill air has no trouble in finding the spaces between the poles that form the walls of the hut. Conversation is soft, singsong Maya starts and dies like puffs of wind. Outside, the constellations of the tropics dawdle across the sky; they seem so close, one feels like raising his hand to push them on their course. Curiosity can hardly be delaying them; they have seen such vigils for many centuries. At daybreak the owner of the land goes to his field ahead of the rest of the party. There, in the center of the field, he burns copal and sows seven handfuls of maize in the form of a cross oriented to the four world directions, and recites this prayer:

> *O god, my grandfather, my grandmother, god of the hills, god of the valleys, holy god. I make to you my offering with all my soul. Be patient with me in what I am doing, my true God and [blessed] Virgin. It is needful that you give me fine, beautiful, all I am going to sow here where I have my work, my cornfield. Watch it for me, guard it for me, let nothing happen to it from the time I sow until I harvest it.*

Another poignant example of how deeply the Maya venerate their heritage was demonstrated by a remarkable event that took place in an underground cavern in Yucatán known as Balankanché. Situated barely four miles east of Chichén Itzá, this tunnellike cave had been explored by archaeologists and local Indians for years. But in 1959 an amateur speleologist and part-time guide at the Mayaland Hotel at Chichén Itzá—José Humberto Gomez—unexpectedly stumbled upon a previously overlooked passageway sealed with tightly cemented stones.

After breaking open the wall, Gomez squeezed through a narrow chamber leading into a maze of winding vaults. At the end of this corridor he found a large grotto, its ceiling covered with glistening stalactites. Near the center of the room these encrustations reached the floor and formed what seemed to be a gigantic pillar supporting the roof. No sooner had he entered the chamber than his flashlight revealed a breathtaking spectacle: scattered about were dozens of pottery vessels, incense burners, miniature *metates* and *manos*, and similar offertory objects too numerous to distinguish in the darkness.

Aware of the significance of his discovery, Gomez notified Fernando Barbachano, the owner of the Mayaland Hotel, who in turn alerted officials in Mérida and the archaeologist E. Wyllys Andrews IV, director of the Tulane University–National Geographic Society expedition then excavating at Dzibilchaltún. When Gomez led investigators back to the cavern to view his findings, the sight confronting them far exceeded their expectations. Recalling his first impression of the grotto, Andrews wrote:

The tiny tunnel suddenly opened into a small chamber facing a vertical wall of slippery rock which could be negotiated only by climbing a rope which Gomez had secured to a stalactite above. From here the going was easier, over piles of fallen rock and along flat passageways of muddy clay, until suddenly we emerged into a great domed chamber. The ceiling was coated with millions of tiny stalactites, the point of water on the tip of each winking back as the pencil rays of our headlamps cut through the blackness. Carved by nature in the great complex of stalactitic growth filling the center of the room was a deep niche which might have been the throne of some god. And we thought immediately of the cave's name: Balankanché in [Yucatec] means "Throne of the Balam" . . . a name given to the native priests in the last days before the Conquest. . . .

As the beams of our lights moved lower we saw that the pitted rock surfaces beneath the "throne" were literally covered with archaeological remains: brightly colored clay incensarios like nothing known before from the Maya area, beautifully carved stone cylinders showing women, warriors, and dancing figures with a wealth of detail, piles of pottery offerings—in short, an archaeological treasure trove.

While we were still standing with our mouths open, Humberto said, "This is only the first chamber." Before we had finished our inspection we saw three more groups of offerings, one even richer than the first. By morning when we staggered out of the cave, it was clear that we had seen one of the most striking and valuable discoveries in many years, and that immediate steps must be taken for its conservation. . . .

Accordingly, a joint effort by Tulane University, the National Geographic Society, and the Instituto Nacional de Antropología e Historia was launched to explore the cave. In spite of almost unbearable working conditions caused by excessive humidity and lack of oxygen, a team of archaeologists, photographers, and artists spent five weeks excavating and studying its contents. More than six hundred artifacts were recovered, and some sections of the cavern had apparently been used as long ago as 1000 B.C. The most fascinating aspect of the discovery, however, was the fact that the hidden grotto revealed by Gomez was actually a shrine to the Toltec rain god Tlaloc, the Mexican counterpart of the Maya deity Chac. Many of the objects in the vault bore Tlaloc's characteristic trademarks—exposed fangs, large ringed eyes, and a scroll-like device on the forehead—and the offerings had undoubtedly been placed in the cavern by the Toltec-Itzá sometime after their intrusion into Yucatán.

Scarcely had work at the cave begun when a young Maya appeared on the scene. Introducing himself to Andrews as Romualdo Hoyil, he turned out to be an important *h-men* or native priest from the nearby village of Xkalakoop. Hoyil expressed eager interest in the newly discovered crypt, explaining how for generations his people had known of the existence of a secret *adoratorio* dedicated to the rain god, though no one had been able to locate it. After viewing the grotto and its offerings, he grew visibly excited and requested permission to conduct special religious ceremonies at the site without delay. "He then explained," Andrews wrote, "that the Chacs, gods of rain, whose sacred precincts had been violated, and the *balams*, guardians of the cave and the water sources, must be propitiated, not only to avoid retaliation on the individuals who had entered, but to insure against possible suffering on the part of the whole population. He insisted that the ceremonies begin the following day, and we, of course, agreed."

Soon after dawn the next morning the participants assembled at the cave. In addition to the scientific staff involved in the explorations, an expert in Yucatecan linguistics named Alfredo Barrera Vásquez, and Romualdo Hoyil, there were thirteen assistant priests who had been specially recruited for the occasion. Hoyil had taken particular care in collecting the necessary offertory items: thirteen hens, one turkey, thirteen black candles, two bottles of anise, thirteen jars of honey, plus copal incense, tobacco, corn, cloves, cumin, and other spices. The assistant priests were to be paid thirteen pesos apiece for their services, while Hoyil himself received fifty-two pesos. (Andrews pointed out the importance of the numbers thirteen and fifty-two in ancient Maya religion, especially fifty-two, which represented the cycle of years in the Calendar Round.) Hoyil announced that the ceremony would require twenty-four hours to complete, and no one would be allowed to leave until it was over. "We shuddered at the thought of twenty-four hours," recalled Andrews, "with twice the users of oxygen abetted by the smoke of incense, offerings, and tobacco. As it turned out our worst fears were short of reality."

Inside the grotto, Hoyil instructed each of the priests to hold a candle and kneel in a circle around the huge stalactitic formation in the center of the room; everyone else was grouped together in the semi-darkness behind them. On a makeshift altar two of the supplicants placed bowls of copal, tobacco, and maize, and when Hoyil was satisfied that the proper ritual code had been observed, the strange ceremony began. Slowly, in a low, solemn voice, the *h-men* chanted a curious prayer:

You then, my Lord! Thrice be honored, my Lord. You I humbly address—oh, my Lord. I am presenting my word to You then, my Lord, K'ulu Balam, greatly named by word, thrice be honored, my Lord, to You I give my word. So the warmth be cooled, my Lord, thrice be honored. . . .

For hours the chanting droned on through a series of twenty-seven rites intended to placate the cave's guardian *balams* and the powerful rain god Chac. At the conclusion of each ritual the celebrants paused long enough to drink a thick, sweet beverage made of corn gruel and honey served in gourds, then the incantations resumed. Everything about the scene—the sound of the half-sung prayers, the smoking incense, the sweat-soaked bodies of the priests illuminated by candlelight—was vividly reminiscent of ceremonies that must have occurred in the grotto centuries ago, when the Toltec-Itzá had gathered there to worship Tlaloc.

During the last act of the ritual, seven small boys ranging from four to eight years old were brought in to serve as imitators of frogs and tree toads, the earthly messengers of Chac who announced the coming of rain. Since this was part of the well-known Cha-Chac ceremony widely practiced in Yucatán, the children had been trained to skillfully reproduce the sounds made by various species, and throughout the remainder of the night they accompanied the *h-men*'s chants with a chorus of high-pitched croaking and clicking, an eerie counterpoint to his monotonous prayers.

When the ceremony finally ended, everyone was given branches cut from a bush to use in "sweeping" evil spirits out of the cavern. As a final gesture the *h-men* symbolically "sealed" its entrance with a chant, ordering it closed to everyone for a period of forty-eight hours. To reenter before then, he warned, would risk the vengeance of its guardian spirits.

Outside the cave a feast prepared by members of Hoyil's village awaited the exhausted participants. For many hours the turkey and thirteen hens designated as sacrifices—which were killed, cleaned, and wrapped in plantain leaves—had been cooking in underground ovens called *pib,* and these were served along with special cakes made of corn dough and spices as part of the festivities. In the tradition of ancient Maya banquets, large quantities of *balché* brewed from fermented maize, *balché* bark, honey, and water were also consumed— its intoxicating properties well suited to bring men and gods into close contact.

And so the deities whose memory haunted the cave of Balankanché had been appeased. For perhaps a thousand years the grotto's secret had lain undisturbed, its existence only dimly recalled in folklore. Yet Romualdo Hoyil had honored the shrine as reverently as he would have done centuries ago, employing rituals he described as "intended for use in chambers hidden beyond the memory of man."

Elsewhere throughout the Maya realm, similar acts of homage take place every day: ageless prayers are recited, copal incense is burned on crude altars, and rituals are enacted in sacred shrines. Ironically, the Maya remain suspended between two contrasting worlds—ancient and modern—clinging stubbornly to threads linking them to remote depths of antiquity, to those unfathomed mysteries buried in the shattered, jungle-shrouded cities of their ancestors.

BIBLIOGRAPHY

No attempt has been made to include all of the works consulted in the preparation of this book. Instead, the references listed below are those I found particularly helpful and are intended to serve as a guide to further reading, with special emphasis on significant research during the last twenty-five years.

Adams, Richard E. W. "Suggested Classic Period Occupational Specialization in the Southern Maya Lowlands." In *Monographs and Papers in Maya Archaeology*, ed. by W. R. Bullard, Jr. *Papers of the Peabody Museum of Archaeology and Ethnology, Harvard University*, Vol. 61, 1970.

———. "The Collapse of Maya Civilization: A Review of Previous Theories." In *The Classic Maya Collapse*, ed. by T. Patrick Culbert. Albuquerque: University of New Mexico Press, 1973.

———, ed. *The Origins of Maya Civilization*. Albuquerque: University of New Mexico Press, 1977.

———, and Robert C. Aldrich. "A Reevaluation of the Bonampak Murals: A Preliminary Statement on the Paintings and Texts." In *Tercera Mesa Redonda de Palenque, Part 2*, ed. by Merle Greene Robertson. Austin: University of Texas Press, 1981.

Andrews, E. Wyllys, IV. "Dzibilchaltún: Lost City of the Maya." *National Geographic Magazine*, Vol. 115, No. 1, 1959.

———. "Excavations at Dzibilchaltún, Northwestern Yucatán, Mexico." *Proceedings of the American Philosophical Society*, Vol. 104, No. 2, 1960.

———. "Archaeology and Prehistory in the Northern Maya Lowlands." In

Handbook of Middle American Indians, Vol. 2, ed. by Gordon R. Willey. Austin: University of Texas Press, 1965.

————. "Dzibilchaltún, A Northern Maya Metropolis." *Archaeology*, Vol. 21, No. 1, 1968.

————. "Balankanché—Throne of the Tiger Priest." *Explorers Journal*, Vol. 49, No. 4, 1971.

————. "The Development of Maya Civilization After Abandonment of the Southern Cities." In *The Classic Maya Collapse*, ed. by T. Patrick Culbert. Albuquerque: University of New Mexico Press, 1973.

Andrews, George F. *Maya Cities: Placemaking and Urbanization*. Norman: University of Oklahoma Press, 1975.

Anton, Ferdinand. *Art of the Maya*. New York: G. P. Putnam's Sons, 1970.

Ashmore, Wendy A., ed. *Lowland Maya Settlement Patterns*. Albuquerque: School of American Research, University of New Mexico, 1981.

Ball, Joseph W. "A Coordinate Approach to Northern Maya Prehistory." *American Antiquity*, Vol. 39, No. 1, 1974.

Becker, Marshall J. "Priest, Peasants, and Ceremonial Centers: The Intellectual History of a Model." In *Maya Archaeology and Ethnohistory*, ed. by Norman Hammond and Gordon R. Willey. Austin: University of Texas Press, 1979.

Berlin, Heinrich. "El Glifo 'Emblema' en las Inscripciones Mayas." *Journal de la Société des Américanistes*, Vol. 47, 1958.

Blom, Frans. *The Conquest of Yucatan*. Boston: Houghton Mifflin Company, 1936.

————, and Oliver La Farge. *Tribes and Temples*. 2 vols. Middle American Research Series, No. 1. New Orleans: Tulane University, 1926.

Borhegyi, Stephan F. "Archaeological Synthesis of the Guatemalan Highlands." In *Handbook of Middle American Indians*, Vol. 2, ed. by Gordon R. Willey. Austin: University of Texas Press, 1965.

Bullard, William R., Jr. "Maya Settlement Patterns in Northeastern Peten, Guatemala." *American Antiquity*, Vol. 25, No. 3, 1960.

————. "Postclassic Culture in Central Peten and Adjacent British Honduras." In *The Classic Maya Collapse*, ed. by T. Patrick Culbert. Albuquerque: University of New Mexico Press, 1973.

Catherwood, Frederick. *Views of Ancient Monuments in Central America, Chiapas, and Yucatan*. New York: Barlett and Welford, 1844.

Chamberlain, Robert S. "The Conquest and Colonization of Yucatán." Washington, D.C.: Carnegie Institution of Washington, Publication 582, 1948.

Charnay, Désiré. *The Ancient Cities of the New World*. New York: Harper and Brothers, 1887.

Coe, Michael D. "La Victoria, An Early Site on the Pacific Coast of Guatemala." *Papers of the Peabody Museum of Archaeology and Ethnology, Harvard University*, Vol. 53, 1961.

———. *The Maya*. New York: Frederick A. Praeger, 1966.

———. *The Maya Scribe and His World*. New York: The Grolier Club, 1973.

———. *Lords of the Underworld*. Princeton: Princeton University Press, 1978.

Coe, William R. "A Summary of Excavation and Research at Tikal, Guatemala: 1956–61." *American Antiquity*, Vol. 27, No. 4, 1962.

———. "Tikal, Guatemala, and Emergent Maya Civilization." *Science*, Vol. 147, No. 3664, 1965.

———. "Tikal: Ten Years of Study of a Maya Ruin in the Lowlands of Guatemala." *Expedition*, Vol. 8, No. 1, 1965.

Coggins, Clemency C. "Painting and Drawing Styles at Tikal: An Historical and Iconographic Reconstruction." Ph.D. dissertation, Harvard University. Ann Arbor, Mich.: University Microfilms, 1975.

Covarrubias, Miguel. *Indian Art of Mexico and Central America*. New York: Alfred A. Knopf, 1957.

Culbert, T. Patrick, ed. *The Classic Maya Collapse*. Albuquerque: University of New Mexico Press, 1973.

———. *The Lost Civilization: The Story of the Classic Maya*. New York: Harper & Row, 1974.

Diehl, Richard A. *Tula: The Toltec Capital of Ancient Mexico*. New York: Thames and Hudson, 1983.

Duby, Gertrude, and Frans Blom. "The Lacandon." In *Handbook of Middle American Indians*, Vol. 7, ed. by Evon Z. Vogt. Austin: University of Texas Press, 1969.

Dutton, Bertha P. "Tula of the Toltecs." *El Palacio*, Vol. 62, 1955.

Ediger, Donald. *The Well of Sacrifice*. Garden City, N.Y.: Doubleday and Company, 1971.

Ekholm, Gordon F. "Transpacific Contacts." In *Prehistoric Man in the New World*, ed. by J. D. Jennings and E. Norbeck. Rice University Semicentennial Publications. Chicago: University of Chicago Press, 1964.

Gallenkamp, Charles. *Maya: The Riddle and Rediscovery of a Lost Civilization*. Rev. ed. New York: David McKay Company, 1976.

———. *Maya: The Riddle and Rediscovery of a Lost Civilization*. 2nd rev. ed. New York: Penguin Books, 1981.

————, and Regina Elise Johnson, eds. *Maya: Treasures of an Ancient Civilization*. New York: Harry N. Abrams, 1985.

Gann, T. W. F. *Maya Cities, A Record of Exploration and Adventure in Middle America*. London: Gerald Duckworth & Co., 1927.

Girard, Rafael. *Los Mayas Eternos*. Mexico, D.F.: Antigua Librería Robredo, 1962.

Gordon, George B. "Prehistoric Ruins of Copán, Honduras." *Memoirs of the Peabody Museum of Archaeology and Ethnology, Harvard University*, Vol. 1, No. 1, 1896.

Hammond, Norman. "The Earliest Maya." *Scientific American*, Vol. 236, No. 3, 1977.

————, ed. *Social Process in Maya Prehistory, Essays in Honour of Sir J. Eric S. Thompson*. New York: Academic Press, 1977.

————. *Ancient Maya Civilization*. New Brunswick, N.J.: Rutgers University Press, 1982.

Harrison, Peter D., and B. L. Turner, eds. *Pre-Hispanic Maya Agriculture*. Albuquerque: University of New Mexico Press, 1978.

————, eds. *Pulltrouser Swamp: Ancient Maya Habitat, Agriculture, and Settlement in Northern Belize*. Austin: University of Texas Press, 1983.

Haviland, William A. "Prehistoric Settlement at Tikal." *Expedition*, Vol. 7, No. 3, 1965.

————. "Ancient Lowland Maya Social Organization." Middle American Research Institute, Publication 26. New Orleans: Tulane University, 1968.

————. "Tikal, Guatemala, and Mesoamerican Urbanism." *World Archaeology*, Vol. 2, No. 2, 1970.

Heine-Geldern, Robert. "The Problem of Transpacific Influences in Mesoamerica." In *Handbook of Middle American Indians*, Vol. 4, ed. by Gordon F. Ekholm and Gordon R. Willey. Austin: University of Texas Press, 1966.

Henderson, John S. *The World of the Ancient Maya*. Ithaca, N.Y.: Cornell University Press, 1981.

Hurtado, Eusebio Dávalos. "Return to the Well of Sacrifice." *National Geographic Magazine*, Vol. 120, No. 4, 1961.

Kelley, David H. "Glyphic Evidence for a Dynastic Sequence at Quiriguá, Guatemala." *American Antiquity*, Vol. 27, No. 3, 1962.

————. "A History of the Decipherment of Maya Script." *Anthropological Linguistics*, Vol. 4, No. 8, 1962.

Kidder, Alfred V., Jesse D. Jennings, and Edwin M. Shook. "Excavations at Kaminaljuyú, Guatemala." Washington, D.C.: Carnegie Institution of Washington Publication 561, 1946.

Knorozov, Yuri V. "The Problem of the Study of the Maya Hieroglyphic Writing." *American Antiquity,* Vol. 23, No. 3, 1958.

Kubler, George. *The Art and Architecture of Ancient America.* 2nd ed. Baltimore: Penguin Books, 1975.

Landa, Diego de. "Relación de las Cosas de Yucatán." Trans. and ed. by Alfred M. Tozzer. *Papers of the Peabody Museum of Archaeology and Ethnology, Harvard University,* Vol. 18, 1941.

Littlehales, Bates. "Treasure Hunting in the Deep Past." *National Geographic Magazine,* Vol. 120, No. 4, October 1961.

Lothrop, Samuel K. *Treasures of Ancient America: The Arts of the Pre-Columbian Civilizations from Mexico to Peru.* Geneva: Albert Skira, 1964.

Lounsbury, Floyd G. "The Inscription on the Sarcophagus Lid at Palenque." In *Primera Mesa Redonda de Palenque, Part 2,* ed. by Merle Greene Robertson. Austin: University of Texas Press, 1974.

MacNeish, Richard S. "The Origin of New World Civilization." *Scientific American,* Vol. 211, No. 5, 1964.

———. "The Food-gathering and Incipient Agriculture Stage of Prehistoric Middle America." In *Handbook of Middle American Indians,* Vol. 1, ed. by Robert C. West. Austin: University of Texas Press, 1964.

McQuown, Norman A. "The Classification of Maya Languages." *International Journal of American Linguistics,* Vol. 22, 1956.

Maler, Teobert. "Researches in the Central Portion of the Usumatsintla Valley: Report of Explorations for the Museum, 1898–1900." *Memoirs of the Peabody Museum of Archaeology and Ethnology, Harvard University,* Vol. 2, Nos. 1 and 2, 1901–3.

———. "Explorations of the Upper Usumatsintla and Adjacent Regions." *Memoirs of the Peabody Museum of Archaeology and Ethnology, Harvard University,* Vol. 4, No. 1, 1908.

———. "Explorations in the Department of Petén: Tikal." *Memoirs of the Peabody Museum of Archaeology and Ethnology, Harvard University,* Vol. 5, No. 1, 1911.

Mangelsdorf, Paul C., Richard S. MacNeish, and Gordon R. Willey. "Origins of Agriculture in Middle America." In *Handbook of Middle American Indians,* Vol. 1, ed. by Robert C. West. Austin: University of Texas Press, 1964.

Marcus, Joyce. *Emblem and State in the Classic Maya Lowlands.* Washington, D.C.: Dumbarton Oaks, 1976.

———. "Lowland Maya Archaeology at the Crossroads." *American Antiquity,* Vol. 48, No. 3, 1983.

Marden, Luis. "Dzibilchaltún: Up from the Well of Time." *National Geographic Magazine,* Vol. 115, No. 1, January 1959.

Marquina, Ignacio, *Arquitectura Prehispánica.* Mexico, D.F.: Instituto Nacional de Antropología e Historia, 1951.

Mason, J. Alden. "The American Collection of the University Museum: The Ancient Civilizations of Middle America." *Bulletin of the University of Pennsylvania Museum,* Vol. 10, Nos. 1 and 2, 1943.

Mathews, Peter, and Linda Schele. "Lords of Palenque—the Glyphic Evidence." In *Primera Mesa Redonda de Palenque, Part 1,* ed. by Merle Greene Robertson. Austin: University of Texas Press, 1974.

Maudslay, Alfred P. *Archaeology: Biologia Centrali-Americana.* 5 vols. London: Porter and Dulau & Company, 1889–1902.

Morley, Sylvanus G. "The Inscriptions at Copán." Washington, D.C.: Carnegie Institution of Washington, Publication 219, 1920.

———. "The Inscriptions of Petén." 5 vols. Washington, D.C.: Carnegie Institution of Washington, Publication 437, 1938.

———. *The Ancient Maya.* Stanford: Stanford University Press, 1946.

———. *The Ancient Maya.* 3rd ed. Rev. by George W. Brainerd. Stanford: Stanford University Press, 1956.

———, and George W. Brainerd. *The Ancient Maya.* 4th ed. Rev. by Robert J. Sharer. Stanford: Stanford University Press, 1983.

Morris, Earl H. *The Temple of the Warriors.* New York: Charles Scribner's Sons, 1931.

———, Jean Charlot, and Ann Axtell Morris. "The Temple of the Warriors at Chichén Itzá, Yucatán." Washington, D.C.: Carnegie Institution of Washington, Publication 406, 1931.

Pendergast, David M. *Excavations at Altun Ha, Belize,* 1964–1970. Vol I. Toronto: Royal Ontario Museum, 1979.

———. "Lamanai, Belize: Summary of Excavation Results," 1974–1980. *Journal of Field Archaeology,* Vol. 8, 1981.

Pollock, Harry E. D. "Architecture of the Maya Lowlands." In *Handbook of Middle American Indians,* Vol. 2, ed. by Gordon R. Willey. Austin: University of Texas Press, 1965.

———. "The Puuc: An Archaeological Survey of the Hill Country of Yucatan and Northern Campeche, Mexico." *Memoirs of the Peabody Museum of Archaeology and Ethnology, Harvard University,* Vol. 19, 1980.

———, Ralph L. Roys, Tatiana Proskouriakoff, and A. Ledyard Smith. "Mayapán Yucatán, Mexico." Washington, D.C.: Carnegie Institution of Washington, Publication 619, 1962.

Proskouriakoff, Tatiana. "An Album of Maya Architecture." Washington, D.C.: Carnegie Institution of Washington, Publication 558, 1946.

———. "A Study of Classic Maya Sculpture." Washington, D.C.: Carnegie Institution of Washington, Publication 593, 1950.

———. "Historical Implications of a Pattern of Dates at Piedras Negras, Guatemala." *American Antiquity,* Vol. 25, No. 4, 1960.

———. "The Lords of the Maya Realm." *Expedition,* Vol. 4, No. 1, 1961.

———. "Sculpture and Major Arts of the Maya Lowlands." In *Handbook of Middle American Indians,* Vol. 2, ed. by Gordon R. Willey. Austin: University of Texas Press, 1965.

Rands, Robert L. "The Classic Collapse in the Southern Maya Lowlands." In *The Classic Maya Collapse,* ed. by T. Patrick Culbert. Albuquerque: University of New Mexico Press, 1973.

Recinos, Adrián, Delia Goetz, and Sylvanus G. Morley. *Popol Vuh: The Sacred Book of the Ancient Quiché Maya.* Norman: University of Oklahoma Press, 1950.

———, and Delia Goetz. *The Annals of the Cakchiquels.* Norman: University of Oklahoma Press, 1953.

Ricketson, Oliver G., and Edith B. Ricketson. "Uaxactún, Guatemala, Group E 1926–1937." Washington, D.C.: Carnegie Institution of Washington, Publication 477, 1937.

Robicsek, Francis. *The Maya Book of the Dead: The Ceramic Codex.* Charlottesville: University of Virginia Art Museum, 1981.

Roys, Ralph L. *The Ethno-Botany of the Maya.* Middle American Research Series, Publication 2. New Orleans: Tulane University, 1931.

———. "The Indian Background of Colonial Yucatan." Washington, D.C.: Carnegie Institution of Washington, Publication 548, 1943.

———. "Lowland Maya Native Society at Spanish Contact." In *Handbook of Middle American Indians,* Vol. 3, ed. by Gordon R. Willey. Austin: University of Texas Press, 1965.

———. *The Book of Chilam Balam of Chumayel.* Norman: University of Oklahoma Press, 1967.

Ruppert, Karl, J. Eric S. Thompson, and Tatiana Proskouriakoff. "Bonampak, Chiapas, Mexico." Washington, D.C.: Carnegie Institution of Washington, Publication 602, 1955.

Ruz Lhuillier, Alberto. "The Mystery of the Temple of the Inscriptions." *Archaeology,* Vol. 6, No. 1, 1953.

———. "Mystery of the Mayan Temple." Trans. by J. Alden Mason. *The Saturday Evening Post,* Aug. 29, 1953.

Sabloff, Jeremy A., and Gordon R. Willey. "The Collapse of Maya Civilization in the Southern Lowlands: A Consideration of History and Process." *Southwestern Journal of Anthropology*, Vol. 23, No. 4, 1967.

———, and William L. Rathje. "The Rise of a Maya Merchant Class." *Scientific American*, Vol. 233, No. 4, 1975.

Sahagún, Fray Bernardino de. *Florentine Codex: General History of the Things of New Spain.* 12 vols. Trans. by Arthur J. O. Anderson and Charles E. Dibble. Santa Fe: School of American Research, 1950–69.

Sanders, William T. "The Cultural Ecology of the Lowland Maya: A Re-evaluation." In *The Classic Maya Collapse*, ed. by T. Patrick Culbert. Albuquerque: University of New Mexico Press, 1973.

Satterthwaite, Linton. "Calendrics of the Maya Lowlands." In *Handbook of Middle American Indians*, Vol. 3, ed. by Gordon R. Willey. Austin: University of Texas Press, 1965.

———, and Elizabeth K. Ralph. "New Radiocarbon Dates and the Maya Correlation Problem." *American Antiquity*, Vol. 26, No. 2, 1960.

Saul, Frank P. "Disease in the Maya Area: The Pre-Columbian Evidence." In *The Classic Maya Collapse*, ed. by T. Patrick Culbert. Albuquerque: University of New Mexico Press, 1973.

Schele, Linda. "Genealogical Documentation on the Tri-Figure Panels at Palenque." In *Tercera Mesa Redonda de Palenque*, ed. by Merle Greene Robertson and Donnan C. Jeffers, 1978.

Sharer, Robert J., and David W. Sedat. "Monument 1, El Porton, Guatemala, and the Development of Maya Calendrical and Writing Systems." *Contributions of the University of California Archaeological Research Facility*, No. 18, August, 1973.

Shook, Edwin M. "Tikal Stela 29," *Expedition*, Vol. 2, No. 2, 1960.

———, and Alfred V. Kidder. "Mound E-111-3, Kaminaljuyú, Guatemala." Washington, D.C.: Carnegie Institution of Washington, Publication 596, 1952.

Smith, Robert E., and James C. Gifford. "Pottery of the Maya Lowlands." In *Handbook of Middle American Indians*, Vol. 2, ed. by Gordon R. Willey. Austin: University of Texas Press, 1965.

Soustelle, Jacques. *Mexico: Prehispanic Paintings* (Preface). New York: New York Graphic Society in cooperation with UNESCO, 1958.

———. *Arts of Ancient Mexico*. New York: The Viking Press, 1967.

Spinden, Herbert J. *Maya Art and Civilization*. Indian Hills, Colo.: The Falcon's Wing Press, 1957.

Stephens, John Lloyd. *Incidents of Travel in Central America, Chiapas, and Yucatan*. 2 vols. ed. by Richard L. Predmore. New Brunswick, N.J.: Rutgers University Press, 1949.

————. *Incidents of Travel in Yucatan*. 2 vols. ed. by Victor W. von Hagen. Norman: University of Oklahoma Press, 1962.

Stierlin, Henri. *Art of the Ancient Maya*. New York: Rizzoli, 1981.

Teeple, John E. "Maya Astronomy." *Contributions to American Archaeology*, Carnegie Institution of Washington, Publication 2, 1930.

Thompson, Edward H. *People of the Serpent*. Boston: Houghton Mifflin Company, 1932.

Thompson, J. Eric S. *Maya Hieroglyphic Writing: An Introduction*. 2nd ed. Norman: University of Oklahoma Press, 1960.

————. *A Catalog of Maya Hieroglyphs*. Norman: University of Oklahoma Press, 1962.

————. "Archaeological Synthesis of the Southern Maya Lowlands." In *Handbook of Middle American Indians*, Vol. 2, ed. by Gordon R. Willey. Austin: University of Texas Press, 1965.

————. "Maya Hieroglyphic Writing." In *Handbook of Middle American Indians*, Vol. 3, ed. by Gordon R. Willey. Austin: University of Texas Press, 1965.

————. *The Rise and Fall of Maya Civilization*. Rev. ed. Norman: University of Oklahoma Press, 1966.

————. *Maya History and Religion*. Norman: University of Oklahoma Press, 1970.

————. "A Commentary on the Dresden Codex." *Memoirs of the American Philosophical Society*, Vol. 93, 1972.

Tozzer, Alfred M. *A Comparative Study of the Mayas and the Lacandones*. New York: Macmillan & Company, 1907.

Vogt, Evon Z. "Some Aspects of Zinacantan Settlement Patterns and Ceremonial Organization." *Estudios de Cultura Maya*, Vol. 1, 1961.

————. "Some Implications of Zinacantan Social Structure for the Study of the Ancient Maya." *Actas y Memorias del XXXV Congreso Internacional de Americanistas*, Vol. 1, 1964.

Von Hagen, Victor W. *Maya Explorer: John Lloyd Stephens and the Lost Cities of Central America and Yucatán*. Norman: University of Oklahoma Press, 1947.

Von Winning, Hasso. *Pre-Columbian Art of Mexico and Central America*. New York: Harry N. Abrams, 1968.

Wauchope, Robert. "Modern Maya Houses: A Study of Their Archaeological Significance." Washington, D.C.: Carnegie Institution of Washington, Publication 502, 1938.

————. *Lost Tribes & Sunken Continents: Myth and Method in the Study of American Indians*. Chicago: University of Chicago Press, 1962.

————. "Southern Mesoamerica." In *Prehistoric Man in the New World*, ed. by J. D. Jennings and E. Norbeck. Rice University Semicentennial Publications. Chicago: University of Chicago Press, 1964.

————. *They Found the Buried Cities*. Chicago: University of Chicago Press, 1965.

Weaver, Muriel Porter. *The Aztecs, Maya, and Their Predecessors*. 2nd ed. New York: Academic Press, 1981.

Webb, Malcolm C. "The Peten Maya Decline Viewed in the Perspective of State Formation." In *The Classic Maya Collapse*, ed. by T. Patrick Culbert. Albuquerque: University of New Mexico Press, 1973.

Willey, Gordon R. "The Structure of Ancient Maya Society: Evidence from the Southern Lowlands." *American Anthropologist*, Vol. 58, No. 5, 1956.

————. *An Introduction to American Archaeology*, Vol. 1, *North and Middle America*. Englewood Cliffs, N.J.: Prentice-Hall, 1966.

————, and William R. Bullard. "Prehistoric Settlement Patterns in the Maya Lowlands." In *Handbook of Middle American Indians*, Vol. 2, ed. by Gordon R. Willey. Austin: University of Texas Press, 1965.

————, and Demitri B. Shimkin. "The Maya Collapse: A Summary View." In *The Classic Maya Collapse*, ed. by T. Patrick Culbert. Albuquerque: University of New Mexico Press, 1973.

————, and A. Ledyard Smith. "New Discoveries at Altar de Sacrificios, Guatemala." *Archaeology*, Vol. 16, No. 2, 1963.

————, and A. Ledyard Smith. "The Ruins of Altar de Sacrificios, Department of Petén, Guatemala: An Introduction." *Papers of the Peabody Museum of Archaeology and Ethnology, Harvard University*, Vol. 62, No. 1, 1969.

ILLUSTRATION ACKNOWLEDGMENTS

All photographs not otherwise credited were taken by the author.

1. Peabody Museum of Archaeology and Ethnology, Harvard University.
2. From *Harper's Monthly Magazine,* January 1859.
3. Reconstruction drawing by Tatiana Proskouriakoff; University of Oklahoma Press.
4. From *Views of Ancient Monuments in Central America, Chiapas and Yucatan,* by Frederick Catherwood, 1844.
6. Drawing by Frederick Catherwood.
7. Drawing by Frederick Catherwood.
10. Photograph by Ursula Parifer; Dumbarton Oaks, Washington, D.C.
11. Photograph by Alfred P. Maudslay.
12. Photograph by Alfred P. Maudslay.
13. Reconstruction drawing by Tatiana Proskouriakoff; University of Oklahoma Press.
14. Photograph by Stuart Rome; National Museum of Anthropology, Guatemala.
15. Photograph by Stuart Rome; National Museum of Anthropology, Guatemala.
16. Reconstruction drawing by Tatiana Proskouriakoff; University of Oklahoma Press.
17. Photograph by Stuart Rome; National Museum of Anthropology, Guatemala.
18. The University Museum, University of Pennsylvania.
19. Photograph by Alfred P. Maudslay.
22. Photograph by Stuart Rome; Sylvanus G. Morley Museum, Tikal, Guatemala.

23. Photograph by Stuart Rome; National Museum of Anthropology, Guatemala.

24. Photograph by Stuart Rome.

25. Photograph by Stuart Rome; Sylvanus G. Morley Museum, Tikal, Guatemala.

26. Photograph by Stuart Rome; National Museum of Anthropology, Guatemala.

27. Photograph by Stuart Rome; Sylvanus G. Morley Museum, Tikal, Guatemala.

28. Photograph by Stuart Rome; National Museum of Anthropology, Guatemala.

30. Photographs by Diego Molina; National Museum of Anthropology, Guatemala.

31. Photograph by Diego Molina; National Museum of Anthropology, Guatemala.

32. Photograph by Ursula Parifer; Dumbarton Oaks, Washington, D.C.

33. Photograph by Stuart Rome; Recinto Prehispánico, Fundación Cultural Televisa A.C., Mexico.

34. Photograph by Ursula Parifer; Dumbarton Oaks, Washington, D.C.

35. Michael C. Rockefeller Memorial Collection, Metropolitan Museum of Art, New York.

36. Photograph by Stuart Rome; National Museum of Anthropology, Guatemala.

37. Michael C. Rockefeller Memorial Collection, Metropolitan Museum of Art, New York.

39. Photograph by Alfred P. Maudslay.

41. Photograph by Alfred P. Maudslay.

44. Sarcophagus: National Institute of Anthropology and History, Mexico; detail: photograph by Merle Greene Robertson; Pre-Columbian Art Research Institute, San Francisco.

45. National Institute of Anthropology and History, Mexico.

46. National Museum of Anthropology, Mexico.

47. National Museum of Anthropology, Mexico.

48. National Museum of Anthropology, Mexico.

49. Reconstruction drawing by Tatiana Proskouriakoff; University of Oklahoma Press.

50. Photograph by Stuart Rome; National Museum of Anthropology, Mexico.

51. National Museum of Anthropology, Mexico.

52. Photograph by Stuart Rome; National Museum of Anthropology, Mexico.

53. Photograph by Alfred P. Maudslay.

54. Photographs by Stuart Rome; Recinto Prehispánico, Fundación Cultural Televisa A.C., Mexico.

55. Photograph by Stuart Rome; Recinto Prehispánico, Fundación Cultural Televisa A.C., Mexico.

56. Photograph by Ursula Parifer; Dumbarton Oaks, Washington, D.C.

58. Reproductions by Augustín Villagra Caleti; National Museum of Anthropology, Mexico.

59. Dumbarton Oaks, Washington, D.C.

60. Photograph by Stuart Rome; National Museum of Anthropology, Mexico.

61. Photograph by Ursula Parifer; Dumbarton Oaks, Washington, D.C.

62. Photograph by Stuart Rome; American Museum of Natural History, New York.

63. Photograph by Ursula Parifer; Dumbarton Oaks, Washington, D.C.

64. Photograph by Stuart Rome; National Museum of Anthropology, Guatemala.

65. Dumbarton Oaks, Washington, D.C.

66. Photograph by Stuart Rome; National Museum of Anthropology, Mexico.

67. National Museum of Anthropology, Mexico.

68. Photograph by Stuart Rome; National Museum of Anthropology, Guatemala.

69. Photograph by Stuart Rome; National Museum of Anthropology, Mexico.

70. National Museum of Anthropology, Mexico.

71. Photographs by Stuart Rome; National Museum of Anthropology, Guatemala.

72. Photograph by Ursula Parifer; Dumbarton Oaks, Washington, D.C.

73. Photograph by Stuart Rome; Royal Ontario Museum, Toronto.

74. Michael C. Rockefeller Memorial Collection, Metropolitan Museum of Art, New York.

75. Dumbarton Oaks, Washington, D.C.

76. Photograph by Stuart Rome; National Museum of Anthropology, Guatemala.

77. Reconstruction drawing by Tatiana Proskouriakoff; University of Oklahoma Press.

78. Middle American Research Institute, Tulane University.

79. From *The Ancient Cities of the New World,* by Desiré Charnay, 1887.

80. Reconstruction drawing by Tatiana Proskouriakoff; University of Oklahoma Press.

81. From *Views of Ancient Monuments in Central America, Chiapas and Yucatan,* by Frederick Catherwood, 1844.

83. Photograph by Stuart Rome; Museum of Anthropology, Mérida, Yucatán.

87. From *Views of Ancient Monuments in Central America, Chiapas and Yucatán*, 1844.

89. Photograph by Stuart Rome; Museum of Anthropology, Mérida, Yucatán.

92. Photograph by Stuart Rome; Museum of Anthropology, Mérida, Yucatán.

93. Photograph by Stuart Rome; Museum of Anthropology, Mérida, Yucatán.

94. From *City of the Sacred Well*, by T. A. Willard.

95. From *Views of Ancient Monuments in Central America, Chiapas and Yucatan*, by Frederick Catherwood, 1844.

96. *Bottom left and right:* Photographs by Hillel burger; Peabody Museum, Harvard University.

97. Reconstruction drawing by Tatiana Proskouriakoff; University of Oklahoma Press.

101. From *Views of Ancient Monuments in Central America, Chiapas and Yucatan*, by Frederick Catherwood, 1844.

104. *Bottom:* From *Views of Ancient Monuments in Central America, Chiapas and Yucatan*, by Frederick Catherwood, 1844.

107. Photograph by Stuart Rome; Museum of Anthropology, Mérida, Yucatán.

108. Photographs by Stuart Rome; Museum of Anthropology, Mérida, Yucatán.

109. Photograph by Stuart Rome; Museum of Anthropology, Mérida, Yucatán.

111. From *Views of Ancient Monuments in Central America, Chiapas and Yucatan*, by Frederick Catherwood, 1844.

112. Dumbarton Oaks, Washington, D.C.

113. Photograph by Richard N. Stewart; National Geographic Society.

114. Photograph by Richard N. Stewart; National Geographic Society.

116. Photograph by Donald Cordry; Arizona State Museum, University of Arizona.

117. Photograph by Donald Cordry; Arizona State Museum, University of Arizona.

INDEX

223

Yaxuná, 83

Yellow, symbolism of, 107

Yucatán, 2, 4, 14, 15, 58, 155; architecture in, 157–58, 160–61, 164, 169, 173, 174, 190–91; chronology of archaeological sites, 159; contemporary Maya in, 199, 201; decline of, 19, 158–60, 169, 187, 188–89, 191–93; Mayapán, 186–91, 192–93; Postclassic survival of, 156–60; Sacred Cenote (Chichén Itzá), 177–85; Spanish conquest and colonization of, 7, 11; Terminal Classic period of, 159; Toltec-Itzá colonization and influences, 161–71, 186, 205

Zaculeu, 195

Zapotec culture, 3, 69, 76

Zavala, Lorenzo de, 24

Zero, concept of, 80

FOR THE BEST IN PAPERBACKS, LOOK FOR THE

In every corner of the world, on every subject under the sun, Penguin represents quality and variety—the very best in publishing today.

For complete information about books available from Penguin—including Puffins, Penguin Classics, and Arkana—and how to order them, write to us at the appropriate address below. Please note that for copyright reasons the selection of books varies from country to country.

In the United Kingdom: Please write to *Dept. JC, Penguin Books Ltd, FREEPOST, West Drayton, Middlesex UB7 0BR*.

If you have any difficulty in obtaining a title, please send your order with the correct money, plus ten percent for postage and packaging, to *P.O. Box No. 11, West Drayton, Middlesex UB7 0BR*

In the United States: Please write to *Consumer Sales, Penguin USA, P.O. Box 999, Dept. 17109, Bergenfield, New Jersey 07621-0120*. Visa and MasterCard holders call 1-800-253-6476 to order all Penguin titles

In Canada: Please write to *Penguin Books Canada Ltd, 10 Alcorn Avenue, Suite 300, Toronto, Ontario M4V 3B2*

In Australia: Please write to *Penguin Books Australia Ltd, P.O. Box 257, Ringwood, Victoria 3134*

In New Zealand: Please write to *Penguin Books (NZ) Ltd, Private Bag 102902, North Shore Mail Centre, Auckland 10*

In India: Please write to *Penguin Books India Pvt Ltd, 706 Eros Apartments, 56 Nehru Place, New Delhi 110 019*

In the Netherlands: Please write to *Penguin Books Netherlands bv, Postbus 3507, NL-1001 AH Amsterdam*

In Germany: Please write to *Penguin Books Deutschland GmbH, Metzlerstrasse 26, 60594 Frankfurt am Main*

In Spain: Please write to *Penguin Books S. A., Bravo Murillo 19, 1° B, 28015 Madrid*

In Italy: Please write to *Penguin Italia s.r.l., Via Felice Casati 20, I-20124 Milano*

In France: Please write to *Penguin France S. A., 17 rue Lejeune, F–31000 Toulouse*

In Japan: Please write to *Penguin Books Japan, Ishikiribashi Building, 2–5–4, Suido, Bunkyo-ku, Tokyo 112*

In Greece: Please write to *Penguin Hellas Ltd, Dimocritou 3, GR–106 71 Athens*

In South Africa: Please write to *Longman Penguin Southern Africa (Pty) Ltd, Private Bag X08, Bertsham 2013*